W9-CNQ-098

I.B.TAURIS SHORT HISTORIES

I.B.Tauris Short Histories is an authoritative and elegantly written new series which puts a fresh perspective on the way history is taught and understood in the twenty-first century. Designed to have strong appeal to university students and their teachers, as well as to general readers and history enthusiasts, *I.B.Tauris Short Histories* comprises a novel attempt to bring informed interpretation, as well as factual reportage, to historical debate. Addressing key subjects and topics in the fields of history, the history of ideas, religion, classical studies, politics, philosophy and Middle East studies, the series seeks intentionally to move beyond the bland, neutral 'introduction' that so often serves as the primary undergraduate teaching tool. While always providing students and generalists with the core facts that they need to get to grips with the essentials of any particular subject, *I.B.Tauris Short Histories* goes further. It offers new insights into how a topic has been understood in the past, and what different social and cultural factors might have been at work. It brings original perspectives to bear on the manner of its current interpretation. It raises questions and – in its extensive bibliographies – points to further study, even as it suggests answers. Addressing a variety of subjects in a greater degree of depth than is often found in comparable series, yet at the same time in concise and compact handbook form, *I.B.Tauris Short Histories* aims to be 'introductions with an edge'. In combining questioning and searching analysis with informed history writing, it brings history up-to-date for an increasingly complex and globalized digital age.

www.short-histories.com

'*A Short History of the Normans* guides the reader expertly and readably through a rich and varied landscape. Dr Hicks grounds her analysis in key primary sources and above all emphasises just how fluid and nuanced was the world in which the Normans operated. Her book is a remarkable accomplishment.'

– Paul Oldfield, Senior Lecturer in Medieval History,
University of Manchester

'Judiciously and intelligently written, this lively and engaging narrative targets novices but is thorough and sophisticated enough to be enjoyed also by advanced scholars. It offers impressive modern assessments derived from many different fields of research, and sheds new light on scholarly debates both past and present. A wonderful book.'

– Sally N. Vaughn, Professor of Medieval History, University of Houston

A Short History of . . .

the American Civil War	Paul Anderson (Clemson University)
the American Revolutionary War	Stephen Conway (University College London)
Ancient China	Edward L Shaughnessy (University of Chicago)
Ancient Greece	P J Rhodes, FBA (Durham University)
Ancient Rome	Andrew Wallace-Hadrill (University of Cambridge)
the Anglo-Saxons	Henrietta Leyser (University of Oxford)
the Byzantine Empire	Dionysios Stathakopoulos (King's College London)
the Celts	Alex Woolf (University of St Andrews)
Christian Spirituality	Edward Howells (Heythrop College, University of London)
the Crimean War	Trudi Tate (University of Cambridge)
English Renaissance Drama	Helen Hackett (University College London)
the English Revolution and the Civil Wars	David J Appleby (University of Nottingham)
the Etruscans	Corinna Riva (University College London)
the Hundred Years War	Michael Prestwich (Durham University)
Irish Independence	J J Lee (New York University)
the Italian Renaissance	Virginia Cox (New York University)
the Korean War	Allan R Millett (University of New Orleans)
Medieval Christianity	G R Evans (University of Cambridge)
Medieval English Mysticism	Vincent Gillespie (University of Oxford)
the Minoans	John Bennet (University of Sheffield)
the Mongols	George Lane (SOAS, University of London)
the Mughal Empire	Michael H Fisher (Oberlin College)
Muslim Spain	Alex J Novikoff (Rhodes College, Memphis)
New Kingdom Egypt	Robert Morkot (University of Exeter)
the New Testament	Halvor Moxnes (University of Oslo)
Nineteenth-Century Philosophy	Joel Rasmussen (University of Oxford)
the Normans	Leonie V. Hicks (Canterbury Christ Church University)
the Ottoman Empire	Baki Tezcan (University of California, Davis)

A SHORT HISTORY OF **THE NORMANS**

Leonie V. Hicks

I.B. TAURIS

LONDON · NEW YORK

Published in 2016 by
I.B.Tauris & Co. Ltd
London • New York
www.ibtauris.com

Copyright © 2016 Leonie V. Hicks

The right of Leonie V. Hicks to be identified as the author of this work has been asserted by the author in accordance with the Copyright, Designs and Patents Act 1988.

All rights reserved. Except for brief quotations in a review, this book, or any part thereof, may not be reproduced, stored in or introduced into a retrieval system, or transmitted, in any form or by any means, electronic, mechanical, photocopying, recording or otherwise, without the prior written permission of the publisher.

Every attempt has been made to gain permission for the use of the images in this book. Any omissions will be rectified in future editions.

References to websites were correct at the time of writing.

ISBN: 978 1 78076 211 1 (HB)
ISBN: 978 1 78076 212 8 (PB)
e ISBN: 978 0 85772 856 2

A full CIP record for this book is available from the British Library
A full CIP record is available from the Library of Congress

Library of Congress Catalog Card Number: available

Typeset by Fakenham Prepress Solutions, Fakenham, Norfolk NR21 8NN
Printed and bound in Great Britain by T.J. International, Padstow, Cornwall

To the Normans special subject students,
the University of Southampton 2007–2012.

Contents

List of Maps, Tables and Illustrations

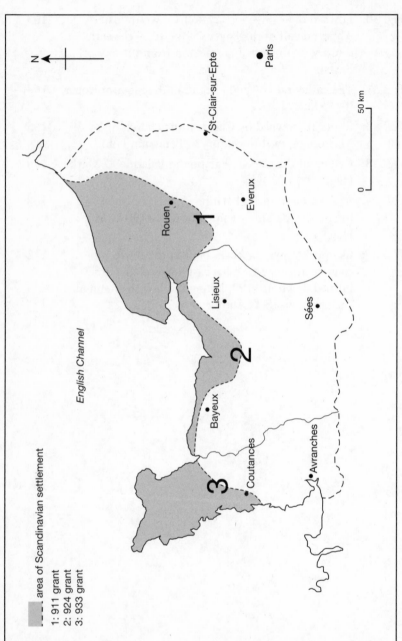

area of Scandinavian settlement

1: 911 grant
2: 924 grant
3: 933 grant

N

English Channel

Paris

St-Clair-sur-Epte

Everux

Rouen

1

Lisieux

Sées

2

Bayeux

Coutances

Avranches

3

0   50 km

Map 1: Settlement of Normandy

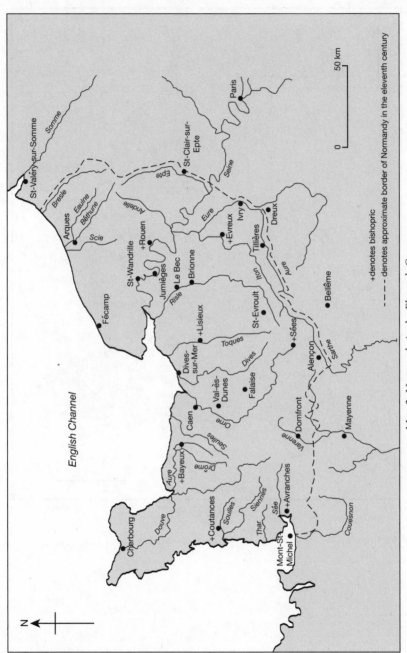

Map 2: Normandy in the Eleventh Century

English Channel

St-Valéry-sur-Somme
Somme
Bresle
Eaune
Béthune
Arques
Scie
Fécamp
+Rouen
St-Wandrille
Jumièges
Le Bec
Risle
Brionne
Andelle
Epte
St-Clair-sur-Epte
Seine
Eure
+Evreux
Ivry
Tillières
Dreux
Iton
+Lisieux
Dives-sur-Mer
Toques
St-Evroult
Aure
+Sées
Bellême
Dives
Falaise
Alençon
Sarthe
Val-ès-Dunes
Caen
Orme
Domfront
Varenne
Mayenne
Seulles
Aure
+Bayeux
Drôme
+Coutances
Soulles
Siennes
Sée
Thar
Couesnon
Cherbourg
Douve
Mont-St-Michel
+Avranches

Paris

+denotes bishopric
- - - denotes approximate border of Normandy in the eleventh century

0   50 km

N

N

Newcastle
Carlisle
Durham

York

North Sea

ENGLAND

Chester
Lincoln
Nottingham

Shrewsbury
Stafford
Peterborough
Norwich

Irish Sea

Ely

Worcester
Cambridge

Hereford
Gloucester

Oxford
London

Salisbury
Winchester
Rochester
Canterbury

Southampton
Battle
Dover

Pevensey
Hastings

Chichester

Exeter

0   100 km

English Channel

Map 3: England

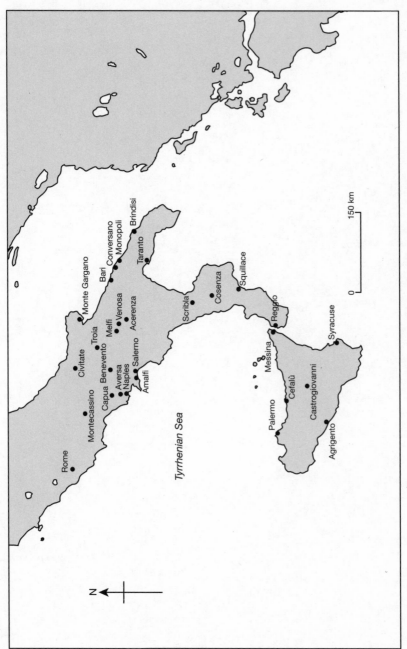

Map 4: Southern Italy and Sicily

Acknowledgements

Writing a book that distils more than two centuries of history in four distinct geographical areas into around 75,000 words has been a challenge and could not have been possible without the help and support of a number of people. When Alex Wright first approached me with the initial idea for the volume, it was Elisabeth van Houts, David Bates and Maria Hayward who encouraged me to put a proposal together: I am grateful to them for their vote of confidence and also to Alex for his patience and support. I should also like to thank the members of the production team for their expertise. I have benefitted enormously from the lively sessions relating to Norman history at the Leeds International Medieval Congress and discussions with the unique body of scholars that comprises the Battle Conference on Anglo-Norman Studies. Nicholas Karn and Mark Hagger read sections of the book and Paul Oldfield and Sally Vaughn read the entire thing and I thank them all for their helpful comments. That not all their suggestions made it into the pages is no reflection on them and all errors remain my own. I am very grateful to Michael Bintley, Mark Hagger and Benjamin Pohl for kindly allowing me to use some of their photographs. Friends and colleagues at both the University of Southampton and latterly Canterbury Christ Church University have offered much moral support, notably Louise Wilkinson. My family has been especially supportive over the course of writing this book and I do not have adequate words to thank them, particularly Ian Hawke who has acted as a willing non-historian reader of various drafts. My final, and greatest, debt is to my special subject students. Teaching the Normans to several groups at the University of Southampton has served to clarify and sharpen much of my thinking on the subject and I look forward to continuing those conversations with the students at Canterbury Christ Church University.

Timeline

841	Viking raid in Seine valley
843	treaty of Verdun
845	Vikings reach Paris
862	Neustrian March granted to Robert the Strong, ancestor of the Capetian dynasty
876	arrival of Rollo in Normandy according to Dudo
888	deposition of Charles the Fat; succeeded in West Francia by Odo
911	traditional date of the foundation of Normandy
922	Frankish king Charles the Simple deposed; succeeded by Robert I
923	Robert I succeeded by Ralph of Burgundy as Frankish king
924	Bessin and Maine granted to the Normans
c.928	death of Rollo; succeeded by William Longsword
933	Avranchin and Cotentin granted to the Normans
c.943	death of William Longsword; succeeded by Richard I
946	attempt by Louis IV, the Frankish king, to seize Rouen
965	rebuilding of Rouen cathedral commences
987	Hugh Capet elected king, marking the end of Carolingian rule in Francia
989	Robert, son of Richard I made archbishop of Rouen
991	treaty between Richard I and King Æthelred II 'the Unready' of England
996	death of Richard I; succeeded by Richard II as duke of Normandy
	Norman peasants revolt

	Robert the Pious becomes king of France
c. 1000	first appearance of Normans in southern Italy as pilgrims and mercenaries
1002	marriage of Emma of Normandy and Æthelred II
1009–10	failed rebellion of Melus against the Byzantines
1013	invasion of England by Swein Forkbeard; Æthelred, Emma and their sons Edward and Alfred flee to Normandy
c. 1013–14	dispute between Richard II and Odo of Blois-Chartres surrounding the border castle of Dreux
1014	death of Æthelred II
1016	Cnut sole king of England and marries Emma of Normandy
1017	Normans join with Melus to fight the Greeks in southern Italy
1019	Rainulf becomes count of Aversa
c. 1020	foundation of Holy Trinity, Cava
1025	work begins on Avranches cathedral
1026	death of Duke Richard II; succeeded by Richard III
1027	death of Duke Richard III; succeeded by Robert the Magnificent
1030	Rainulf granted Aversa; castle built
1030s	elder sons of Tancred of Hauteville make their way to southern Italy
1031	Henry I becomes king of France
1035	death of Duke Robert the Magnificent; William II (later the Conqueror) duke of Normandy
	death of Cnut
1037	death of Archbishop Robert of Rouen; Mauger elected
1038	Byzantine attempt to reconquer Sicily with Norman mercenaries
1042	Edward, son of Æthelred and Emma, becomes king of England
	William II starts to rule independently in Normandy
	William Iron Arm ruling in Apulia
1043	William II captures the castle of Falaise from Thurstan Goz
c. 1044	castle built at Squillace by William Iron Arm
1045	death of Rainulf of Aversa

1046	death of William Iron Arm; succeeded by Drogo
c. 1046/47	Robert Guiscard arrives in southern Italy
1047	battle of Val-ès-Dunes
1049	Leo IX elected pope
1050	marriage of Duke William and Matilda of Flanders
1051	Robert of Jumièges appointed archbishop of Canterbury
	Godwine family exiled
	according to the D version of the Anglo-Saxon Chronicle, William II visits England
	death of Drogo; succeeded by Humphrey in Apulia
1052	rebellion of William of Arques, count of Talou in Normandy
1053	17 June: battle of Civitate
1054	Henry I of France defeated at Mortemer
	death of Pope Leo IX
1055	Mauger deposed as archbishop of Rouen and Maurilius elected
	Victor II elected pope
1056	death of Emperor Henry III; succeeded by Henry IV
1057	battle of Varaville
	death of Humphrey; Robert Guiscard succeeds in Apulia
1058	Richard, nephew of Rainulf of Aversa becomes prince of Capua
1059	Nicholas II elected pope and recognizes Norman possessions in southern Italy
	synod of Melfi
1060	Philip I king of France
1061	Alexander II elected pope following death of Nicholas II
	start of conquest of Sicily
1062	William II takes Maine
1063	battle of Cerami
1064	Harold Godwineson crosses the Channel to visit William II of Normandy
1066	5 January: death of Edward the Confessor; succeeded by Harold Godwineson as king of England
	dedication of the abbey of La Trinité in Caen
	20 September: battle of Fulford
	25 September: battle of Stamford Bridge; Harald Hadraada and Tostig Godwineson killed

	14 October: battle of Hastings
	25 December: coronation of Duke William II of Normandy as king of England
1067	death of Maurilius, archbishop of Rouen; John of Avranches elected
	construction of Chepstow castle begins
1069	death of Ealdred, archbishop of York; succeeded by Thomas of Bayeux who begins rebuilding York minster.
1069–70	Harrying of the North
1070	Penitential Ordinance; deposition of Stigand as archbishop of Canterbury and election of Lanfranc
	rebuilding of Canterbury cathedral begins
1071	fall of Palermo
1073	Gregory VII (d. 1085) elected pope following death of Nicholas II
1075	so-called Barons' Revolt in England
	Robert Guiscard and his nephew Robert of Loritello excommunicated by Gregory VII
1076	execution of Earl Waltheof
	construction of Colchester castle begins
1078	death of Richard I of Capua; succeeded by his son Jordan
1079	death of John, archbishop of Rouen; William Bona Anima elected
1083	death of Matilda of Flanders
1085	death of Robert Guiscard; succeeded in Apulia and Calabria by Roger Borsa
	William the Conqueror commissions Domesday Book
1086	presentation of Domesday Book to King William
1087	September: death of William the Conqueror; succeeded by Robert Curthose as duke of Normandy and William Rufus as king of England
1090	rebellion in Rouen led by Conan against Robert Curthose
	death of Jordan of Capua; succeeded by his son Richard II
1091	end of conquest of Sicily
1093	Anselm elected archbishop of Canterbury
	work begins on Durham cathedral
	consecration of the newly rebuilt Winchester cathedral

1095	preaching of the first crusade by Pope Urban II
1096	Robert Curthose joins the first crusade
	massacre of the Jews in Rouen
1098	Bohemond becomes prince of Antioch
1099	capture of Jerusalem by the crusaders
1100	death of William Rufus; Henry I king of England
1101	death of Count Roger I of Sicily; succeeded by Simon
1105	death of Simon in Sicily; succeeded by Roger II
1106	28 September: battle of Tinchebray where Henry I defeats his brother Robert Curthose and beomes duke of Normandy as well as king of England
	death of Richard II of Capua; succeeded by his brother Robert I
1108	Louis VI king of France
1111	death of Roger Borsa; succeeded by William
	death of Bohemond: succeeded by his nephew Tancred as prince of Antioch
1112	death of Tancred
1120	death of Robert I of Capua; succeeded by his brother Jordan II
1126	Bohemond II, son of Bohemond, becomes prince of Antioch
1127	death of William; Roger II, heir to Hauteville, lands on the mainland of Italy
	death of Jordan II of Capua
1130	Christmas: coronation of Roger II as king of Sicily
	death of Bohemond II
1132	work begins on Roger II's Capella Palatina in Palermo
1133	Bayeux Inquest
1135	death of Henry I
1135–53	period of civil war between King Stephen and Empress Matilda, known as the Anarchy
1138	death of Pope Anacletus II; Innocent II elected
	battle of the Standard
c. 1141	death of Orderic Vitalis
1143	foundation of La Martorana
	death of Innocent II
1144–53	various north African territories captured by the Sicilian Normans

1154	al-Idrīsī's *Book of Roger* completed
	death of King Stephen; Henry II king of England.
	death of Roger II of Sicily; succeeded by William I, 'the Bad'
1156–60	Sicilian kingdom loses north African territories
1162	La Zisa, Palermo, built
1166	death of William I of Sicily; succeeded by William II, 'the Good'
1175	Meath established as an Anglo-Norman lordship in Ireland
1177	Ulster established as an Anglo-Norman lordship in Ireland
1180	Philip II Augustus king of France
1189	death of William II of Sicily
	death of Henry II of England; succeeded by Richard I
1190	massacre of the Jews in York
1194	Emperor Henry VI conquers Sicily
1199	death of King Richard I of England; succeeded by John
1204	loss of Normandy by King John to the French king Philip II Augustus
1220s–30s	deportation of Muslims from Sicily

Table 1: Simplified genealogy of the counts and dukes (in bold type) of Normandy 911–1204

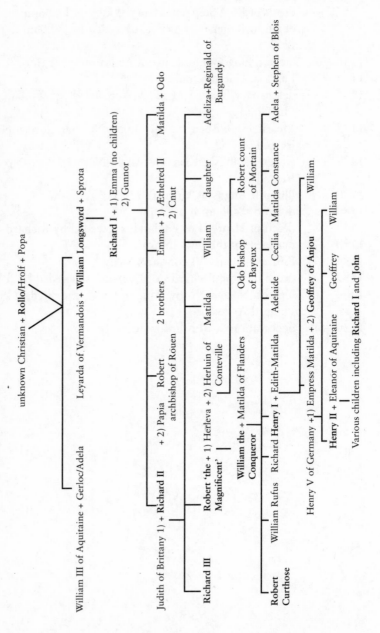

Table 2: Simplified genealogy of the kings of England in the eleventh century with regnal years

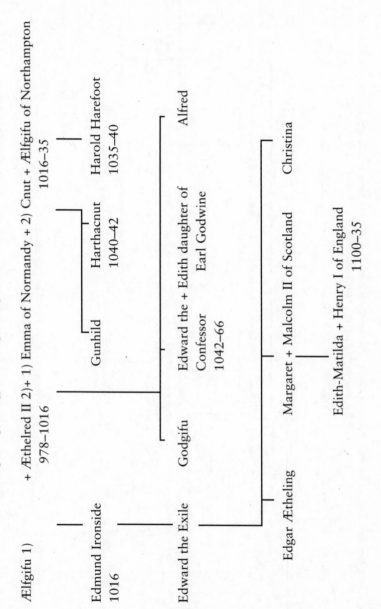

Table 3: Simplified genealogy of the descendants of Tancred of Hauteville (including kings of Sicily in bold and princes of Antioch in italics) and descendants of Anquetil, brother of Rainulf of Aversa

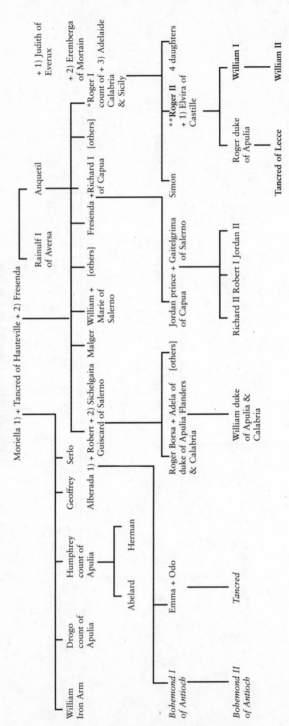

* Roger I also had children by a concubine
** Roger II had a further two wives

Introduction

The story of the Normans begins with a dream. Rollo, the chief of a small band of Viking adventurers,

> seemed to behold himself placed on a mountain far higher than the highest, in a Frankish dwelling. And on the summit of this mountain he saw a spring of sweet-smelling water flowing, and himself washing in it, and by it made whole from the contagion of leprosy [...] and finally, while he was still staying on top of that mountain, he saw about the base of it many thousands of birds of different kinds and various colours, but with red wings extending in such numbers and so far and so wide that he could not catch sight of where they ended, however hard he looked. And they went one after the other in harmonious incoming flights and sought the spring on the mountain, and washed themselves, swimming together as they do when rain is coming; and when they had all been anointed by this miraculous dipping, they all ate together in a suitable place, without being separated into genera or species, and without any disagreement or dispute, as if they were friends sharing food. And they carried off twigs and worked rapidly to build nests; and furthermore, they willing yielded to his command in the vision.[1]

We will return to this episode in the final chapter, but in Dudo of Saint-Quentin's *History of the Normans*, Rollo took heed of the omens in the dream and founded a territory that became the duchy of Normandy, uniting various groups under his lead. Later chroniclers recounted how Rollo's descendants and those of his followers conquered and ruled kingdoms in England and Sicily and led armies on crusade.

Rollo himself is a bit of an enigma. Viking society in the ninth and tenth centuries was primarily an oral culture, so the written

1

Fig.1: Rollo's tomb in Rouen cathedral (modern copy of destroyed thirteenth-century original)

sources that describe his origins were all written later and, for the most part, by churchmen writing within the Frankish historical milieu. Two traditions broadly emerged: one, led by Dudo, placed Rollo in Denmark; the other, based on much later saga evidence, gave him a Norwegian background and the name Rolf or Hrolf Ganger. These sagas are Orkneyinga saga, written at the turn of the twelfth and thirteenth centuries, and the *Heimskringla* of Snorri Sturluson, a historical saga of the Norwegian kings composed in *c.* 1220. The *Heimskringla*, although late, contains echoes of earlier traditions through the inclusion of skaldic poetry – verse written by the skalds (court poets) of the previous era. The poem in question here was written by Rolf's mother, Hild, and laments his outlawry and exile from Norway.[2] This would place him among the significant group of people forced out of their homeland by the ambition and growing power of the Norwegian king Harald Finehair (d. *c.* 932). Rolf's compatriots would go on to settle Iceland and establish Viking colonies elsewhere in York and the Scottish isles.

Rollo/Rolf was simultaneously just one of many Viking leaders who had been raiding the North Sea littoral, including the coasts of Scotland, England, modern-day Belgium and the Netherlands, and France for a century prior to the foundation of Normandy in 911. Annals written close to the time of these raids show that rulers initially tried to resist the incursion of the Norsemen by force and when that failed, they tried to buy them off or give them land to settle in the hope they could resist future attacks. What is crucial to the story of the Normans and what marks them out as different is the fact that none of these settlements on mainland Europe were as long-lived as Normandy. This region survived as an autonomous principality within the Frankish (later French) kingdom until 1204 when Philip II Augustus of France captured it from King John of England.

This book deals in the main with the story of the Normans in the tenth and eleventh centuries as they established territories in Normandy, England, southern Italy and Sicily, and the Holy Land. It is important to note here that the sphere of Norman activity was much wider. Following the invasion and conquest of England in 1066, William the Conqueror and his successors began to push into lands held by the Welsh princes and the Scottish kings before crossing the Irish sea and establishing an Anglo-Norman colony along much of the east coast of Ireland in the 1170s. As well as founding principalities in the Mediterranean and Middle East, Normans fought the Muslims in Spain and, under the kings of Sicily, temporarily conquered part of north Africa. Robert Guiscard, duke of Apulia, also spent the last years of his life campaigning in the Balkans. In a short book, it is clearly not possible to incorporate everything and so the focus is primarily on Normandy, England and southern Italy and Sicily, as these areas have material that makes it possible to highlight points of comparison and difference in the experiences of the Normans.

Previous histories of the Normans have tended to focus on one aspect of their past, for example the conquest of England or the settlement of southern Italy. This is hardly surprising, as both events and the processes they engendered led to long-lasting changes and developments in those countries, some of which are discussed later in this volume. One of the main aims here is to highlight differences between the Normans' experiences. In so doing, this volume questions the idea of the Normans as a single *gens* or people and emphasizes their adaptability and the fluidity of what it meant to be Norman, a theme more fully explored in the concluding chapter. One of the other key differences to note is the centrality of the sources about the Normans. At times this book is about how historians read sources and how those readings change as we revisit familiar material with new questions and perspectives. As such I have placed a strong emphasis on social and cultural aspects of the Norman past, drawing on chronicles, archaeological evidence and material culture. This book should, therefore, be seen as part of an on-going dialogue between the historians writing now and our medieval predecessors.

In terms of solidifying their place in the political geography of the early Middle Ages, the people who became the Normans had one other great advantage: they commissioned, inspired and otherwise generated a large amount of historical writing. In the main these histories were written by churchmen who were often aware of, and used, each other's work. We would be unwise, however, to think that the fact that the historians were clerics led to a homogeneous outlook. They wrote from a variety of perspectives, notably to explain who these people who became known as the Normans were, to justify the settlement or conquest of various territories and to make sense of cataclysmic events like the conquest of England in 1066 or the first crusade. The religious background of many writers meant that some of the works considered here paid particular attention to the Normans' role in God's divine plan for humanity, for example the *Ecclesiastical History* of Orderic Vitalis or Geoffrey Malaterra's *Deeds of Count Roger*. It is also important to note that just because the majority of writers were male, women's voices were not necessarily excluded. Histories written by women were very rare: the Byzantine princess Anna Comnena's biography of her father Emperor Alexius is a notable exception. They were, however, crucial eyewitnesses, guardians of family memory and otherwise provided important information for the chroniclers as well as commissioning works themselves.

It is possible to group various medieval chroniclers depending on subject matter and date. We noted that the history of the Normans, in the sense of a written record of how an individual or group understood events to have occurred, began with Dudo of Saint-Quentin. Dudo himself was not a Norman, but a canon from a community in Vermandois who originally found himself in Normandy as an ambassador from the count of Vermandois to the court of Richard I. Dudo was, however, steeped in Frankish traditions of scholarship and thus well placed to provide the descendants of Rollo with the foundation history they lacked. Although he was initially commissioned by Richard I in 996, most of his work was completed in the early decades of the eleventh century under his son, Richard II. Dudo's chronicle is the only source we have for much of Normandy's earliest history. Like all narrative sources, it cannot be taken at face value and it was not the author's intention to provide an account of what actually happened. Dudo combined legends, history and poetry, drawing on classical scholarship in his account of the Normans' Viking antecedents and first three rulers (Rollo, William Longsword and Richard I). Dudo's history formed the basis of much of the later writing.

William of Jumièges, a monk of the abbey of Jumièges in the Seine valley that had close connections with the ducal house, edited, revised and expanded Dudo's history to include accounts of the dukes up to William II, later the Conqueror. He initially wrote his chronicle in the closing years of the 1050s or early 1060s before taking up his pen again after the conquest of England in 1066 to include an account of William's campaigns up to 1070. Known in Latin as the *Gesta Normannorum ducum*, which translates as *Deeds of the dukes of the Normans*,[3] William's work provided opportunities for later historians to hone their skills. As well as numerous anonymous continuators, it was interpolated and expanded by two of the twelfth century's most significant monastic chroniclers, Orderic Vitalis and Robert of Torigni, who continued the history into the reign of Henry I.

The last of the major eleventh-century historians considered here is William of Poitiers. Rather than writing a history of all the Norman dukes or continuing the work of Dudo and William of Jumièges, William of Poitiers composed a biography of just one duke, William the Conqueror. He was well placed to do this, as he was a chaplain at the ducal court and either witnessed events himself or could talk to eyewitnesses to other happenings. Like Dudo, William of Poitiers was schooled in the classical tradition and he drew on this learning extensively to provide a florid and at times sycophantic account of William's life. For some reason, William stopped writing in the early 1070s:[4] historians have since speculated that he had fallen out of favour so chose to remain silent.[5] The *Gesta Guillelmi* as it exists today is incomplete and survives only in a post-medieval copy; the original was almost certainly destroyed in the Cotton Library fire of 1731.

Towards the end of the eleventh century, medieval historians were beginning to write chronicles concerning the Normans in southern Italy. Our information about some of these individuals is rather vague. The first account was written by a monk of the famous abbey of Montecassino called Amatus around 1080. Amatus recorded the arrival of small groups of Norman adventurers in Apulia and their gradual take over of Apulia, Calabria and Sicily. Like all accounts, this chronicle presents significant problems for the historian. Not only does it not survive in its original manuscript, but the earliest copy we have is in a French translation of the fourteenth century. Enough, however, survives in other near-contemporary works, notably the early twelfth-century Montecassino chronicle written by Leo Marsicanus, for scholars to be sure that the fourteenth-century translation is reasonably faithful to the original.[6] Amatus was ambivalent in his attitude towards these new arrivals. He was initially critical of their attitude towards the Church and the appropriation of ecclesiastical lands; however, once the Normans became benefactors and protectors of his monastery, his tone became far more positive.

The other two historians of the early Norman settlement of Italy were Geoffrey Malaterra and William of Apulia. Geoffrey, writing in the 1090s, was certainly a monk (in the monastery of Sant'Agata at Catania on Sicily) and possibly a Norman immigrant, though his origins are by no means certain. He could equally well have been a native of Italy or from the county of Perche to the south of Normandy.[7] Geoffrey's history is less a history of the Normans and more the achievements of one man in particular, Count Roger of Sicily, brother of one of the most charismatic and ruthless southern Italian Normans, Robert Guiscard.[8] Written to explain and justify the conquest of Calabria and Sicily and with a court audience firmly in mind, Geoffrey's *Deeds of Count Roger* contains a mix of history, exhortation and humour which suggests parts of it were designed to be read aloud and to entertain.

William of Apulia's origins are even more obscure. It is likely he was a Lombard, although William is a name traditionally associated with the Normans. It is also possible that he was a layman, rather than a cleric, as there are far fewer religious motifs in his work than that of his colleagues.[9] He also wrote in an entirely different genre, namely poetry in Latin hexameters detailing the deeds of Robert Guiscard, and his poem dates from the late 1090s.[10] Like Dudo and William of Poitiers, William of Apulia's work was a learned history full of allusions to Greek and Latin authors and sophisticated in its structure.

The Norman Conquest of England was a deeply traumatic event. By the end of 14 October 1066 the greater proportion of the English aristocracy lay dead on the field of Battle. Aside from brief notices in the Anglo-Saxon Chronicle (annals that record events year-by-year, though they could be written up much later),[11] sustained historical writing and explanation had to wait for a generation or so after. The most comprehensive among these were William of Malmesbury, Henry of Huntingdon and Orderic Vitalis – the so-called Anglo-Norman historians, as all three men were of mixed English and French or Norman parentage.

We have already mentioned Orderic Vitalis as he was one of the interpolaters of William of Jumièges's *Gesta Normannorum ducum*.[12] Orderic was born in Atcham near Shrewsbury, grew up in the shadow of the new Norman buildings and received his initial education from a local priest. At the age of ten, his French father sent him to the monastery of Saint-Evroult on the southern border of Normandy to become a monk. He never saw his family again. Orderic felt the sense of exile keenly, but found purpose in his monastic vocation and history writing. His *Ecclesiastical History* began initially as an account of the monastic community of Saint-Evroult, but rapidly expanded to include the history of the Normans in Normandy, England and southern Italy, an account of the first crusade, and a sacred history of the world. As such it is vast in scope and provides a wealth of detail regarding Norman society, including the role of women. Unfortunately its very size made it unattractive to copyists in the Middle Ages and Orderic is more renowned now than he was in his own time. Although writing firmly in the context of Norman Benedictine monasticism, Orderic was critical of the Normans' actions and character. He particularly condemned William's use of extreme violence during the Harrying of the North in 1069-70. The *Ecclesiastical History* was written over a long period of time from *c.* 1114 to shortly before his death in *c.* 1141.

William of Malmesbury was also a monk, but at the English abbey of Malmesbury. He wrote several works of history including

Fig.2: The abbey of Saint-Evroult in Normandy, home to Orderic Vitalis: the ruins date from the thirteenth century

the *Deeds of the Kings of the English*, the *Deeds of the Bishops of the English* and a shorter *Historia novella*, which dealt with the civil war of the mid-twelfth century.[13] William has been called the greatest historian of the twelfth century. He travelled extensively to make use of libraries in various religious houses as well as drawing on the reserves of his own scholarship. Like Orderic, his attitude towards the Normans is ambivalent and at times directly hostile. For example, he was conscious of what the new rulers had done to improve and ornament the Church, but he was critical of their behaviour in other aspects of life. Unlike Orderic and William, Henry of Huntingdon (d. *c.* 1157) was a secular cleric – an archdeacon in Huntingdon. Henry's starting point was the Anglo-Saxon Chronicle and his writing follows that annalistic (year-by-year) format.[14]

The twelfth century also saw a change in genre in the writing of the Norman history. In the eleventh and early twelfth centuries, chronicles were written in Latin and usually in prose, though authors could and did include poetry within their texts, notably Dudo and Henry of Huntingdon. In the second half of the twelfth century, King

Henry II of England commissioned writers to produce not only verse chronicles, but verse chronicles in the vernacular Norman-French. The first of these writers was Wace, a canon of the cathedral of Bayeux and the author considered in detail here. Unfortunately, Wace was a slow writer and Henry an impatient king. Tired of waiting, Henry sacked Wace and passed the task onto Benoît of Sainte-Maure, who also failed to complete the task. There might well be more to Wace's loss of the commission: Martin Aurell argues that Wace failed to place enough emphasis on the sacral nature of the Norman dukes, whereas Charity Urbanski notes that Wace cast doubts on Henry I's (Henry II's grandfather) claim to the throne of England and dukedom of Normandy.[15] These verse histories contain more elements of the romance and *chanson de geste* traditions, suited to a court audience. They were also, at least in the case of Wace, serious works of history designed to provide examples and models of behaviour to follow as well as to make politically sharp points.

The history of the Normans is not merely recorded in the pages of chronicles, but also preserved in material culture. In one case, a narrative of the Norman Conquest of 1066 was sewn. In the Bayeux Tapestry, probably commissioned by Bishop Odo of Bayeux, William the Conqueror's half-brother, and embroidered in Canterbury, we can read the Norman story of Edward the Confessor's promise of the throne to William, Harold's treachery in seizing that throne after Edward's death, preparations for the invasion and the battle itself. This unique artefact has become synonymous with the Normans and extensively parodied in modern political cartoons. Napoleon studied it ahead of a planned invasion and its value as propaganda was recognized by Himmler during the Nazi occupation of France in World War II. The conquest in reverse – Operation Overlord, the Allied D-Day landings in June 1944 – has also been depicted in a similar vein.

The Normans left behind them some of the most visible reminders of the medieval past we have in the areas in which they settled. The eleventh century saw a flourishing of monastic foundations across the duchy exhibiting magnificent Romanesque architecture that still survives today. Most notable are the twin abbeys of Saint-Etienne and La Trinité in Caen, founded by William and his wife Matilda of Flanders. The Normans encouraged this style of building across the Channel, initially through Edward the Confessor's Westminster

Abbey and then later with the building of castles and cathedrals post-1066. Durham cathedral, the White Tower and Chepstow Castle all stand as very visible reminders of the changes wrought by William and his sons. Norman history is also inscribed upon the landscape and we can think here particularly of Castle Acre in Norfolk, a planned Norman settlement with town, castle and priory around which an older Roman road was re-routed to display the assemblage to its best advantage.

In contrast, the architecture associated with the Normans in southern Italy and Sicily reflects less a narrative of conquest and more a blending of the different cultures – Greek, Latin and Muslim – that Count Roger and his successors found there. The first Norman king, Roger II, oversaw the construction of the Capella Palatina in Palermo that exhibited influences from the Romanesque style so familiar in northern Europe, Muslim craftsmanship in terms of pavements and ceilings, and a Greek taste for mosaic work. Members of Roger's court, notably the admiral George of Antioch, also commissioned mosaics, the most famous being the depiction of the king's coronation by Christ in George's church, La Martorana. These images raise an interesting question. Throughout this introduction, and indeed, throughout much historiography, we speak of the Normans as if they were one people. Books are written entitled *The Normans* or *The Normans in Europe*, big research projects refer to 'The Norman Edge' or websites hosted by academic institutions refer to 'The Norman World', but are we right to think in this way? Do the people who produced such wonders as the Sicilian mosaics have anything meaningful in common with those who invaded England? Should we be thinking less of the 'Norman people' and more of the 'Norman peoples'?

The final chapter of this book will attempt to unpick these questions in more detail, set against the development of modern historical writing on the Normans. It is unsurprising that historians living after the Middle Ages have found in the pages of chronicles and in viewing buildings inspiration to research and write. In the Anglophone world particularly, the story of the Normans has been told with an eye on 1066. The idea of the Norman Yoke during the Civil War was very strong, namely that the Normans had invaded and deprived the English of their liberties and freedoms. Later groups of historians, both in Britain and also in continental Europe, studied these people with regard to the development of institutions and law.

Ideas surrounding race, ethnicity and identity of the Normans have been more recent concerns, particularly following Ralph Davis's publication of *The Norman Myth,* which put forward the idea that Norman identity was a creation of the twelfth-century chroniclers, notably Orderic Vitalis. These views have been subsequently revised and challenged. Historians have also spoken of a 'Norman empire', which was then abandoned in favour of a 'Norman diaspora'. Most recently cultural and social history has come to the fore, asking questions about gender (how society views and constructs ideas about men, women and the roles and qualities associated with each sex), marriage and social interaction.

What this rich body of scholarship shows is that there is not, nor can be, one definitive history of the Normans. The story of the Normans is one that was told many times during the Middle Ages and countless times since by successive generations of historians. Each generation stretching back to Dudo of Saint-Quentin, who wrote the first official history of the Normans, through to historians writing today has provided its own gloss and own version or interpretation of the events that led to the foundation of Normandy in 911 and later conquests. During the Middle Ages, the Normans were written about both positively and negatively, but rarely from a neutral perspective. They have inspired admiration and condemnation, have been looked to for emulation and examples of what not to do. Post-medieval historians are more measured in their tones, but trenchant views exist as will be seen below. This book does not, therefore, seek to be comprehensive: it aims, as its title suggests, to tell *a* history of the Normans. In contrast to other volumes in this area, it does so with particular regard for the medieval Norman historical tradition embedded within modern social and cultural history. It is comparative in scope, considering the areas of Europe in which the Normans settled. The first three chapters comprise an examination of Normandy, England and southern Italy focusing on the Rollo, William the Conqueror and the Hauteville brothers, Robert Guiscard and Roger. Chapters 4 to 6 consider aspects of Norman history thematically, notably society, the Church, and cultural exchange, before Chapter 7 discusses how Norman history has developed and where it might go in the future. It is, however, in the region that became known as Normandy that the story starts and so in Normandy we must begin.

1

ROLLO AND THE SETTLEMENT OF NORMANDY

After a number of years raiding up and down the rivers of northern France, reaching as far as the city of Chartres, or so Dudo says, Rollo met Charles the Simple, king of the Franks, at Saint-Clair-sur-Epte. Here, Dudo of Saint-Quentin tells us, Charles granted Rollo the land around Rouen between the Epte and the sea in hereditary right. Not content, Rollo pressed for more, citing the fact that the land could not sustain his followers as, although fertile, it was largely uncultivated. Charles then offered him Flanders, dismissed by Rollo as marshy, before suggesting the land to the west (the Avranchin and Cotentin) as an alternative. In return, according to Dudo, Rollo was to convert to Christianity and accept baptism, as well as to marry Charles's daughter Gisla. To seal the bargain, he 'immediately put his hands between the hands of the king', but considered it beneath his dignity to kiss the king's foot and deputed one of his followers to do this on his behalf. Instead of bending down to kiss the king's foot, this man raised Charles's leg, thus throwing the unfortunate monarch onto his back, to the great amusement of the Vikings.[1] The significance of this act, and whether it meant that Rollo held his land from the king, has been widely debated.[2] What is more important is that, according to Dudo's account, the land that Duke William II (the Conqueror) held as Normandy on the eve of 1066, from the rivers Bresle in the east to the Couesnon in the west, and from the sea to

13

the borders with Maine, came into being in one moment through a grant made by the Frankish king and legitimized by conversion and marriage.

Dudo's account contains many of the elements traditionally associated with the settlement of Viking war bands in other parts of northern Europe, notably England and Frisia (encompassing modern-day the Netherlands and part of Germany): land in exchange for a cessation of violence, acceptance of Christianity, and also marriage into the ruling elite.[3] Rollo was the epitome of the Viking turned respectable. Writing a century after these events had taken place, very little Dudo says is substantiated by sources from the tenth century beyond the grant of land to Northmen operating in the Seine. Although the outline of events was based on the annals of Flodoard of Reims and oral history from the ducal house, much else of what Dudo wrote, particularly his borrowings from the *Aeneid*, led many historians to dismiss his work as little more than fiction prior to the publication of Eleanor Searle's important article, 'Frankish Rivalries and Norse Warriors'.[4] Nonetheless, Dudo's history became the basis for the writing of subsequent medieval historians like William of Jumièges and Orderic Vitalis. We need, therefore, to understand why our limited sources present us with such radically different pictures of Norman settlement and why Dudo wrote what he did.

This chapter looks at the settlement of Rollo and his Vikings in the Seine valley and the creation of what became the duchy of Normandy. It will also consider how historians writing in the modern era have changed the way they read the medieval sources. We will begin with a discussion of the settlement of Normandy as presented by the tenth-century sources and analyse Dudo's account in more detail in order to understand why he wrote as he did, before moving to the circumstances of the creation of Normandy and how Rollo's dynasty was established and survived. This chapter ends with a consideration of Richard I's foundation of a religious community on the site of the ducal castle at Fécamp. First of all, however, it is necessary to review the ninth century context in order to understand the circumstances that made it possible for Rollo and his followers to settle.

THE NINTH-CENTURY CONTEXT

In order to place the settlement of Normandy in a wider context, we must begin almost a century before and set the story of Charles's grant to Rollo against the struggles between the descendants of the Carolingian emperor Charlemagne and the Viking raiders.[5] After Charlemagne's death, his empire began to disintegrate as his sons struggled for dominance. The division was formalized in the treaty of Verdun of 843, which split the empire between the three sons of Louis the Pious, though this did not prevent future infighting every time a particular ruler died. The result was a steady decline in royal authority and control of territory with successive weak kings leading to the eventual division of Francia into east and west kingdoms following the deposition of Charles the Fat in 888.[6] In addition to dynastic squabbles, more and more Northmen made an appearance on the rivers of Francia as the century progressed, sometimes spending longer periods of time in proto-settlements over winter. The Frankish annals, short accounts of events written according to the year in which they took place, record Viking raids in the Seine valley as early as 841. In this year the annals of Saint-Bertin note:

> Danish pirates sailed down the Channel and attacked Rouen, plundering the town with pillage, fire and sword, slaughtered or took captive the monks and the rest of the population and laid waste all the monasteries and other places along the banks of the Seine, or else took large payments and left them thoroughly terrified.[7]

This account is corroborated by the annals of one of those monasteries, Saint-Wandrille. These name the Viking leader as Oskar, and note that the monks of Saint-Denis on the outskirts of Paris ransomed sixty-five captives from the community's lands. The towns and monasteries of the Seine valley were, however, too attractive a target and when, after a series of raids, the Vikings reached Paris in 845, King Charles the Bald paid them '7000 pounds of silver' to go away and leave his people alone.[8] The mid-ninth century saw an increase in the frequency and scale of the Viking raids in Francia, possibly encouraged by Lothar I as a means of undermining his brother Charles's power. In 841, the annals of Saint-Bertin record that Lothar granted the Frisian town of Walcheren (in what is now the southern Netherlands) and its surroundings to the Viking Harald in order to secure his support. This was an act that earned him the condemnation of the annalist for putting Christians under the rule of 'men who worshipped demons'.[9]

The descendants of Charlemagne also had to deal with another dangerous threat that would prove significant in the creation of Normandy: the Bretons, a group that had never been part of the Carolingian empire. Like the Vikings, this group took advantage of the decline in royal authority following the death of Charlemagne. In 862, to counter this threat and also to bolster defence against Viking incursions, Charles granted an area of land known as the Neustrian March to a powerful noble, Robert the Strong. This was a buffer created by Charlemagne between the empire and the Breton territory, part of which comprised Normandy. Robert was not wholly successful as the Bretons acquired the Avranchin and Cotentin in what is now Lower Normandy in 867 and advanced further east towards Bayeux. The grant of the Neustrian March to Robert, however, had a much wider political significance and one in which the 'Normans' would play a significant part. Robert's descendants founded the dynasty, known to history as the Capetians, that eventually in 987 succeeded the Carolingians as rulers of Francia after the crown had passed between the two families for a century. The settlement of Rollo and his Vikings in the Seine valley therefore took place against a backdrop of dynastic struggle, competing interests and the fragmentation of royal authority. Anyone able to exploit these fault lines and negotiate the resulting complex web of alliances would do very well.

THE SETTLEMENT OF NORMANDY ACCORDING TO THE TENTH-CENTURY SOURCES

Our understanding of the settlement of Normandy is complicated by the fact that Dudo's is the only account of the treaty of Saint-Clair-sur-Epte that exists and was written around eighty years later. The original treaty, if it ever existed, no longer survives. Contemporary entries in the Frankish annals and some of the later charters of Charles the Simple do, however, survive and through these it is possible to arrive at a narrative of Norman settlement that helps place Dudo's version in context.

The date of Rollo's arrival in the area around Rouen is a matter of conjecture. The eleventh-century historical tradition, following Dudo, places his appearance around 876,[10] but it is more likely his activity in the Seine valley dates from the early tenth century. Historians place the formal land grant sometime between 905/906, when the last Carolingian charters showing direct evidence of government in Normandy were issued under Charles the Simple, and 918 when a charter refers to the grant retrospectively.[11] In lieu of a firm date, 911, the date given by Dudo, has been taken as the traditional moment of the foundation of the duchy. The 918 charter provides a suggestion for why this territory was given to Rollo. This document records that Charles the Simple made a grant of land previously belonging to a defunct abbey to the monastery of Saint-Germain-des-Prés near Paris 'except that part of the abbey['s lands] which we have granted to the Normans of the Seine, namely to Rollo and his companions for the defence of the kingdom'.[12] This excerpt probably means that the land was granted to Rollo in order that he could defend it from raids by other groups of Vikings. In other words, he had entered into some form of reciprocal arrangement with the king and this may well have involved a formal recognition of Charles's overlordship. Terms like 'vassal' and 'homage' that occur in modern historical writing are not unambiguous, however, and the evidence does not permit any certainty in understanding how and by what conditions Rollo held the grant.[13] The area covered by the treaty is not specified, but Flodoard, a canon of the cathedral of Reims, records in his *History of the Church of Reims* that Rollo was given Rouen and the *pagi* (Carolingian administrative units) on the coast and surrounding the city: Talou, Caux, Roumois and parts of the Vexin and Evrecin.[14] This is by no means the huge swathe of land that Dudo records, nor was it exceptional, as Vikings had already settled in Frisia.[15] What was unusual was that the settlement in Normandy lasted whereas the others fizzled out.

Flodoard of Reims provides additional information regarding the settlement of the Normans. Although he was writing at quite some geographic distance from the English Channel, Flodoard suggests Rollo and then William Longsword accrued their territory in three separate grants as they took advantage of political divisions elsewhere in the Frankish realm. In this narrative, the Normans acquired Maine and the Bessin in 924 and then, under Rollo's son

William Longsword, 'the territory of the Bretons, which is situated on the sea-coast', namely the Cotentin and the Avranchin in 933.[16] This was the territory the Bretons themselves had been granted in 867. This tripartite grant is accepted as the most likely version of events, but grants of land do not necessarily translate into the ability to exercise authority over that territory and can mask longer-term developments as will be discussed below.[17] What we can say is that, according to the Frankish sources, Rollo was granted land in the Seine valley in return for service to the king and that gradually the Normans acquired more territory through a series of raids and negotiations. The process by which they were able to rule this territory effectively was, however, a slow and bumpy one.

Flodoard's opinion of the Normans is also a point of difference between his writing and that of Dudo. These Vikings were not innocent victims of plots by the Franks as depicted in Dudo's account of the assassination of William Longsword, but truce breakers, greedy for land. Flodoard does not make much of a distinction between the Seine valley Norse and those elsewhere as he recounts episodes of raiding, pillaging and devastation. His *History of the Church of Reims* also sheds fascinating light on the settlers' relationship with the Christian faith. The archbishop of Reims, Harvey, was asked for advice by his counterpart in Rouen, Guy, on how to deal with the Northmen who converted, relapsed and converted again. If Rollo had been active in the Seine valley earlier than the first decade of the tenth century, it is possible that he was one of the lapsed Scandinavian converts.[18] Flodoard's Vikings of the Seine are a very different people indeed from the pious converts we find in Dudo's later account.

DUDO'S ACCOUNT

Dudo's *History of the Normans* formed the basis of all the major Norman historical writing in the duchy from the mid-eleventh century onwards. Placing Dudo in his context and understanding why he wrote what he did and for whom is crucial. If Dudo is read less for 'facts' and more for what he was trying to achieve in creating a history for the descendants of Rollo, his account becomes far more interesting: it reflects the ambitions of the Norman rulers, his own concerns, and fits into a wider political discourse in late tenth- and early eleventh-century Francia. Having said that, it is easy to see why scholars in the past dismissed episodes in the *History* as fantasy, as there are certainly passages which, if read literally, strain credulity. A good example is his account of the origins of the ancestors of Rollo. In terms of geography, he places the Danish ancestors of the Normans initially on the island of 'Scanza' and thence to 'Dacia', the Roman province on the Danube, a long way from the northern homelands of the Danes.[19] In doing this he drew on sources from the world of late antiquity, notably Jordanes's history of the Goths. This is not simply a case of Dudo muddling up his geography, but, as Ewan Johnson notes, a device to situate the Normans within a classical schema that gave them some antiquity as a people.[20] Dudo goes on to describe the customs of the Scandinavian people, including a graphic description of human sacrifice to the god Thor, which again owes more to the writings of classical authors than it does to any original information. Finally, he links the Danes with the Trojans and ancient Greeks, notably from Antenor from whom, he claims, they were descended. Claiming descent from classical peoples was a common device in medieval historical writing. What is important here is that the Franks, the people among whom Rollo and his Vikings settled, also claimed descent from Antenor. Dudo was providing the Normans with a genealogy that did not emphasize their difference from the Franks, but their similarity, or at least an ideal that he thought they should aspire to.

In understanding how and why Dudo provided such a different account, it is necessary to think about for whom he was writing. He was initially commissioned to write a history of the Normans by Duke Richard I, and this was completed under his successor, Richard II. He was well educated and, as we have seen, drew on classical traditions. His position at the ducal court, initially as an ambassador and then as a ducal chaplain, enabled him to garner information and memories from eyewitnesses, including members of the ducal family. Interestingly though, the dedicatory letter at the beginning of his history is addressed not to the dukes, but to Bishop Adalbero of Laon (d. 1030). The seeming disjuncture between the subject matter (the settlement of the Normans) and the addressee (a Frankish bishop) has led historians to advance a number of theories for Dudo's audience and reasons for writing. On the whole most scholars agree that this was a history written very much in the Carolingian tradition; however, Eleanor Searle argued that Dudo should be read as something approaching a Latin saga, 'the victory song of the Norse people'.[21] Searle is right that the history presents a narrative that culminated in a pious duke (Richard I) governing a stable duchy with the succession assured, but her suggestion does not account for everything found in Dudo, particularly the letter to Adalbero. The description of the work as a saga is a step too far. On the one hand Dudo can be read as providing a history for his Norman patrons that suggests they were divinely ordained to take over the land of Normandy and rule justly. It is also possible, if Geoffrey Koziol is correct, to see in the *History of the Normans* a process of coming to terms with the failure of the descendants of Charlemagne to hold on to power and the rise of the Capetians.[22] Without sitting on the fence too much, Dudo both justified and legitimized the settlement, while also explaining it in a framework that made sense for a Carolingian audience. The count of Vermandois, who had initially sent Dudo as an ambassador to the ducal court, had after all refused to recognize the coronation of Hugh Capet and the final passing of the crown from the Carolingian to Capetian dynasty. If we follow the idea that Dudo's is essentially a Carolingian history, it is possible to see how he endeavoured to explain recent developments within their Frankish context.

In this light, Dudo's account of the treaty of Saint-Clair-sur-Epte makes more sense than as a literal account of what happened. We have already noted that many of the elements that go to make up this account can be found elsewhere. The period of Viking settlement coincided with the conversion period in northern Europe, as gradually the Scandinavian kings accepted Christianity for a wide variety of reasons and in turn began to impose it on their people. The Vikings who settled in Francia and England, among other places, were quicker to adopt this new religion than their kin in the homelands of Scandinavia. By doing so, they worked in a frame of reference that was familiar and acceptable to the people among whom they had settled. Rollo's baptism was therefore a recognition of this new reality, though his conversion as presented by Dudo is not unproblematic in the wider context. As stated above, Guy, archbishop of Rouen, had needed to seek advice regarding the repeated apostasy of the Seine valley Vikings, one of whom might well have been Rollo.[23] We see nothing of this in Dudo's account. Guy is not mentioned; instead, we read that the archbishop of Rouen was called Franco. This is pure invention on Dudo's part, but the alternative, a Viking convert not wholly committed to his new faith, was not in keeping with the narrative of legitimate succession Dudo need to present. He therefore had to invent a scenario in which Rollo's baptism could be presented as final. The marriage to Gisla is equally mendacious as not only did the marriage likely not happen, but Gisla, as a daughter of Charles the Simple, either did not exist or was far too young to marry.[24] What Dudo has done here is to borrow the idea of a Frankish marriage from an earlier example: Gisla the daughter of Lothar II, who was married to Godefrid as part of the settlement of Vikings around Walcheren in 882.[25] The union of Rollo and a Frankish princess is a form of acceptance of the Viking leader.

Finally we need to consider the grant of land itself. According to Dudo's account, the region that became the duchy of Normandy, stretching from Eu in the east to the Cotentin peninsula in the west, was covered by the 911 treaty, rather than in the successive grants of land recorded in Flodoard and the other Frankish sources. Again clues lie in the narrative itself. In Dudo's history Charles the Simple's grant was the culmination of the prophetic dream that led Rollo to Normandy in the first place. This was the migration of a band of Vikings to the promised land and from paganism to Christianity, reflecting another theme evident in much medieval historical writing, that of divine providence. The working out of God's purpose in the world was seen in the progress of human history. If God's plan was that Rollo should settle in Normandy, then it follows that the land under the control of the Normans by the time Dudo was writing was granted as a whole. Bearing in mind that the history was commissioned by Richard I and finished under Richard II, Dudo's version of the treaty provided for the antiquity of Normandy. According to Felice Lifshitz, Richard I commissioned this history from Dudo in order to provide justification for and to ease the succession of his son Richard II in light of continuing troubles on the borders.[26] While the timing of the history's completion argues against that reading, it is highly likely that an emphasis on the antiquity of Normandy eased worries about the legitimacy of Rollo and his successors' occupation of the land, when set in the context of the survival of the dynasty, somewhat against the odds. Certainly, the survival of Normandy is all the more remarkable when one considers that Rollo's son, William Longsword was assassinated by a rival count and that William's son, Richard I was only a child at the time of his succession.

THE CREATION OF NORMANDY

The evidence recording the grant of land to Rollo raises the question of whether the creation of Normandy was a deliberate act on the part of Charles the Simple or whether it was a territory that emerged out of a temporary, politically expedient alliance with a group of Vikings. The diploma of 918 discussed above reveals that Rollo was granted land in return for defending the kingdom, presumably from subsequent Viking raids. The creation of Normandy was a result of Rollo, William and Richard I's abilities to exploit the opportunities offered to them, to build on the work of their predecessors and to negotiate a complex web of alliances. In this section it is essential to look beyond the written sources to archaeology and place-name evidence and examine the population and resources of the Seine valley in the tenth century to understand how Rollo was able to form a base as well as looking at some of the dangers posed to the dukes by their enemies, both internal and external. This is a controversial topic and one which has occasioned very differing interpretations.

The river Seine was navigable a long way inland beyond Paris, though access varied depending on the tides and time of year. This allowed the Viking raiders easy access to the wealth of the monasteries and cities as recorded by the Frankish annals for the mid-ninth century. Dudo also stated that the land was depopulated and desolate. Might these factors together explain how a relatively small war band could instigate a take-over of the region? After the successive raids prior to the 880s, many of the religious communities went into exile, taking their relics with them. Jacques Le Maho, the main proponent of the depopulation thesis in modern historiographical debate, has suggested that monasteries like Jumièges and Saint-Wandrille initially maintained links with their port sites along the Seine, leading to continuity in economic activity, but as the raids escalated, the monastic communities migrated further away beyond the borders of what would become Normandy and their lands were taken over by the king. Odo, son of Robert the Strong, enjoyed some success against the Vikings, preventing them from taking Paris and also clearing them from the Seine valley. As this area was closed to them, the Norse war bands raided the Cotentin, forcing the religious communities there and the bishop of Coutances to seek sanctuary further east within the walled city of Rouen.[27] Around this time, Le Maho also suggests that, under royal command, the population of the Seine valley made a tactical withdrawal to the city of Rouen which was more easily fortified and defended and where we see the vestiges of Carolingian institutional authority in the use of the title of count and the royal mint. Archaeological evidence supports the continued presence of some organizing body as the northern defensive wall was partly reconstructed and the Gallo-Roman street plan reorganized to accommodate new houses and settlements. Excavation in the area of the cathedral and the Lycée Camille-Saint-Saëns revealed evidence for metal and bone working suggesting that the manufacturing centres had relocated from the river ports to the city, leaving the harbour sites essentially empty.[28]

If this thesis is correct, then those raiders who chose to settle prior to 911 would have found little opposition in taking land. Le Maho points to the existence of one 'Hunedus', a Viking who sailed down the Seine in 896 and who, he suggests, obtained permission from Charles the Simple to settle in the valley. Le Maho also turns to Dudo and his account of Rollo's early activity. On reaching Saint-Vaast, one of the harbour sites associated with Jumièges, Rollo received a delegation from the archbishop of Rouen, who asked him to spare the city as only non-combatants lived there. The place name evidence would support some form of Scandinavian settlement prior to the treaty of Saint-Clair-sur-Epte: twenty settlement sites associated with economic activity on the river seem to have received new Scandinavian names in the early tenth century, compared with five that retained their Frankish names. This concentration suggests a rapid change of population over a short space of time and is interpreted by Le Maho as evidence for the impact of Scandinavian settlement. In addition Laurent Mazet-Harhoff has considered what evidence we do have in constructing a plausible Scandinavian mental map of the Seine valley. The key topographical point, known as the 'Wind's End' in the nineteenth century, marked the transition from sail to rowing. It was located near Jumièges and was quite possibly the site of a shipyard.[29]

Le Maho's theory is neat, but almost certainly pushes the evidence too far and Janet Nelson urges caution in accepting it uncritically. The main issue here is the speed at which the Norman takeover and settlement would have needed to take place and a tendency to regard it as an event, rather than a process. The evidence is patchy at best. Place names can rarely be dated with the precision demanded here and the textual sources are mainly hagiographical – writings about the lives of saints and the miracles associated with them – in nature and written with a particular agenda in mind. In addition we have little archaeology to support Scandinavian settlement happening at the speed Le Maho believes: it is on the whole scanty and limited. Anne Nissen-Jaubert has summarized our knowledge of Scandinavian settlement in France based on archaeology and concludes that the lack of substantial remains show a process of assimilation and acculturation to Frankish ways. She also draws on place name evidence to support her hypothesis, as many of the Scandinavian toponyms in Normandy are Anglo-Scandinavian in origin. Some of the Viking settlers then were already at one remove from their homeland and so Norse influences would be weaker. In addition, most artefacts that have been tentatively identified as Scandinavian lack proper stratigraphic contexts to date them accurately. For example, the identification of swords found during dredging work in the Seine is based on locations associated with Viking activity documented in written sources.[30]

A better way of thinking about this topic is how Rollo and his followers – a small group of people – were able to establish dominance in this area. Much like the arrival of the Great Winter Army in England in the mid-ninth century, settlement followed acts of violence.[31] If the existing powers were weak, then Viking leaders like Rollo could offer an alternative. In the case of the Seine valley, if the population really was concentrated in Rouen by this point, then that tight focus might well have facilitated the Normans filling a power vacuum and providing a measure of stability to a fractured region, allowing farmers, merchants and so on to operate in a degree of safety. Pierre Bauduin, whose work has done much to elucidate the development of Normandy on its eastern borders, also stresses the importance of process and argues we should place the origins of the duchy in the context of attempts to establish greater stability in a region fragmented by rival powers. He also suggests that the Franks and Norse of the Seine valley found some way of living together that was not predicated on conflict.[32] This would allow for a gradual acceptance of Scandinavians settling in the area and the idea that Rollo was given land in return for defending it against other Vikings fits in well.

A key factor in Rollo's ability to consolidate and his descendants to expand their authority was the city of Rouen itself. Rouen was originally a Gallo-Roman foundation and became the seat of the archbishop from the Merovingian era onwards. It was the regional capital set in a strategically significant location on the river Seine protecting the route into Paris. There is some discussion among historians of the Normans as to the extent to which Rouen was a viable town in the early tenth century, as discussed above. Here we must not be misled by Dudo, who stresses the desolation of Normandy as a whole and the ruins of Rouen in particular. Lifshitz, in contrast, has argued for continuity in the presence of the archbishops and, by extension, representatives of the Carolingians.[33] If we follow Le Maho's suggestion of a strategic withdrawal within its walls, then a remarkable degree of wealth and resources would have been contained within it. Numismatists (people who study coins) have suggested that the mint was still active in the city, as well as in other urban centres in Normandy.[34] Such a concentration would have provided a sound economic basis on which to develop the ducal capital, especially if Lifshitz is correct in her assertion that the archbishops continued to maintain a presence in the city. There is no reason to assume, either, that this redevelopment was solely due to a brief resurgence in royal power in Francia. Elsewhere – York being the primary example – the Vikings themselves acted as spur to economic development. Following the work of Le Maho and Bernard Gauthiez, we can point to developments within the city that were important for ducal power and authority.[35] It is likely that the early Norman rulers, who took the title 'count of Rouen', used the site of the Carolingian palace mentioned by Dudo for their residence, which was located in the south-west angle of the city wall. Connected with this site was a chapel dedicated to St Clement, a popular patron among Scandinavian communities. As the counts became more secure in their territory and possibly in keeping with a

Fig.3: The city of Rouen as it is now

self-image presented by Dudo, Richard I or II (we cannot be certain as to who) built a new castle in the south-eastern corner of the city wall on the modern place de la Haute-Vieille-Tour. Importantly, building on the Romanesque cathedral also began in 965–70 under Richard I and was carried forward by his son Archbishop Robert. What we see here is a strong link between the person of the duke and the archbishop, the temporal power with the spiritual. The focus on Carolingian places of power within the city demonstrates a willingness to adapt to existing structures: the Normans were not trying to reinvent Rouen wholesale. The importance of Rouen as a capital that we find in Dudo and the other Norman historians also shows just how far the descendants of Rollo had come, from their marauding, pagan ancestors.

THE SURVIVAL OF NORMANDY

Having a sound economic basis and a hinterland that was at least not openly hostile was not solely enough for the dukes to establish their authority. They also had to negotiate the different interests and enmities that surrounded them. The long-term survival of Normandy was by no means guaranteed. Not only did the early Norman rulers face opposition from royal forces, but also from the counts bordering their territory and other Viking leaders elsewhere in northern France, including the Loire Valley and the areas around Bayeux and the Cotentin (not yet under direct ducal control as they were far removed from the centre of power in Rouen). We will consider three examples here that reflect internal relations, but also relations between powerful nobles on the borders of Normandy and the Frankish kings.

The first examples concern Rollo's son William Longsword's ability to exercise authority in Normandy beyond the immediate confines of Rouen, as seen through Dudo's account of the rebellion of Riulf. The rebellion of Riulf is interesting as not only does it raise questions about the scope of the count of Rouen's authority, but also because it gets to the heart of Norman identity, which will be considered in more detail in Chapter 7.[36] The identity of Riulf is uncertain. Dudo's modern translator suggests he was Frankish, while Searle suggests he was one of the many Scandinavian chieftains who had settled in Normandy. Whatever his identity, Riulf was alarmed at the young count's cultivation of Frankish nobles at the expense of his Norman followers and encouraged other local leaders to form a mutual assistance pact to resist him. It is important to note that William did not have an automatic right to rule through inheritance, but depended for his authority on designation as heir by Rollo, probably in consultation with advisers, when he was still alive. If his followers did not deem him capable, then he could be challenged. Riulf asked for land 'up to the river Risle'. William replied that the land was not his to give and offered them honoured places in his court as counsellors. This was not enough for the rebels, who eventually forced William into battle, whereupon they were defeated.

The fact that William had to meet a rebellion at the beginning of his reign points to two matters of importance. The first is that there were other powers within Normandy vying for control. The second is that his authority really did not extend much beyond Rouen. Searle has located Riulf's sphere of activity as the region around Evreux, accepting the twelfth-century evidence of Orderic Vitalis. While this tradition is late, the proximity of Evreux to Rouen indicates why

Riulf's rebellion might have been considered a serious threat. Of course, Dudo was typically vague, as a powerful neighbouring chief negated his interpretation that Normandy existed in its final form from 911 onwards.

The dukes also had to manage relations with neighbouring nobles on their frontiers. A case in point, and one which is seen as a crisis for Norman power, is the death of William Longsword, murdered on an island in the river Somme at the behest of Count Arnulf of Flanders.[37] This episode is told by Dudo, but also referred to in an important contemporary source, the *Planctus* (a memorial poem), probably commissioned by William's sister Gerloc who was married to the duke of Aquitaine.[38] It has been used variously by historians to argue that the Norman settlers were not accepted as equals by the Franks (Searle), that Franks were not to be trusted (Lifshitz) and by others to indicate that the early rulers were active in pursuing policies to extend and consolidate their borders, just like other counts in the Frankish realm.[39]

The events leading up to William's death revolve around a dispute between Arnulf and one of Arnulf's men, Herluin of Ponthieu. Arnulf had previously captured one of Herluin's castles

Fig.4: William Longsword's tomb in Rouen cathedral (modern copy of destroyed thirteenth-century original)

at Montreuil, and after failing to find redress from other quarters, Herluin turned to William to help regain his land. In this he was successful, but William's actions provoked Arnulf into seeking revenge. He eventually arranged William's murder under the guise of a peace treaty. Having tricked the count into staying behind on an island in the Somme while his followers went on ahead, Arnulf's men slew him. Dudo portrays William as an innocent martyr, a victim of perfidy and treachery, but the situation was perhaps a little more complex. Previously, Rollo had been defeated on this border, limiting expansion eastwards. Struggles on the border were not just a means of increasing territory, but also ensuring the safety of the patrimony, the land granted to Rollo and his successors. It is likely that Arnulf and other figures in the Frankish realm were wary of this new power on their doorstep and sought to do something about it. In addition, Elisabeth van Houts has recently argued that Arnulf might well have felt vulnerable following marriage alliances between Rollo's children and Frankish nobles. William Longsword married Leyarda of Vermandois and his sister, Gerloc, married William I of Poitou and III of Aquitaine, taking the name Adela on her marriage. Arnulf's family was not favoured in this way by alliances with the ducal house despite their geographical proximity.[40] Removal of a ruler with expansionist ambitions was therefore one way of achieving security, especially as the designated heir was a young boy. If the creation of Normandy in the way historians have come to understand was indeed unintentional, then the murder of William presented an opportunity to reverse the Norman advance to the advantage of other powerful nobles. Alternatively, the threat of Viking raids had decreased to such an extent that the need for a buffer zone was no longer necessary and Louis IV was willing to support other vassals against the Norman rulers, despite the role played by William Longsword in negotiating his return from exile.

Relations with the king of the Franks are also crucial for understanding the history of early Normandy: after all Charles the Simple and his successors had not intended to create a semi-independent duchy in the northern part of their realm, but to provide a means of defence against Scandinavian raiders. According to Dudo, Richard I had to face two encounters with Louis, the man whom his father had helped become king.[41] Following the death of

William Longsword, Louis travelled to Rouen, where he granted the young Richard 'the land to hold by hereditary right of inheritance from his grandfather and father', but not before the citizens of Rouen believed that the king had acted in bad faith and imprisoned their leader. The situation was resolved by Bernard, one of the leading Normans and close adviser to the dukes. Louis then took Richard back to his court, where various Norman accounts tell us that the boy was mistreated and had to flee in the dead of night with his guardian. Louis later invaded Normandy. Dudo goes to great lengths here to stress that the king could not be trusted and the unity of the Normans in facing this threat, but he also tells us that victory was achieved in part by aid given earlier by 'Harold, king of Dacia' – in other words, a Danish king. This designation does not imply that Harold was from Denmark, but it is more likely that he was one of the Danish Viking leaders from either the region around Bayeux or the Cotentin peninsula. Dudo's ambiguity is deliberate as he did not want to suggest the existence of powerful rivals to Rollo's descendants.

The partial but contemporary account written by Flodoard, in contrast, records more elements of dissent among the Normans and notes particularly the presence of two Viking leaders, Turmod and Setric, whom he suggests forced Richard into paganism and plotting against the king. Later in his annals he notes the arrival of new Norse bands from over the sea.[42] Searle has argued that the counts of Rouen were by no means pre-eminent among the Viking leaders in Normandy at this time and that powerful chiefs were just as capable of using the succession of Richard as an opportunity to further their own interests as was the king of the Franks. In this argument, the Danish Harold of Dudo's account is perhaps not such a benign figure. Power in the early Middle Ages depended on personal authority and ability, much more than an appeal to any notion of an hereditary principle that was yet to be established. Richard might have been designated as the next count by William, but he still needed the acceptance of other powerful nobles in the region. Turmod and Setric were, however, killed by Louis. Dudo, naturally, would not be too keen to foreground people who possibly posed a threat inside the duchy; he was far more interested in the external threat posed by the Franks.

Trouble flared up again in 946 when the king invaded Normandy and attempted to seize Rouen with the support of Arnulf of Flanders (the same man who murdered William Longsword) and the German emperor, Otto I.[43] Frankish politics was at the heart of this dispute, but other Scandinavian interests also had a part to play. Not only did Louis and perhaps other Viking leaders take advantage of William's death to advance their cause, but so too did Hugh the Great, grandson of Robert the Strong. In the years immediately following William's death, both Dudo and Flodoard record in varying degrees of detail and emphasis that Hugh made gains in Normandy. By 946 Dudo and the later chroniclers suggest that Louis was alarmed at the rise of the Normans, but in actuality, he was most concerned with the increase in power wielded by Hugh the Great and the potential this carried with it for destabilizing his own position, especially once Hugh had allied himself with Richard I. Richard was able to defeat and repel Louis and, as a consequence, secure his hold on the territory comprising Normandy. The descriptions of his encounters with Louis and his survival, following Dudo's account, shows the ability of Richard and his advisers to negotiate the complex web of allies and enemies all looking after their own interests and so secure the territory of the Normans.

THE CHARACTER OF NORMANDY: CONTINUITY VS DISCONTINUITY

Following these difficult initial years of his reign, Richard, a very long-lived duke who died in 996, could set about securing and expanding his authority across the lands granted to his father and grandfather. This is not to say that he did not have to fight any more battles – Count Theobald of Chartres proved to be a tricky neighbour – but he laid much of the ground work for the relatively coherent political unit in the east of Normandy that emerged by the end of Richard II's reign.[44] In three generations, the people who settled in the Seine valley had gone from Viking pirates to powerful rulers with their own history crafted for them by Dudo. Historians have put forward various theories as to how and why this came about. Key here are the debates about whether what the Normans had achieved or did marked a fundamental rupture with the Carolingian way of doing things, or whether they merely stepped into the place of the old Carolingian counts and took over the same institutions and mechanisms of power. As documentary evidence that would elucidate this more clearly is largely absent until towards the end of the tenth century, it is necessary to consider the problem from a point of view of comparison with other areas of Francia.

Let us first look at the evidence used by historians to stress the existence of continuities between the Carolingian province of Neustria and what became Normandy. Lucien Musset and Jean Yver emphasized structural continuity.[45] The rulers used Carolingian titles, namely 'count', and once the church was re-established it was done so along the lines of the Carolingian dioceses. Normandy, which may have been created from scratch due to the coherence of the land grants of 911 onwards, can still be compared to Flanders and Aquitaine, principalities created to counter the threat of incursions and expansion to the north-east and south-west. The grants to Rollo, as Bates has shown, were not unique in this context and therefore at least partially legitimate in the way that those who favour continuity suggest.[46] That is to say they were recognized by the king. In addition, numismatic evidence argues for the continuation of the mint at Rouen and in other areas of Normandy, with Carolingian coin-types adopted by Rollo and his successors.[47]

The main proponent of the discontinuity thesis is Searle. She argued that the absence of Carolingian officials or nobles in Normandy at the time of the treaty of Saint-Clair-sur-Epte presents a powerful case against assuming that Rollo and his successor adopted the Carolingian system; there would have been no folk memory or means of operating these institutions. The Normans fundamentally ruptured the political context of the tenth century. For Searle the creation of Normandy was something that the Frankish kings never meant to do and was an act of coercion and violence. Yet, as we have seen, Charles the Simple was still issuing charters as late as 905 that suggest the existence of Carolingian forms of administration in the region. If Rollo was active for a significant period of time in Normandy prior to 911, the supposed date of the treaty, and an archbishop was involved in negotiation and conversion, then surely these facts militate against a complete rupture. Much of Searle's argument is also dependent on long-lasting ties with Scandinavia (which will be examined in more detail in later chapters) and assumptions about the nature of kinship.

Certainly, to argue for direct continuity with Carolingian institutions is to minimize the impact the Normans had on this part of France in terms of establishing themselves as a significant power. We still have to deal with Searle's idea that the Frankish kings never meant to create a virtually independent principality on their doorstep. What we see in the success of Rollo and his descendants is a ruthless ability to take advantage of the opportunities offered, and through the patronage of men like Dudo, to create a history that legitimized that exploitation and set it in a context that was familiar to the people they governed and their political neighbours. Certainly she is right to assert that the creation of Normandy was not a deliberate policy and possibly a short-term solution to the problem of Viking incursions. However Searle pushes her thesis too far and minimizes the gradual evolution of institutions, law and custom in the area that became Normandy, an evolution that was given a boost after 1066 when William the Conqueror and his successors had to work out how to govern Normandy as duke, while ruling England as king. What we may be seeing then in the creation of Normandy, as Jean Dunbabin has suggested in an examination of the whole of the Frankish realm under the later Carolingian kings, is a series of improvisations to manage a situation in which grants of land supposedly freely given by the king could hide a great deal of coercion and duress on the part of Rollo and his followers.[48]

FROM PAGAN RAIDERS TO CHRISTIAN PRINCES: FÉCAMP AND DUCAL SELF-PERCEPTION

Dudo of Saint-Quentin ended his history with a description of the ducal palace, originally built by William Longsword, and religious community at Fécamp refounded by Richard I as a community of canons after it was destroyed by the Vikings and then later established as a Benedictine abbey.[49] This episode brings to a conclusion the story of Rollo's migration and the settlement of the now Christian *gens Normannorum* in their promised land. Archaeological evidence from the site and Dudo's praise of Richard shed fascinating light on the way that the counts perceived themselves and were perceived. Dudo uses the Beatitudes from the Gospel of Matthew to enumerate the qualities of a good ruler as made manifest in Richard. He stresses his piety and gifts to the church, as well as his humility in wishing to be buried outside the church building. Dudo uses the Latin word *tumulus* for his grave and Searle has interpreted this to mean a burial mound not unlike those of his Viking ancestors.[50] Here then is a Christian Northman, the culmination of the Normans' divinely pre-ordained journey. If we turn to the archaeological evidence, a different picture again emerges. The layout of the palace is known primarily from the excavations of Annie Renoux in the 1970s and 1980s. In common with other ducal sites, Fécamp started out as a fortified enclosure with the initial buildings constructed from timber and then later in stone. Although the existing hall dates from the twelfth century onwards, an earlier stone structure on a different alignment survives underneath it dating from the time of Richard I, in conjunction with a large wooden building some distance away. Renoux argues that this complex is very much in the tradition of earlier Carolingian villas or Anglo-Saxon palaces, rather than borrowing Scandinavian forms.[51] It would seem in this respect that Richard was stressing an identity that sat within a firmly Frankish political context. Fécamp was also strategically important as it was located on the coast and so ideally placed for maintaining links

Fig.5: The abbey church of Fécamp. The current building dates from the twelfth century and the west front is post-medieval

Fig.6: The remains of the ducal place at Fécamp, dating from the twelfth century

with Scandinavia and developing them with England. What we see here then is the hybrid identity as foretold in Rollo's dream. The Normans at the end of the tenth century were neither Frankish, nor Scandinavian, but Norman, able to operate within a political context familiar to Dudo, yet maintaining links with the Scandinavian world.

By the end of Richard I's reign, there existed something that would come to be called Normandy as a recognizable entity in the minds of contemporaries, even though ducal authority in the west was limited and patchy and the borders elsewhere flexible and permeable. Dudo's work presents a duke who, if not wholly accepted by the Frankish elite, was, by the end of his reign, sufficiently similar to cause no significant alarm and, crucially, one whose occupation and rule of the territory was both legitimate and justified. Dudo's account contrasts with the slow and piecemeal advance west and the contractions of ducal authority in times of crisis. Historians therefore have two versions of the early settlement of Normandy: Dudo's creation of a recognizable province from the reign of Rollo; and the far more patchy and difficult birth as reflected back through the ducal acta that survive from the late tenth century onwards, the annals of Flodoard and the material evidence. Despite these problems, Richard had survived the early death of his father and the struggles of his minority. It is in his reign that we begin to see a number of developments, continued by his son Richard II, that enabled Normandy to become the powerful duchy of the eleventh century, which we shall pick up on in later chapters. Family in key positions either through marriage or through being given land on the borders began to strengthen the duke's authority in different parts of the duchy, far removed from Rouen (discussed further in Chapter 4). Richard appointed his son, Robert as archbishop of Rouen. Robert's abilities enabled him to re-establish the secular church throughout the duchy (Chapter 5). Although pretty much absorbed into the Frankish milieu by the turn of the tenth and eleventh centuries, Normandy still maintained some links with Scandinavia, as well as forging closer ones with England (Chapter 6). Finally, in the reception of Dudo's history and its use by later writers, we begin to see the development of ideas of what it meant to be a 'Norman' (Chapter 7).

2

WILLIAM OF NORMANDY AND THE CONQUEST OF ENGLAND

When thinking of Duke William II of Normandy, known variously to history as the Conqueror and the Bastard, several images spring to mind.[1] For Wace, writing a verse chronicle in the twelfth century, William was destined for greatness from the moment of his conception. His mother, called Arlette by Wace, tells Robert the Magnificent 'My Lord [...] I dreamt that a tree which was growing up towards the sky was emerging from my body. The whole of Normandy was covered by its shadow.'[2] William of Jumièges in the *Gesta Normannorum ducum* recounts how the duke dealt with the challenge to his authority during the siege of Alençon by mutilating the defenders of the town who, according to Orderic's later interpolations, mocked his mother's supposed low birth.[3] Following the invasion of England in 1066, Orderic provided his readers with a memorable and powerful image of conquest with the king sitting in full royal regalia within the smoking ruins of York Minster on Christmas Day 1069 having put down a rebellion. Finally Orderic, never a chronicler to miss underlining any possible moral, shows the king at the moment of his death deserted by his followers, his possessions looted and, in a final indignity, his corpse bursting as it was crammed into too small a sarcophagus.[4]

These anecdotes surrounding the life of William tell us a great deal about how chroniclers viewed their world and the events and people in it. There is admiration for William, respect, fear and implied criticism. All agree that William was extremely successful and, by the standards of the eleventh century, not overly brutal, except in the case of the Harrying of the North in 1069–70. He was, however, a man for whom violent action was a means to an end and a way of life and who would have to account for those actions before God, the ultimate judge. Even aside from the battlefield his actions might contain a violent edge. A well-known charter of 1069 recording a grant of land to La Trinité-du-Mont in Rouen tells how William picked up a knife and made as if to stab the abbot's hand, saying 'thus ought the land to be given'.[5] It is a powerful and arresting image of a man, whom William of Malmesbury presents as a physically imposing individual, even if the king became more than a little corpulent towards the end of his reign:

> He was of a proper height, immensely stout, with a ferocious expression and a high bald forehead; his arms extremely strong so that it was often a remarkable sight to see no one able to draw his bow, which he himself, while spurring his horse to a gallop, could bend with taut bowstring. He had great dignity both seated and standing.[6]

Violence was nothing, however, without the ability to negotiate the political and social networks of western Europe of the eleventh century. Here William was a shrewd and astute operator, especially when it came to planning the invasion of England. Yet at the same time he was a pious individual and devout Christian concerned with the welfare and reform of the Church in his territories as the chroniclers all agree. The abbey churches of Saint-Etienne and La Trinité (founded by Matilda of Flanders, his wife) testify to this side of his character and are examined in more detail in Chapter 5.

The subject of William the Conqueror and the conquest of England is a vast one with an ever-expanding historiography. We can do no more than scratch the surface here and highlight some of the important and significant aspects of his rule in Normandy and the debates surrounding 1066. To that end it is necessary to consider how William, who succeeded to the duchy when he was aged just seven or eight, was able to secure and expand his position and territory, why he was interested in the throne of England, how he planned the invasion and the question of whether the conquest of England created a Norman empire.

FROM 1035 TO 1066: SURVIVAL, CONSOLIDATION AND EXPANSION

William became duke when Robert the Magnificent died on the return journey from a pilgrimage to Jerusalem. Prior to departing Normandy, Robert, in common with established Norman custom, designated William as his heir and ensured that his nobles swore allegiance to the young boy.[7] According to the narrative sources, Robert's death and William's extreme youth ushered in a period of political uncertainty and violence in which rival nobles sought to consolidate their position at the expense of ducal power. William of Jumièges writing in the 1050s comments on the number of castles built without permission and from which powerful families could control their territories.[8] The account of the miracles of St Vulfran completed 1053–4 also mentions the disorder. Orderic Vitalis, whose narrative of the early years of William's reign was written in the first two decades of the twelfth century, points out the violence that surrounded the duke from a young age setting the murder of the duke's steward, Osbern, in the same chamber where both he and William were asleep. Orderic was writing many years later and in a monastery on the southern border of Normandy that suffered a great deal from outbreaks of civil unrest in the years that followed the death of the conqueror. This might well have coloured his account. The period of William's minority as one of disorder is, however, a view that gained wider currency.

Historians, notably David Douglas, have traditionally regarded William's character as having been forged in these troubles from which he emerged as an extremely able military commander, with steely determination and a pronounced ruthless streak.[9] His ability to conquer and pacify England was directly linked to his experiences dealing with rebellious nobles once he assumed power. Recently, this view has been questioned, notably by David Bates and Mark Hagger.[10] We should view the political disruption up to 1042, when William began to rule independently, against a background of struggle for control of the duke, rather than attempts to kill him or otherwise remove him. The key point in this analysis would be the death in 1037 of Archbishop Robert of Rouen, originally appointed to that see by Richard I, who provided continuity from one reign to another since 996. With Robert gone, there was no comparable figure who could hold the competing factions together. As well as the

Fig.7: Falaise was Duke William II's birthplace. The building now standing dates from the twelfth century onwards. The round tower was built in the early thirteenth century by the French king, Philip II Augustus

steward Osbern, William's guardian Count Gilbert of Brionne was killed in a dispute with Ralph de Gacé (son of Archbishop Robert). Bates points to contested territory as the root cause, while Hagger suggests that in addition, Ralph might have thought he should have been chosen as the duke's guardian instead.

The year 1042 is taken as the date from which William could exercise effective and independent rule by most modern historians: it is necessary then to consider the circumstances in which this occurred. William's first military engagement according to William of Jumièges was in 1043 when he captured Falaise from Thurstan Goz, vicomte of the Hiémois in the south of Normandy, and forced him into exile.[11] The background to Thurstan's rebellion was apparently the concessions made by the duke to the French king Henry I as a result of the settlement surrounding the disputed castle of Tillières-sur-Avre (c.1043) that seemingly rendered parts of the Hiémois vulnerable to raids through the destruction and subsequent rebuilding of the castle by the king.[12] It might well have been shortly after Henry's invasion that William was able to assume independent control. As Bates highlights, the decisions in this dispute were taken by 'the Normans' and William is described as a 'boy'.[13] In contrast, once William heard that Thurstan was fortifying the castle against him, he organized the army and besieged the town. The duke's first biographer, William of Poitiers, points out that at this stage he was beginning to rule wisely and to rid his court of people who had offered bad counsel in the past. Decisive action in the form of countering Thurstan's rebellion would have encouraged his nobles to see William as a viable leader. To offer leadership in a military engagement in 1043 suggests that William was already exercising authority independently.

That is not to say that William did not face any more threats during his reign. The 1040s may have seen him assume independent rule and begin to establish peace and order in Normandy, but he continued to encounter opposition, often from his own family members, into the 1050s. For example, his uncle William, who was count of Talou and held the castle of Arques, rebelled in 1052, while in the run up to the battle of Val-ès-Dunes in 1047 his cousin Guy of Burgundy was to prove a significant opponent. In terms of kinship,

Fig.8: The castle of Arques near Dieppe, held by William II's uncle William of Arques. The ditches and some of the walls date from the eleventh century

Guy was the son of Adeliza, sister to the short-lived Richard III (the elder brother of Robert the Magnificent) and wife of Reginald I of Burgundy. William had granted Guy land in the form of the castles of Vernon and Brionne, but crucially, he was not included in the duke's closest circle of advisers, despite the fact that both men had been brought up together in Robert's household.[14] William also faced opposition from a broader cross-section of Norman society, including men who felt threatened by or objected to the duke's gradual assertion of his authority in the west of Normandy where he had installed men who were loyal to him, but not necessarily from the area. These conspirators included Nigel of the Cotentin, Ranulf vicomte of Bayeux and Haimo 'toothy' (recorded by William of Poitiers), alongside Grimoult of Le Plessis-Grimoult, Serlo of Lingèvres and Ralph Taisson. It is important to remember, as Hagger has discussed, that these men were not all rebelling for the same reason, but all had grievances. For example, Guy was unhappy with his position at court, Haimo was probably supporting his exiled kinsman Thurstan Goz, and Ranulf wanted lands in Guernsey restored to him.[15]

On a plain to the south-east of Caen, William confronted an army comprising a collection of dissatisfied nobles, each with their own grievance, including his cousin, Guy, at Val-ès-Dunes. Significantly, William was aided substantially in this enterprise by King Henry I of France. Indeed, rather than the young duke, it would seem that King Henry was the hero here. It is also a timely reminder that, although Normandy was a semi-independent principality, it was still connected by ties of over-lordship to the kingdom of France. The dukes of Normandy wielded immense power, but still had to respond to calls for aid from their sovereign or risk breaking faith. Such an occasion had arisen during the rule of William's father, Robert, who had gone to the aid of the king. Seigneurial ties like these worked both ways. In return for supporting his, or occasionally her, king, a lord could expect support and protection of his/her lands in return. Henry was not slow to remember the service rendered by Robert and came to support William, who had also campaigned on his behalf and had been given his arms by him. The battle is recorded by William of Poitiers, for whom it is a significant event in his biography of William (he downplays Henry's role), and also by William of Jumièges in the *Gesta Normannorum ducum*. Wace later used these accounts to provide a suitably embellished version for a court audience. The key point is that William emerged victorious and able to consolidate his hold on the duchy.

Just how significant the battle of Val-ès-Dunes was in terms of power relations in northern France is reflected in subsequent military engagements in which the king of France, rather than a threat from within the duchy, was the main enemy. William's victory at Val-ès-Dunes not only allowed him to secure Normandy, but to turn his attention to land beyond his borders. Expansion of the Norman lands had ceased under Richard II, but frequent border skirmishes meant that, in some areas at least, attack could be construed as the best form of defence. William had turned his attention to Maine in the south. Alarmed by the rise of the young and ambitious duke, the count of Anjou and the king of France had to take action, especially as the latter's forces had been defeated in a skirmish at Mortemer in the east of the duchy in 1054. In 1057 Henry, along with Geoffrey, count of Anjou, led a small force into Normandy to push back William and his ambition. As they advanced northwards, William's forces cut them off from the rear in the Dives estuary at Varaville as the invading force tried to cross the river in marshy territory. With part of his army trapped on the other side of the river, Henry could, according to chroniclers keen to stress the duke's prowess, only watch helplessly as his troops drowned in the rising waters of the incoming tide and were carried out to sea.[16]

Varaville marks the point of the last attempted French invasion of Normandy during the reign of William II, but throughout the 1050s and the early 1060s William was actively campaigning. During the 1050s and 1060s he campaigned in Brittany; in the Vexin, finally taking the castle at Thimert after a protracted siege; and on the borders of Maine to the south, eventually taking the county in 1062. Through these actions he increased his influence to the west of the duchy and gradually accrued territory in the south. This was necessary in order counter the threat of Geoffrey of Anjou (d. 1060) and to safeguard his patrimony. A great deal of the first part of the *Gesta Guillelmi* relates to this activity, stressing the prowess and abilities of the duke as he conquered difficult territory and brought important towns like Alençon and Domfront under his control. It is a good example of how writers of history in the Middle Ages sought to praise and extol their subjects. Poitiers's account of William's

Fig.9: Looking across the battlefield at Varaville, near Dives-sur-Mer, Normandy

campaigning in the south of Normandy makes a good case study. It is noticeable that Poitiers focuses on the difficulties the duke faced, which served to underline his exceptional abilities in overcoming them. During the siege of Domfront, he describes the landscape as follows: 'The site of the fortified town prevented any sudden attack by force or by skill, for the roughness of the rock discouraged even foot soldiers, except those able to approach by two steep and narrow paths.' William was in such control of this inhospitable territory that he could ride about freely, hide in 'secret places' and scout in order to protect his foragers. He was also able to engage in that most aristocratic of leisure pursuits – hunting – underlining, as Poitiers states, 'the ease by which he operated in enemy territory'.[17]

It was not just through his military activities that William was able to establish effective rule of Normandy. His marriage to Matilda, daughter of the powerful duke of Flanders and niece of the French king, Henry I, was an advantageous and fortunate match. Matilda acted as supporter, representative and companion until her death in 1083. In addition, the alliance helped secure William's eastern frontier and demonstrated recognition on the part of neighbouring lords that he was ruling effectively and independently. He also strengthened his relationship with the Church. Following his victory at Val-ès-Dunes in 1047, William had proclaimed the Truce of

God within the borders of Normandy. The Truce sought to restrict violence and prohibit private warfare of the type seen in the 1030s and early 1040s.[18] William of Poitiers, always keen to show the duke in the best possible light, summed up his achievements in establishing peace. The duke upheld the law, protected orphans, widows and the poor and established peace so that 'strangers, seeing that in our country horsemen go to and fro unarmed, and that the road is safe for every traveller, have often wished to have a similar blessing in their regions'.[19] On the eve of 1066 William II was thus one of the most powerful and militarily capable war lords in northern Europe, and Edward the Confessor, the childless king of England and related to the duke through his mother, Emma, was on his deathbed.

THE NORMANS AND ENGLAND

Normandy and England already had political and cultural connections prior to the invasion in 1066. We cannot take Dudo's story of Rollo spending time at Æthelstan's court at face value, but place-name evidence indicates that some of the Viking settlers in Normandy originally came from the Danelaw area of England, rather than direct from Scandinavia.[20] Evidence also exists, in the form of a letter from Pope John XV dated to 991, for a treaty between the duke of Normandy and the king of the English. This treaty aimed to prevent their people harming each other, which has been interpreted as a measure to prevent Viking war bands attacking England finding shelter in Norman harbours.[21] The English king, Æthelred II tried to invade Normandy in the early years of the eleventh century after this treaty was apparently breached.[22] Of most significance for this chapter is, however, the marriage of Richard I and Gunnor's daughter, Emma, to Æthelred. Emma was Æthelred's second wife and with him she had two sons, Edward, known to history as the Confessor and his brother, Alfred: both boys were therefore related by blood to the Norman dukes through the female line. English politics was greatly disrupted following the invasion of the Danish king, Swein Forkbeard, in 1013. Æthelred, Emma and their sons fled to Normandy where they were welcomed at the ducal court. Æthelred and his son by his first marriage, Edmund Ironside, tried to repel the invaders, but in this they were unsuccessful. Æthelred was killed in 1014 and Edmund, despite initially sharing the throne with Swein's son, Cnut, died in 1016. Emma then either chose or was forced to marry Cnut (Rodolfus Glaber states that the marriage brought peace between Richard and Cnut)[23] while her sons remained in Normandy under the protection of their uncle, Duke Richard II, and later Robert the Magnificent.

This period of exile in Normandy was very important, both for Edward and the ducal court. Edward seems to have been regarded highly and was recognized as the rightful king by his Norman relatives. In a charter dated to 1033–4 in favour of the abbey of Mont-Saint-Michel, Edward is referred to as 'king of the English' and his name appears in the witness list alongside the title 'rex'. He also appears in the witness list for a charter of Robert the Magnificent in favour of Fécamp, again as 'king'.[24] William of Jumièges also includes an interesting detail in the *Gesta Normannorum ducum*. He states that Robert adopted Edward and Alfred as brothers, interpreted by van Houts as a sworn or blood-brotherhood, and sent an embassy to Cnut to try to persuade him to allow the æthelings to return to England.[25] William's source might well have been Robert of Jumièges, a former abbot of the monastery and bishop of London who returned to the community after he was banished from England when Edward was forced to restore the powerful Godwine family, which included Edward's successor, Harold, to power.[26] Robert had previously been appointed as archbishop of Canterbury at the expense of Earl Godwine's candidate. When diplomacy failed, William tells us that Duke Robert decided to launch an invasion in support of his cousins, but the fleet was held at Jersey by strong winds and the plans were abandoned. This evidence demonstrates that the Norman dukes themselves had a strong interest in forming an alliance with England.

Edward had become accustomed to Norman advisers during his time in exile. After he eventually returned to England in 1042 following the death of Cnut's sons Harthacnut and Harald Harefoot, he introduced Normans to his court alongside English nobles and within the church, notably Abbot Robert of Jumièges who became bishop of London.[27] It is also highly likely that his rebuilding of Westminster Abbey in the Romanesque style was influenced by edifices he saw on the continent, for example the abbey of Jumièges. During his time in Normandy, his advisers Robert of Jumièges and

Abbot John of Fécamp may well have pushed Edward's ambitions for the kingship.[28] This is not to say that Edward's court in England was 'Norman' – certainly the English Church had had a cosmopolitan make-up prior to Edward's accession, with bishops from different parts of Europe – but it is clear he maintained some links with the country of his exile and valued the connections that he had made there.

None of this explains why William sought the crown following the death of Edward, who had failed to produce children of his own, and on what grounds. Despite the large amount of scholarship given over to this topic, we cannot avoid the fact that the evidence remains inconclusive and contradictory. Historians have taken up trenchant positions with regard to what might have been going on at Edward's court in relation to the succession: did he or did he not promise the throne to William of Normandy and was this promise then superseded by a later offer to Harold, son of Earl Godwine? How far were these promises based on customary law in either Normandy or England? Was Edgar ætheling, probably in his early teens at the time of the conquest, but a direct descendant of Æthelred's son Edmund Ironside, ever a viable candidate?

At the heart of this debate is how someone could become king in eleventh-century England and, indeed, what qualities were deemed important in a king. Primogeniture, the hereditary principle of the eldest son succeeding his father, was not automatic at this point in time. Although eldest sons did succeed and blood claims were important, there were other factors in king-making. In the first place candidates needed to be deemed worthy, but that might still result in a choice having to be made from a selection of potential heirs, as was the case following Cnut's death in 1035. Although the English crown was not fully elective, potential kings needed the support of the *witangemot*, that is the leading nobles of the kingdom, in order to secure their position. Deeds enacted during the previous reign, for example Harold's securing of the Anglo-Welsh border, would count for a great deal in this scenario, especially when compared to an untried, yet royal-blooded teenager (Edgar). Heirs could be designated during a particular ruler's lifetime, termed a *post obitum* grant as it took effect after death, or alternatively, granted the throne as part of a deathbed bequest, *verba novissima*.[29] It is these last two means of becoming a king, and how the sources present the evidence for them, that concern us here.

Following the Norman sources, notably William of Jumièges and later, William of Poitiers, Edward intended William to be his heir in return for support for his claim at the Norman court during his exile. Poitiers records that the leading men of Edward's court accepted this decision and that Robert of Jumièges was sent to Normandy to convey the outcome to William. A son and grandson of Earl Godwine were given as hostages in order to ensure good faith. At a later date, 1064, Harold was sent on his now infamous trip across the Channel, depicted on the Bayeux Tapestry, to confirm that William would succeed Edward.

Additional English evidence in the form of a short extract in the 'D' version of the Anglo-Saxon Chronicle gives some support to the notion that Edward might have offered William the throne. In the entry for 1051 it records:

> Then soon Earl William came from beyond the sea with a great troop of French men, and the king received him and as many of his companions as suited him, and let him go again.[30]

In the event, however, Harold was nominated as Edward's heir on his deathbed. This might well be what is shown in the deathbed scene on the Bayeux Tapestry and also in a passage in the *Life of St Edward*:

> stretching forth his hand to his governor, her [Queen Edith's] brother, Harold, he said, 'I commend this woman and all the kingdom to your protection. Serve and honour her with faithful obedience as your lady and sister, which she is, and do not despoil her, as long as she lives, of any due honour got from me.[31]

Interestingly, even though it contradicted his carefully constructed narrative of William's claim, William of Poitiers also noted that Harold was promised the throne at Edward's death.

There is much in both versions that does not bear detailed scrutiny in terms of the order of events or their interpretation. George Garnett has recently described the case for William's claim as essentially a fabrication based on a document put together by Lanfranc, abbot of Caen and later archbishop of Canterbury, in order to obtain papal support and justify the conquest in the long term and that William's claim had basis neither in Norman nor English law.[32] Although this argument is a tempting one, it does not explain why William of Poitiers included the deathbed promise to Harold. Following Garnett's suggestions means we have to accept either that the Norman court and papal curia contained some quite gullible people, or that Lanfranc and Pope Alexander II saw an opportunity to promote their own agenda and present an entirely concocted claim.[33] The fact that this claim, fictitious or otherwise, proved responsible for a large degree of bloodshed did not go unremarked. In a letter to William dated April 1080, Pope Gregory VII noted how his support for the conquest (prior to his election as pope) had led others to insinuate 'that by such partisanship [I] gave sanction for the perpetration of great slaughter'.[34] If we consider – as Stephen Baxter and Brian Golding have – the merits of the sources against the political context of Edward's reign, then it is highly likely that both William and Harold believed they had been promised the throne by Edward at some stage. The only way this matter would be resolved, therefore, was on the field of battle.[35] There was, of course, precedent for this: Swein and Cnut had claimed the throne by right of conquest in 1013 and 1016.

The reason Harold posed a threat to William's claim lies in the position his father, Earl Godwine, and his family held in mid-eleventh-century England. Godwine had risen to prominence in the reign of Cnut and continued to be a key figure after his death. Edward married Godwine's daughter, Edith and promoted his sons. In 1051, however, the family was forced into exile following an outbreak of hostilities surrounding the appointment of Robert of Jumièges as archbishop of Canterbury over the head of Godwine's nominee and the granting of a castle at Dover to Eustace of Boulogne. Having freed himself of the powerful earl's influence, Edward might well have felt strong enough to look elsewhere to secure the succession, namely across the Channel to Normandy. Much hangs on the interpretation of the Anglo-Saxon Chronicle evidence and when it was written. For some scholars, this passage was written later, after the conquest.[36] It is, however, essential to bear in mind the context in which this version of the chronicle was composed. The evidence suggests that it was produced in the household of Archbishop Ealdred of York, who was at Edward's court around the time of William's visit. Even if this entry is a later insertion, then it was almost certainly based on eyewitness testimony.[37] Scholars have also argued that the political situation in Normandy at this time meant that it would have been impossible for William to visit England, as his own position was not secure. By late autumn it was much improved and there is no reason to suppose he could not have made the journey then.

After the Godwines were restored to power, Edward's position would have been weaker and so, by extension, would William's claim to the throne. As Harold grew in favour and also in ability through his campaigns on the Welsh borders, alongside the fact that his brothers were granted powerful earldoms, it seems that Edward looked to the family for his successor: he might well not have had a choice. How then do we explain the supposed visit of Harold to Normandy, which all the sources agree had disastrous consequences for Harold personally and the kingdom more broadly? Eadmer, a monk of the cathedral priory of Christ Church Canterbury and confidant of Archbishop Anselm, provides some clues in his history of the recent events in England, though this was written fifty years after the conquest. As part of the reconciliation package between Edward and the Godwines, hostages from the family were handed over and sent to Normandy for security. In 1064, Harold wanted to secure their release and set out in the face of King Edward's unease to do so. What follows is the familiar story of his shipwreck, capture by Guy of Ponthieu and his release secured by Duke William. Eadmer states that his relatives' freedom was conditional on swearing to support William's claim after Edward's death and entering into marriage alliances with the ducal family. It is impossible to know for certain what went on in Normandy in 1064, but if William did feel he had a claim, then he would certainly have used this visit to his advantage and taken any opportunity to press it. What we can say is that Edward's policies did not secure a peaceful succession after his death and that two very ambitious men with resources to support them felt that they should be king of the English.

THE CONQUEST

On hearing that Edward the Confessor had died and that Harold, son of Earl Godwine had taken the throne, William of Poitiers, Duke William's biographer, recorded that he sought the counsel of his men and resolved 'to avenge this injury with arms and claim his inheritance by force of arms'.[38] Poitiers's implication is that William had a claim to the throne of England and that force was necessary and right to enforce it. There were dissenting voices who argued that the undertaking would be too great and too expensive, though Poitiers dismissed their arguments as 'specious'. His biography is, however, problematic and has been described as 'nauseatingly sycophantic' by one historian.[39] It certainly aims to present William in the best possible light and to justify the conquest, but it is inconceivable that the duke would have embarked on this campaign without seeking advice and planning thoroughly. Not only did he have to garner sufficient provisions, ships and men to launch the invasion, but also ensure that Normandy was left in safe hands and its borders secure.[40]

William of Poitiers stated that it was the quality of the men at William's court that meant Normandy could be kept secure. Later in the biography he notes that Matilda of Flanders had been entrusted with the protection of the duchy aided by Roger of Beaumont; Orderic Vitalis added William fitzOsbern and Roger of Montgomery, a man who had proved his ability on the southern borders of Normandy. William of Jumièges notes that Robert Curthose, William and Matilda's eldest son, was ruling in the duke's absence. It is quite possible that Robert was nominated as William's successor in Normandy prior to the invasion, so ensuring the potential for a smooth handover should he be killed in combat, much as William's own father had tried to do prior to his pilgrimage. The magnates and some of the leading clergymen also provided ships for the invasion as seen in a document known as the Ship List, with Matilda financing William's flagship, the 'Mora'.[41] The Bayeux Tapestry depicts the felling of trees for ship timber and provisions, arms and horses being loaded into the fleet. William was also keen to secure divine favour. In 1066 the abbey of La Trinité in Caen was dedicated and his youngest daughter Cecilia given to the community as a child oblate. She later became its abbess. He also sought the approval of Pope Alexander II, who provided him with a papal banner, possibly shown on the Bayeux Tapestry's depiction of the flagship.[42] The pope's motives in offering support are not wholly clear, though we may speculate that he was keen to remove Archbishop Stigand of Canterbury from his position. Stigand was a

Fig.10: Duke William II's flagship, 'The Mora', detail of the Bayeux Tapestry –
eleventh century (with special permission from the city of Bayeux)

problematic figure who had not resigned his see of Winchester on
becoming archbishop. Such behaviour was unacceptable to a papal
curia increasingly in the control of the reformers seeking to eradicate
such abuses. Papal support did, however, perhaps encourage men to
join the campaign, especially those from outside Normandy. William
of Poitiers reported that the army that faced Harold included
Bretons, Flemings, Aquitainians and men from other areas of what
is now France.

After the planning, negotiations and waiting for the weather (the
fleet was held in the Dives estuary until conditions were favourable),
William crossed the sea, landed in late September and proceeded
to raid Harold's ancestral lands while he was away fighting in
Yorkshire. Nearly as much ink has been spilled since 1066 as blood
was on the field itself in attempts to analyse and describe the events of
14 October 1066.[43] Medieval accounts of battles can be notoriously
difficult to interpret. No one source gives what undergraduates like
to call an 'accurate' picture of events. Why should it? Each account
was written from a different perspective, for a subtly different
audience and often at great chronological and geographical remove.
They were all written, composed or designed in different genres and

this also affects their interpretation: for Hastings reports survive in a biography, chronicles, a poem and pictorially. No eyewitness account in the sense of a narrative written by someone who was actually on the field of battle exists, not that it would make any difference. However, writers like William of Poitiers, the duke's biographer, drew on first-hand accounts when writing their own works and later chroniclers reused the material of their predecessors, adding their own interpretations where appropriate.

Military historians have got somewhat caught up in trying to determine tactics and an exact order of events. Academic papers on the battle contain trenchant views on the ordering of lines, the respective generalship of William and Harold, and the effectiveness of Norman cavalry against the defensive tactics of the English shield-wall.[44] Much of this interest stems from the fact that the battle itself was an extremely unusual event in the eleventh century. Many of what are termed 'battles' in the sources and modern historical writing (for example, Varaville and Val-ès-Dunes discussed above) were more like skirmishes and involved a small number of men at arms. Rulers did all they could to avoid a pitched battle like that between the armies of William and Harold; they were expensive in terms of equipment, but more importantly, the loss of men. This desire to avoid unnecessary bloodshed is the reason given by some of the Norman accounts, notably that of William of Poitiers, for the duke's challenge to Harold of single combat, a more judicial way of settling disputes. Of course, Harold's supposed refusal served to show him in a more negative light and to add further legitimacy in Norman eyes for the Normans' invasion.

One way to approach the accounts of the battle is to think about what it is we actually do know beginning with the place and the tactics used. The military engagement fought between William and Harold on 14 October 1066 has gone down in history as the 'Battle of Hastings'. It was not, however, fought at that town, but most probably at the place now known as Battle roughly ten miles inland from where William landed at Pevensey. This is the site on which William gave orders to build an abbey that served to commemorate his victory and to do penance for the bloodshed inflicted on both sides. This site is recorded variously in the sources as 'Senlac' or the place of the 'hoar apple tree':[45] the latter is found in the Anglo-Saxon Chronicle and suggests that Harold mustered his forces at a known

Fig.11: Battle Abbey, looking across the battlefield to where the Normans were positioned

meeting place identifiable by a distinctive tree.[46] This location meant that the English could take up a defensive position on high ground and withstand the Norman cavalry charge. The various accounts also tell us something of the tactics and arms used by the two sides. The English fought in a formation known as a shield wall whereby soldiers lined up on foot with their shields overlapping. Providing discipline held, this was very hard to break. In contrast, the Norman ranks contained both foot soldiers, including archers, and cavalry. Fighting on horseback was an important part of Norman warfare, though the animals were also used as a means of traversing ground quickly by both sides in preparation for battle. The importance of horses to the Normans is underlined in the Bayeux Tapestry. It depicts the Normans leading their mounts on to the waiting ships in preparation for crossing the Channel and later scenes show them safely stowed, their heads peering over the sides of the vessels. This cannot have been a particularly pleasant crossing for either the men or the animals.

The specific details of the battle are, however, much murkier and imprecise and are further muddled by the later chroniclers' tendency to copy one another's work. Orderic Vitalis, for example, was heavily reliant on William of Poitiers's biography of Duke William for his section on the immediate events of the conquest. Poitiers's section in the *Gesta Guillelmi* is regarded as the earliest written account of the battle, with the Bayeux Tapestry also accepted as an early source. To these two we can, on the Norman side, add the *Carmen de Hastingae Proelio*, a Latin poem that describes the battle. There is some debate as to the dating of this work, but on the whole, an eleventh-century date is now accepted. The accounts in eleventh-century English sources like the Anglo-Saxon Chronicle and Eadmer's *Historia* written in the early twelfth century, give little information beyond Harold's death and its dreadful implications for the country. What is notable is that while the accounts might agree on the broader events of the battle – it lasted all day, it was bloody, Harold died – many differences surface as to the manner in which it was conducted. The reasons for this are perhaps best shown on the Bayeux Tapestry. This artefact presents a narrative in linear form, meaning that events that might have occurred simultaneously are depicted sequentially. The viewer can, however, see the hail of missiles very clearly and, intruding into the border, the dead bodies of the English and Norman soldiers, some of them decapitated. As the battle progresses, looters emerge to strip the bodies. Horses and men tumble before a steep hill or ditch; archers continue to loose arrows from the lower margin. For all its cartoon-like appearance, it is a grim spectacle of the confusion and chaos of war.

Two particularly contested issues illustrate this confusion regarding events and tactics perfectly: the number of feigned flights and the manner of Harold's death. The feigned flight is a manoeuvre in which the cavalry pretends to flee in order to encourage the defenders to break ranks and pursue the mounted soldiers. In so doing it is then possible for the cavalry to isolate and kill their pursuers. As the English had formed their defensive shield wall on high ground, it was particularly difficult for the Normans to break through. William of Poitiers recorded that part of the Norman army was so discouraged at being unable to prevail that the 'footsoldiers and the Breton knights and other auxiliaries on the left wing turned tail'.[47] The Bretons were the butt of many jokes in the eleventh and twelfth centuries for their supposed barbaric nature and dishonourable behaviour, so it is no surprise that Poitiers used them in this way. He did, however, find it necessary to excuse their conduct by stating the army believed the duke to be dead. William rallied his troops, who then turned on the pursuing English and killed them. Later in the battle, this trick was deployed again, perhaps twice more, to good effect. Only by luring the defenders from the high ground were the Normans able to advance. For William of Poitiers this was a chance to show how the duke could turn adversity into success. By contrast, Henry of Huntingdon and William of Malmesbury, who were both writing in the early twelfth century, recorded that the feigned flight was, in one respect, disastrous for the Normans as it resulted in many of them falling into 'a large ditch cunningly hidden', though another section of the army was able to break through.[48] This might be a reference to the notorious 'mal fosse' incident in which Norman and/or English (depending on the account) all fell into a ditch and perished horribly. Like the feigned flights, this incident moved around; sometimes it is reported in the middle of the battle as, for example, on the Bayeux Tapestry, and at other times at the end.

There is also little agreement in the sources as to the manner by which Harold met his death. The earliest written account, William of Poitiers's *Gesta Guillelmi*, is not specific. Poitiers merely states that Harold died, but is not forthcoming as to how and when during the battle. As Marjorie Chibnall states in her footnotes, this is perhaps because no one who survived the battle actually knew. Alternatively, Poitiers did not have access to people who did know. The other chroniclers provide conflicting accounts: was Harold shot through the eye with an arrow, or was he hacked to pieces by a group of knights? The earliest written source to mention the arrow was not composed in either England or Normandy, but southern Italy, by Amatus of Montecassino during the 1080s. Later twelfth-century English accounts, notably Henry of Huntingdon and William of Malmesbury, also record Harold met his fate by an arrow, but the earlier English narratives are silent on this point. Other eleventh-century accounts, notably the *Carmen* and the Bayeux Tapestry present different versions. The *Carmen* records that Harold was cut down by four men, including one who sliced off part of the king's thigh and carried it some distance.[49] This event is alluded to by William of Malmesbury who named the man as Eustace of Boulogne and describes the act as dishonourable.[50] The Bayeux Tapestry offers three alternatives. In the scene captioned 'Harold interfectus est', there are two figures that could be Harold. One is depicted with an arrow in his eye and the other is shown being cut down by a mounted knight. Of course what we might see here is a sequence of events: Harold shot and then hacked down. The picture is further complicated by the fact that the tapestry has undergone repairs over the course of its long history and some scholars have questioned whether or not the arrow is genuine.[51] Modern historical writing is full of arguments for and against either event, reflecting a deep desire to know for certain what happened to the last 'English' king. Did he die a hero or was the manner of his death deliberately dishonourable, reflecting his status among the Norman sources as a traitorous perjurer?

Although many accounts of the battle survive, we can never know precisely what happened. But to think in these terms is to start from the wrong place. Does it matter how many feigned flights there were? Does it matter whether the battle started with trumpets or the Song of Roland or when a minstrel juggled swords between the opposing armies?[52] Does it matter how Harold was killed, as after all, it does not make him any more or less dead? Ultimately it does not and the answers are, in any case, unknowable. Medieval warfare was as confusing and as bloody as anything in modern history and perspectives on what happened, when, and how will differ. So how

Fig.12: The death of Harold, detail of the Bayeux Tapestry – eleventh century
(with special permission from the city of Bayeux)

should we best think about the events of 14 October 1066? Eadmer is admirably concise: 'a furious battle was joined; Harold fell in the thick of the fray and William as conqueror possessed himself of the kingdom.'[53]

For the English, Hastings was the second major battle they had fought within the space of a couple of weeks, the first being Harold's defeat of the Norwegian king Harald Hadraada at Stamford Bridge in Yorkshire. Hastings was also bloody. It is important to stress that, by the evening of 14 October 1066, most of the leading men of England lay dead or dying on the field, including Harold and his brothers Gyrth and Leofwine. His youngest brother, Tostig, had fled England following an unsuccessful rebellion in 1065, and died with Hadraada at Stamford Bridge. The Normans also sustained heavy losses. The violence did not end with the death of Harold and women whose male relatives had been killed fled to nunneries to avoid rape and forced marriage.[54] Military campaigning continued with the suppression of various rebellions in the south-west, the Welsh borders, the Fens and particularly the North until 1071. The process of consolidation of the conquest took much longer as land was transferred from English lordship to that of the Normans and high-ranking churchmen were replaced by William's appointees, some of which is discussed in later chapters. In the rest of this chapter we will focus on how the conquest was understood and explained following William's victory and whether or not it brought about a Norman empire.

RECEPTION OF THE CONQUEST

The battle of Hastings was in all senses a shocking event and those writing history in the eleventh and twelfth centuries needed to find a way to explain it. This was not an event that just affected England and Normandy, but one that had wider European ramifications that are sometimes overlooked in the modern scholarship surrounding William's reign. This section considers how writers from different perspectives thought and wrote about the Norman Conquest and the differences between them. Key here is the purpose of history writing in the Middle Ages, including the need to provide examples of good and bad behaviour and the idea of divine providence, that is God's purpose worked out in human affairs. As we shall see, the notion of providence played a large part in attempts to make sense of or explain the conquest.

The Norman sources, particularly William of Poitiers's *Gesta Guillelmi*, were keen to stress that the root cause of William's invasion and conquest was Harold's perfidy in seizing the throne after the death of Edward the Confessor. The implication here is that Harold was never a legitimate king. This point is made explicit in Domesday Book's point of reference being the time of King Edward (1065), ignoring the reign of Harold completely. Harold was an oath breaker and as such, he and his people, were punished through military force. This theme is picked up in the Latin poem, the *Carmen de Hastingae Proelio*, culminating in Harold's burial, not interred by his mother in a religious foundation, but buried on the cliff top near Hastings.[55] The narrative of the Bayeux Tapestry also portrays Harold as untrustworthy. We see him swearing oaths on holy relics, but then seated on the throne during his coronation crowned not by Ealdred of York as recorded in some of the English sources, but by Stigand, the uncanonical pluralist excommunicated by successive popes. William's conquest was legitimate as Harold's assumption of the throne was not. The change of regime was heralded by the appearance of Halley's Comet, shown on the Bayeux Tapestry above Harold's coronation and mentioned in some of the chronicles. Comets and other astronomical phenomena were taken as portents of change, often of a political nature. Narratives surrounding the first crusade mention their appearance as the crusaders left Europe.

Although the activities of the Normans are strongly associated with an upsurge in historical writing, the English sources of the eleventh century say very little about the events of 1066 and the aftermath of the conquest. The vernacular annals that historians know as the Anglo-Saxon Chronicle record the events, but in terms of analysis, they are brief and were also written after the events. The 'D' version, which takes a northern perspective, records that once the surviving nobles and Archbishop Ealdred had submitted to William, the new king taxed the country, sailed back to Normandy and left Odo and William fitzOsbern in charge, who 'built castles here and far and wide throughout this country, and distressed wretched folk, and always after that it grew much worse'.[56] Our other main source, written this time in Latin, from the English perspective is the *Vita Edwardi* commissioned by King Edward's wife Edith. The *Vita* was written between 1065 and 1067, straddling the events on the field at Battle. Edith lost four of her brothers that year, either at Battle or Stamford Bridge, yet, as van Houts has shown, 'the battle [Hastings] is only hinted at' in this composition.[57] Neither do we find monasteries on the whole recording lists of the dead. Van Houts suggests this silence, or only brief acknowledgement of the events, stemmed from a profound sense of shock and trauma following the battle. The chroniclers did not write or analyse the events because they could not; they were still coming to terms with what had happened. It is not until the twelfth century that chroniclers based in England began to tackle the events of the conquest when men like William of Malmesbury and Henry of Huntingdon commenced their histories. In their work, we see very strongly that William and his army were instruments of God sent to punish the English for sinful behaviour. Malmesbury notes that the English passed the night before the battle 'without sleep in drinking and singing' and later criticized the morals of the nobility more broadly.[58] Orderic Vitalis, although writing in a Norman monastery, also introduced a moralizing aspect to the history. He was, however, also very critical of William's behaviour in the north as well as those who became rich as a result of the suffering of the English.[59]

As noted above, the conquest of England in 1066 had wider European ramifications and was indeed written about in chronicles outside Normandy and England. A duke had managed to launch an invasion and seize the throne of another kingdom. William therefore became a wider object of interest and the European accounts show that his reputation spread widely. Van Houts has analysed historical writing from the German Empire, Flanders, France, Italy and Scandinavia in order to consider the wider reception of the conquest.[60] Some of the themes that we have already examined emerge, notably the role of Harold as an oath-breaker and the importance of divine providence. The European accounts also note the degree of violence involved. Although some historians praised the military achievements of William and his Normans, or the reforms that he made to the Church, others were critical of the suffering he caused, for example Frutolf of Magdeburg.[61] Perhaps the most interesting accounts are those from Scandinavia. For most of his reign William faced the threat of invasion from particularly the Danes. After the revolt of 1069, this never transferred into actuality, but the threat was serious enough in 1085 that William seems to have made plans for the billeting of mercenary troops in the kingdom and indeed, the Domesday inquest might well be seen in this context. The Danish king Sven Estrithson was a kinsman of Harald Hadraada and a nephew of Cnut and so might well have had a strong interest in England. Aelnoth of Canterbury, an English monk in exile in Denmark, writing in around 1112 wrote that Sven planned to invade in revenge for the death of Harald and that England was suffering under 'the tyranny of the Romans and the French'.[62] Perhaps the most poignant source of all though is the poem written by the skald Thorkill Skallason. Thorkill was in the service of Earl Waltheof, one of the few surviving English noblemen post-1066 and who was married to William's niece Judith. Waltheof was executed for his supposed part in the 1075 rebellion, even though chroniclers like Orderic record that he informed the king of the plot. Thorkill noted that 'it is true that killing in England / will be a long time ending.'[63] He was right.

DID THE CONQUEST CREATE A 'NORMAN EMPIRE'?

In the past historians from Haskins onwards have spoken of a 'Norman world' or a 'Norman empire' stretching from Scotland to Sicily.[64] Connected with this idea is the notion that the Normans were an all-conquering people who enjoyed particular success in the military sphere: following the creation of Normandy, Normans went forth and colonized southern Italy, conquered Sicily, conquered England and then turned their attention to Wales, Scotland and Ireland. Through participation in the first crusade, they also founded the principality of Antioch. More usually, the term 'Norman empire' is taken to mean the Anglo-Norman realm of Normandy and England. Chief among the proponents of empire was John Le Patourel, whose book *The Norman Empire* published in 1976 set the tone for much of the discussion. Le Patourel argued that Norman expansion was a continuous process that had begun with the settlement of Rollo in the Seine valley, but that the empire was made up of the link between England and Normandy. The empire could only exist when England and Normandy were ruled together by the same man. The death of Henry I and subsequent rupture of the Anglo-Norman realm in the civil war between Stephen and Matilda meant that empire came to an end.[65] The existence of a 'Norman empire' has been taken for granted in some contemporary scholarship without any attempt to define it and the term can be used rather uncritically.[66] This is in part due to a historiography that speaks of Norman 'achievement' and 'conquest'. Neither the words 'Norman' nor 'empire', however, have an immutable definition and are deeply contested. We will deal with the question of what it meant to be Norman later, but we will consider empire here.

Most recently David Bates has looked again at the problem of the Norman empire seeking to set the question within a wider historiography of empire stretching across chronological boundaries. He takes Le Patourel as his starting point alongside an article he himself published in 1989.[67] Bates's key points are that an empire must have a 'single ultimate source of authority' and a centre – in this case filled by the person of William the Conqueror and the duchy of Normandy. In his analysis, the conquest of England and subsequent endeavours of William, his son Henry I and his great-grandson Henry II to rule Normandy, England and the gradually expanding Anglo-Norman realm together, need to be seen not as an attempt to rule a unified kingdom, but as a plurality of different realms within a wider polity. In other words, kings exercised hegemonic power over a vastly divergent range of territories and recognized those territories' differences. In this respect, Bates prefers the term 'empire of the Normans'. For Bates, this empire survived because it was based on cross-Channel networks from the start, such as the estates granted by William to his followers, trade, and exchange of personnel, for example between monasteries and cathedrals. These networks allowed the empire to survive periods of civil war, particularly in the mid-twelfth century as different institutions and individuals had interests either side of the Channel. At the centre of the creation of this empire was William himself and his ability to enforce power and the duchy of Normandy as a primary political focus and a strong central core from which territories could be governed.

Two ways to approach the question are to look for evidence that people in the eleventh and twelfth centuries saw connections between the events of their own times with those of past ages relating to concepts of empire and also for demonstrations of power on the part of the central authority. The conquest of England in 1066 and its consolidation in the years following was violent and although scholars have noted that William's use of force was in keeping with the norms of the eleventh century, certainly writers felt uneasy or ambivalent about the level on occasions. Orderic, writing in the early twelfth century, but having grown up in Shropshire 1075–85, was particularly condemnatory about William's violent suppression of the north. He was damning, where previously he had refrained from direct criticism of William's actions. The violence during the Harrying was so devastating, so extreme, that Orderic could not commend the king, but only remand him to God for judgement as he could find no excuse or reason for William's cruelty.[68] William of Malmesbury also presents us with a picture of the north reduced to rubble:

> As for the cities once so famous, the towers whose tops threatened the sky, the fields rich in pasture and watered by rivers, if any one sees them now, he sighs if he is a stranger, and if he is a native surviving from the past, he does not recognize them.[69]

Domesday Book records large parts of Yorkshire as 'waste', though this may mean only that the land was not returning an income.[70] The Evesham Chronicler wrote that many refugees came to the gates of his monastery in a state of starvation.[71] Against this background of devastation, Orderic states that William sent for his royal regalia and wore his crown in the ruins of York minster. As Ann Williams has written, this left no one in any doubt about who was king of the English.[72] From this point on the earls who had survived 1066 were replaced with Normans. This is what Bates, using the language of sociology, terms 'hard power' – visible and direct: 'the exercise of power without consent'.[73] Authority and empire were also created and exercized through the medium of 'soft power' demonstrative of a way of life deemed to be superior. In this category we might place new forms in church building, or the performance of liturgy, as well as changes in eating habits or courtly activity introduced by the Normans. In this respect, the religious roles performed by William as part of kingship, for example the ceremonial crown wearings at Christmas, Easter and Pentecost, or the singing of special liturgies such as the *Laudes regiae* that accompanied such occasions, can be seen as indicative of soft power and as creating an environment in which hard power (the exercise of violence) was deemed more acceptable.[74]

Connections with past ages and ideas of empire are particularly evident in the chronicle writing and elements of architecture. Medieval authors certainly had an idea of 'empire' derived from their knowledge of Rome and reading of the classical authors. Writers like William of Malmesbury also had a deep knowledge of Bede and elaborated on the close connection between the English and Rome, especially in an ecclesiastical context that predated the Norman invasion. Both William and Henry of Huntingdon included a great deal of geographical detail relating to the different invasions in Britain from the Romans on. In their narratives, the Normans were the final group in a series of people sent to inflict punishment on the English for past sins. As we have seen, divine anger was one of the explanations used to rationalize the events following 1066. William of Poitiers made explicit links between William the Conqueror and Rome in his comparisons of William with Julius Caesar. On the return march south following the Harrying of the North in 1069–70, William's army complained bitterly as they trudged through Cheshire and Shropshire about the landscape, the weather, the food and the enemy, while the king himself 'maintained a calmness worthy of Julius Caesar'.[75] It is important to note that these ideas were not confined to an English context. There is also a strong association between Normans and the Roman Empire in writing associated with Normandy. We see this especially in the comparisons of Rouen with Rome or the idea that the duchy's capital was a new Rome, as van Houts's recent study of two poems by Stephen of Rouen and an anonymous author shows.[76]

Architectural developments post-conquest also reference a vocabulary of empire as we can see in some of the earliest castles to be built in England and Wales following the conquest. The castle at Colchester was built on the site of the temple of Claudius and reused both Roman building material and copied Roman building techniques. The pre-conquest chapel dedicated to St Helena, the mother of Emperor Constantine, but also believed to be the daughter of the legendary King 'Cole' (Cunobelin), the founder of Colchester, was retained. William's keep at London, the White Tower, was situated within the corner of the Roman city wall. On the borders of his newly acquired territory, William installed his close adviser, William fitzOsbern as earl of Hereford. In this capacity, fitzOsbern built a castle at Chepstow (though some dating suggests it was

Fig.13: Colchester castle built on the site of the Roman temple of Claudius, eleventh century

actually the king who constructed it), the great tower of which incorporated Roman remains and sculptural detail.[77] However, we should not just look to Rome, but to Normandy itself and other parts of Europe. In terms of building, the Norman rulers imported a large quantity of Caen stone, a soft butter-coloured limestone that is easy to carve, into England following the conquest. This stone was used extensively in facings for castles and cathedrals and for carving the fine sculptural detail around windows, doorways and on pillars. It was a commodity that was clearly highly prized for individuals went to great lengths to import it into England. The styles employed in building castles and cathedrals also echoed building traditions elsewhere in northern Europe, for example Carolingian and Ottonian styles, both associated with ideas of empire. In terms of visuality, then, the buildings of the conquest made direct links between the Normans and ideas of empire in the past and their contemporary present.

It is clear that in aspects of our source material we can see concepts that relate to ideas of empire. This does not mean, however, that scholars who research and write about the Roman or British empires

Fig.14: The exterior of the great hall at Chepstow castle begun in the eleventh century

for example would necessarily recognize it as such. The Normans were not unique in borrowing ideas from the Roman past. As noted above, there was already a strong tradition within English historical writing of linking the English people to Rome. In other medieval societies, notably in Carolingian Francia under Charlemagne or Ottonian Germany, kings adopted the title of emperor for a variety of reasons including to strengthen ties between ruler and pope or to give legitimacy to a new dynasty. Certainly Bates is right to stress the importance of the person of the Conqueror and the centrality of Normandy in the creation of an Anglo-Norman real, but how far his definition of 'empire' is applicable after William's death is debatable. It was, nonetheless, founded on the exercise of violence, sometimes naked, sometimes implied, but never far from the surface. In addition its geography was limited to either side of the English Channel. In no way did any potential empire of the Normans include the land seized in southern Italy and Sicily, nor did it include the principality of Antioch in the Holy Land from the 1090s onwards. In speaking of the Normans in those areas, we should think in terms of a diaspora and look as much for the differences in experience as the similarities. Their reasons for leaving their homeland were different, their social status was less elevated and certainly in the case of southern Italy, the takeover was not a planned campaign. It is to that diaspora that we turn in the next chapter.

3

NORMANS IN THE MEDITERRANEAN: THE HAUTEVILLE CLAN AND OTHERS

Writing in the 1080s, Amatus of Montecassino recorded that Normans began to migrate from Normandy to other parts of the world at the beginning of the eleventh century:

> Abandoning little in order to acquire much, these people departed, but they did not follow the custom of many who go through the world placing themselves in the service of others; rather like the ancient warriors they desired to have all people under their rule and dominion. They took up arms, breaking the bond of peace, and created a great army of foot soldiers and horsemen.[1]

He was, of course, writing with hindsight and knew that not only had the Normans taken over part of southern Italy and Sicily, but also that they had conquered England. Events do not quite bear out Amatus's description, though it does serve to underline the reputation the Normans had acquired. The fame of the southern Italian Normans was also in the mind of the twelfth-century chronicler William of Malmesbury. He recorded that William the Conqueror used to spur himself on by calling to mind the deeds of Robert Guiscard, instrumental in establishing Norman rule, 'saying it would be disgraceful to show less bravery than one whom he so surpassed in rank'.[2] Just as the conquest of England gave rise to a great deal of historical writing that sought to explain how and why William had been able to kill Harold on the field of battle and seize the throne, so too did the activities of the Normans in the Mediterranean, particularly in relation to the conquest of southern Italy and Sicily. Three independent chronicles from, or for, a Norman perspective survive, written by Amatus of Montecassino, Geoffrey Malaterra and William of Apulia.

The Norman takeovers of England and southern Italy did, however, differ in many crucial aspects, not least of which was the rank of the people involved as William of Malmesbury's comparison of Duke William and Robert Guiscard underlines. Whereas the invasion of 1066 was launched by the duke of Normandy himself, the settlement of southern Italy was part of a wider aristocratic diaspora of men seeking a role and position within society.[3] The focus of this chapter is on the Hauteville family, even though its members were just some among many other Normans who migrated. It was men like Robert Guiscard and Roger who were able to negotiate the competing factions and command the writing of history. Geoffrey Malaterra noted the humble beginnings of the dynasty in a reference to the place they hailed from:

In that province [Normandy] there is a city which is called Coutances, in the vicinity of which is an estate called Hauteville. We speculate that this villa was referred to as 'high' [haute] not so much for the prominence of the hill upon which it sits but as an omen of the most noteworthy deeds and prosperous achievements that would be accomplished by those who would inherit it.[4]

These men and their descendants from a backwater of Normandy went on to found the duchy of Apulia, kingdom of Sicily and principality of Antioch, though in the mid-twelfth century Bernard of Clairvaux, the great Cistercian abbot, could still regard King Roger (Robert Guiscard's nephew) as an 'upstart'.[5] We can imagine the insult was double-edged, referring not only to the circumstances of his kingship, but also the humbler origins of his ancestors.

THE CONQUEST OF SOUTHERN ITALY

The conquest of southern Italy has often been compared to the conquest of England and written about in terms of Norman expansion. It would be wrong, however, to think of these two events along similar lines. The conquest of England under William the Conqueror was a planned, single event with a primary goal in mind: to take the throne of England. As discussed in Chapter 2, he acquired widespread diplomatic support, papal backing and persuaded his men to embark on the hazardous crossing to England. The conquest of southern Italy took place over several decades, did not have one single leader and, crucially, had no overarching plan that would result in Norman colonization of the region. In the early stages of settlement there was no indication that the Hauteville family would become pre-eminent. The Normans, and indeed people from other parts of France who also went seeking their fortune, comprised disparate groups in the service of the competing factions that made up the political landscape of the Mezzogiorno.[6] The Hautevilles were not actually the first to migrate to the south and, although the chronology is uncertain, there is evidence that contact between Normans and southern Italians began at the turn of the tenth and eleventh centuries when Norman pilgrims on their return journey were recruited as mercenaries by the Lombard princes.

One of the reasons why the Normans were so successful in southern Italy lies in the fractured political nature of that region in the early Middle Ages. While the inhabitants of Normandy during the period of Scandinavian raids in the ninth and early tenth centuries can be identified as broadly Frankish, the population of southern Italy was made up of a variety of different ethnic, political and religious groups. We might think of Italy has having its roots firmly in the Roman imperial past, but Apulia and Calabria maintained a distinct Greek identity culturally and linguistically. After the fall of the Roman Empire in the west, these provinces became part of the Byzantine Empire, which saw itself as the continuation of the true Rome in the east, ruled from Constantinople. The western coastal region, known as the Campania, was ruled by the descendants of Lombards who had settled there from 568 onwards following the collapse of the Roman Empire.[7] This area was further split into three principalities based around Benevento, Capua and Salerno, along with the duchy of Naples and many city states, in whose contending princes the Normans found willing employers and allies.[8] Sicily, in contrast, had been conquered by the Arabs from 827 and had remained under Islamic rule since. These different regions were not even homogeneous within themselves and were further divided along religious, ethnic and linguistic grounds. Sicily might have been subject to Islamic rulers, but the island contained large Greek-speaking populations which followed the rites of the eastern church as well as Latin Christians whose loyalty was to Rome. All this made for a very volatile mix and the arrival of the Normans provided support for those unhappy, initially with Byzantine rule, to assert their independence.

The chronology of contact between the Normans and the inhabitants of southern Italy is confused. The written sources suggest that the Normans arrived in Italy for very different reasons. Geoffrey Malaterra, as noted below, wrote that poverty and the need for land were primary factors in migration. According to Amatus of Montecassino and William of Apulia, the initial contact between Normans and Lombards was through pilgrimage. Amatus records an incident that most likely took place in c. 1000. A band of around forty pilgrims returned from Jerusalem via Salerno where they volunteered to fight for Prince Guaimar to help him repel a Muslim raid. The Normans were so successful that Guiamar begged them to say. The group refused but took back costly gifts including citrus fruit, nuts, purple cloth and various bits of harness for horses to encourage their compatriots to make the journey south.[9] William's account differs in details. He places the Norman pilgrims at the shrine of the Archangel Michael at Monte Gargano. Here they were recruited by a Lombard, Melus, to fight against the Greeks.[10] This campaign has been dated to 1017, by which point Normans had already been involved in engagements elsewhere.[11] In this case, too, the Normans returned home, but came back to Italy with reinforcements. Pilgrimage is certainly a very likely explanation for the appearance of the Normans on the peninsula early in the eleventh century, although their subsequent deeds as mercenaries, as Graham Loud notes, might have been overstated.[12] Their presence, given the increased interest in Jerusalem in the west from the late tenth century onwards and the presence on Monte Gargano of a shrine to the Archangel Michael, a saint who was a particular favourite of the Normans, makes their presence distinctly plausible.[13]

If pilgrimage might be considered a 'pull factor', encouraging involvement in southern Italy, then some Normans also found themselves pushed out of their homeland through the process of exile, or, as was the case with the sons of Tancred, through the need to seek their fortunes. The case of the brothers is instructive. The Hauteville patriarch was Tancred, an aristocrat of the middle rank whose landholdings were not extensive. With the benefit of hindsight and with a demanding patron to please, Geoffrey Malaterra describes Tancred's lineage as 'outstanding'. His sons certainly went on to do great things, but the reasons for that lie in necessity rather than high politics. Tancred's family was large: he had five sons with his first wife Muriella (William, Drogo, Humphrey, Geoffrey and Serlo) and at least seven sons with his second wife Fresenda, including Robert Guiscard and Roger, and a daughter, also Fresenda, who later married Jordan of Capua. His fief, however, was small. As partible inheritance was the norm in the early eleventh century, the brothers, so Malaterra tells us, decided that some of their number would leave Normandy to seek their fortune elsewhere to avoid the family holdings being divided up to the point where they would no longer sustain a household.[14]

The process of exile is worth considering in some detail as it serves to highlight the temporary nature of some Norman migration to southern Italy from the time of Duke Richard II, underlining the fact that the takeover was not planned. Exile was a punishment that was either handed down by the dukes of Normandy to rid themselves of troublesome persons, or something people undertook voluntarily to avoid further penalties. In other words, it was a formal or informal process by which fear of authority might cause people to flee. The Burgundian chronicler Rodolfus Glaber, writing in the 1030s and 1040s, records that the Norman Rodulf fled the anger of Duke Richard II and travelled to Rome where he was recruited by Pope Benedict VIII to fight the Greeks.[15] Orderic gives the example of Hugh Bunel, who murdered the infamous Mabel of Bellême after she had seized his lands and then fled before the duke's justice could catch up with him.[16] In contrast, Duke William played a more active role in other cases, notably disinheriting and forcing Arnold of Echauffour and Hugh of Grandmesnil into temporary exile in 1058.

It is the twelfth-century chronicler Orderic Vitalis who provides the most information about the exiles, both in his interpolations in William of Jumièges's *Gesta Normannorum ducum* and the *Ecclesiastical History*. Some of these exiles were closely connected with the monastery of Saint-Evroult, and as Johnson notes, the inclusion of their stories is an important part of Orderic's 'attempts to explain the past and present' both of his abbey and the duchy of Normandy.[17] Arnold and Hugh were both members of the family that founded the community. More surprising to modern eyes is that their relative, Robert, the abbot of Saint-Evroult, also fled Normandy with a group of his monks and his two sisters Judith and Emma. For some individuals, exile was a temporary banishment, so there was always the possibility that, once the political temperature had cooled, those individuals could return to their lands. This was the case for Arnold and Hugh, but in contrast Abbot Robert did not return to Normandy permanently, even after his reconciliation with William in 1077. By this point he had become abbot of a new community at Sant'Eufemia in Calabria. His sister Judith had also married Count Roger. Hugh Bunel stayed for a while in Italy and then went on to Jerusalem where Orderic tells us he acted as a translator for the crusaders.[18] As Johnson notes, exile for some people would have entailed giving up everything, thus making return to Normandy impossible.[19] In this context, their situation was similar to individuals like the sons of Tancred, who, having nothing to lose and everything to gain, made their home and carved out land on the peninsula.

It is important to stress here that the first Normans to make their mark in the politics of southern Italy did so in the service of primarily the Lombard princes as discussed above, and also the papacy. This meant that they were not a unified group and, indeed, could find themselves fighting other Normans in the service of different lords. The Lombard princes were keen to use Normans in their own disputes with each other, for example. The first Norman base in southern Italy was founded at Aversa under Rainulf. Amatus states that the town was granted to Rainulf by Duke Sergius of Naples in 1030 following his dispute with Pandulf IV of Capua. Rainulf also married Sergius's sister, but when she died, he swapped sides to support Pandulf! Rainulf cannot be identified with precision, but it is possible that he was a brother of one of the Norman exiles, Gilbert Buatère.[20] Rainulf also helped Guaimar of Salerno to take Sorrento. As Loud notes, however, other groups caused difficulties. Pandulf IV had established some Normans on lands belonging to the abbey of Montecassino, but they despoiled them, damaging the community's economic interests.[21] Guaimar took the opportunity offered by a Byzantine request for troops to fight in Sicily by sending 300 Normans, including William Iron Arm and Drogo of Hauteville, to rid himself of potential trouble.[22]

It was around this time, the 1030s, that the elder sons of Tancred also began to make their presence felt on the peninsula. The land that the Hauteville brothers chose to travel to was the province of Apulia in southern Italy. William Iron Arm and Drogo were the first of the siblings to arrive and they took service, first with the prince of Capua and then with Guaimar of Salerno, and acquitted themselves very well. The Norman takeover was slow and piecemeal, but began to gather pace in the 1040s. Gradually the Normans were in a position to choose their own leaders, notably Rainulf of Aversa and William Iron Arm, from among their number. They also planned a division of territory as recorded by Amatus following the campaigns in Apulia under Rainulf's leadership in 1043:

> Before they came to a division [of the land], they took care to endow Count Rainulf with territory that they had conquered [...] The remaining lands which they had acquired and which they would acquire the Normans divided among themselves in good will, peace and concord. In this manner William received Ascoli; Drogo had Venosa; Arnolin had Lavello; Hugh Toutebove had Monopoli; Rodulf had Canne, Walter [son of Amicus], Civitate; Peter [son of Amicus], Trani; Rodulf, son of Bebena, Sant'Arcangelo; Tristan, Montepeloso; Hervey Grumento; Asclettin, Acerenza, and Rainfroi, Malarbine.[23]

Not all the places listed by Amatus were in Norman hands at the time of the division, but the 1040s and 1050s did see an increase in raiding and consolidation of their hold on territory as they pushed further north into the Lombard principalities and south into Calabria. This period marks a sea change in the Normans' involvement in the region. Up to this point individuals had taken service with the Lombard princes. Instead, the new arrivals joined with their relatives and compatriots who had already carved out a place for themselves. According to Geoffrey Malaterra, the younger Hauteville brothers learned that their siblings 'were ascending to the heights of honour and dominion through their valiant efforts'.[24] As soon as they were old enough, some of them also journeyed to southern Italy, including Robert Guiscard who arrived *c.* 1046/47 and Roger.

The Normans were still, however, disunited and in this light Amatus's list is interesting for a number of reasons. Not only does it show William and Drogo of Hauteville rising to prominence, but also Walter and Peter, the sons of Amicus, who were the strongest rivals to the increasing power of the Hauteville clan. For example, following William's death, they challenged Drogo's right to succeed to his land. The size of the Hauteville family still continued to be a significant factor. After Humphrey died, Robert Guiscard disinherited Humphrey's son Abelard. Once Abelard was older, he allied with Walter's son, Amicus, to try to regain his patrimony. Kinship was absolutely no guarantee of loyalty.

The conquest of the southern Italian mainland as recorded by Amatus and Geoffrey is carefully mapped in their chronicles. This is particularly noticeable in the accounts of Rainulf's Aversan campaigns and Robert Guiscard's expeditions in Calabria alongside his brother, Roger. We noted the importance William of Poitiers placed on emphasizing the difficulties faced by Duke William II in consolidating his rule on the southern frontier of Normandy and how his ability to overcome them emphasized his qualities as a ruler. Geoffrey in particular did something similar with his description of the Calabrian campaign. In many respects, Roger was seeking to prove himself able to conquer and hold territory alongside his older brothers. Geoffrey states that Roger was only equipped with sixty knights, but despite this he was able to achieve victory through strategic use of the landscape. For example, he established camps and fortifications in elevated positions less prone to diseases, as at Vibona, and used his command of the area around Scalea to harass his brother Robert when the two fell out over resources. Both Amatus and Geoffrey were careful to plot the campaigns, listing the towns taken in turn and so providing an itinerary of conquest.[25] This description also served to underline the achievements of men like Rainulf, Robert and Roger.

The growing power of the Normans and their despoliation of other people's lands resulted in an alliance between the Lombards, the pope and the German emperor, all of whom had interests in the region that were potentially damaged by the various Norman advances. It is important to underline that the Normans were still not particularly united at this point. They had cooperated when they needed to, but otherwise each man was concerned with consolidating his own territory. Even the Hauteville brothers fought among themselves. This disunity might well have contributed to the level of violence experienced by the inhabitants of Apulia and Calabria. Narrative sources like Amatus's *History* and the Montecassino chronicle alongside charter evidence bear witness to the level of deprivation suffered by those under Norman control. Abbot Richer tried to expel the Normans from the lands of Montecassino as 'they did much harm to the poor'.[26] Key to the escalating tensions between the Lombards, papacy and emperor on the one hand and the Normans on the other was the city of Benevento. The emperor, Henry III, claimed overlordship and in the face of the recalcitrant prince, persuaded Pope Clement II to excommunicate the city and allowed the Normans to continue their attacks on the principality in 1047. In 1051 the Beneventans surrendered to the new pope, Leo IX, who tried to broker peace with the Normans:

> He was concerned above all to establish harmony between the natives of the region and the Normans, who the princes of the kingdom had originally welcomed to aid them against the foreign peoples, but whom they would not willingly endure when they became very savage tyrants and ravagers of their homeland.[27]

Nonetheless, the Normans continued their attacks. This led to the murder of Drogo and several other Norman leaders, but also the realization among other parties with interests in the region that something had to be done to halt the takeover.

As Loud notes, the campaign mounted by Leo in alliance with Emperor Henry and forces from the Lombard principalities, was the 'only concerted effort made to defeat the Normans in southern Italy'.[28] The Normans were faced with a mighty coalition and, had it been successful, might well have seen the end of independent Norman ambitions in the region. What it did achieve was a degree of unity among the Normans, albeit temporarily. Count Humphrey of Apulia (the third-eldest Hauteville brother after William Iron Arm and Drogo) took command of an army that included not just the Hautevilles, but also the sons of Amicus and Count Richard of Aversa. Battle was still by no means inevitable. The Normans were short of food and tried to negotiate, but to no avail. On 17 June 1053, the armies met near Civitate and the Normans won a decisive victory, with Robert Guiscard playing a leading part.[29] They also captured Pope Leo. This victory paved the way for more rapid advances in territory, particularly in Calabria by Robert Guiscard and in the Lombard principalities by Richard of Aversa. Although the Normans continued to face problems notably famine, disease and resistance, they were in a much stronger position with regard to their main rivals for supremacy in the region, the pope and the emperor. Henry III died in 1056 leaving a minor as his heir, and the death of Leo IX in 1054 marked the beginning of a period of instability within the papacy. By 1059 the Normans were in a position to have their conquests recognized by Pope Nicholas II. Richard was recognized as prince of Capua and, later at the synod of Melfi, Robert as duke of Apulia. In return, Robert swore fealty to the pope and crucially he also did this as future duke of Sicily. The consolidation of Norman rule continued on the mainland with further campaigns in Calabria and Apulia and the need to suppress uprisings, including from other Normans unhappy with Robert's increasing supremacy, but now there was new land to be conquered across the Straits of Messina.[30]

THE CONQUEST OF SICILY

Parts of Sicily had been under Muslim control from 827, though the conquest progressed slowly: Rometta, the last town to fall, did so only in the mid-960s. The prolonged campaigns meant that parts of the island, notably the west, had had significantly more exposure to Muslim rule than the east. The ethnic, cultural and religious landscape of Sicily was thus very mixed. By the early eleventh century the Islamic authority on the island had fragmented during a period of internal disorder related to the rise of the Zirid dynasty in north Africa. In 1038 the Byzantines sought to profit from the unrest and an invasion was launched under their general Maniakes with Norman mercenary involvement.[31] Although this expedition was unsuccessful, it does seem that later the pope and Robert Guiscard viewed the conquest of Sicily as desirable. How that conquest has been interpreted is a matter of great debate among historians, particularly whether it is helpful to think of this event as 'Norman' and how far it should be viewed as a crusade.

As noted above, Robert Guiscard had sworn fealty to the pope as future duke of Sicily in 1059. This would suggest that the idea of a Norman-led expedition to the island had at least been discussed some years prior to the first invasion in 1061. This contrasts with Geoffrey Malaterra's assertion that it was Roger who came up with the idea in 1060 because he saw that Sicily was under Muslim, rather than Christian, control:

> Informing himself about Sicily, which was under the control of the infidels, and noticing how narrow the sea was that separated it from Calabria, Roger, who was always avid for domination was seized with the ambition of obtaining it.[32]

Geoffrey was, of course, writing a court history for Roger and so his desire to stress the count's involvement and credit him with the initial idea should be read in this light. It is clear from subsequent events, however, that Roger was the driving force behind the conquest, with Robert as his nominal overlord. Although the first campaign took place in 1061, the conquest was not completed until the 1090s. There are several reasons for this. The Norman leaders may have had their conquests recognized by the pope and other political powers in southern Italy, but that did not mean that all opposition to their takeover ceased in 1059. Robert Guiscard faced a number of rebellions against his rule not only from Lombards, but also disaffected Normans who did not want to recognize his overlordship or thought that he had seized lands unjustly. This included his own nephews, Abelard, son of Humphrey, and Geoffrey of Conversano. Other groups had bided their time and took the opportunity to attack Guiscard's lands, notably the princes of Capua, descendants of Rainulf of Aversa. As a result Robert was not always in a position to support his brother's campaigns in Sicily as the situation on the mainland demanded his presence and resources. Like southern Italy, Sicily itself was torn by internal divisions and competing interests between Muslims and non-Muslims and among the Arab rulers themselves, which both aided and hindered the Norman takeover. As Alex Metcalfe notes, the initial campaigns can be seen as very much within the context of civil war on the island. In 1061 Robert and Roger allied with the disaffected emir, Ibn Thumna, who had taken power in Syracuse.[33] It is highly likely that alliance with Muslim factions increased the chances of a successful Norman conquest, given the limited troops available on the mainland.[34] At times Roger also found himself in opposition to Christian groups, notably the Greeks at Troina. Malaterra records that the citizens of the town resented military impositions such as the billeting of troops and were concerned for the virtue of their womenfolk. While Roger was campaigning elsewhere, they tried to overthrow the Norman garrison, with whom his wife, Judith, was staying. Roger came back only to find himself besieged over winter for a period of four months.[35]

There were other factors that also served to delay the subjugation of Sicily recorded in the pages of Geoffrey Malaterra's *Deeds of Count Roger*. These relate to the terrain and fauna encountered by the Normans. One infamous incident involved the Normans setting up camp on a hillside outside Palermo in 1064 that turned out to be home to a colony of tarantulas, which 'bothered the army a great deal'. In the description that follows it must be remembered that Malaterra probably did not know much about the habits of these particular arachnids. The spiders bit the Normans, who then swelled up; these symptoms could only be relieved by farting.[36] There is more than an element of comedy here, as Malaterra also noted that the encounter 'provided a silly sort of entertainment for those who managed to stay far enough away' from the tarantulas, and no doubt it did several decades later as the old campaigners reminisced about their exploits in the court of Count Roger. Less amusing were the extremes of climate encountered. Malaterra tell us that Roger had to suspend campaigning during the summer heat and in the mountains the winter could be bitter. In 1063 Roger returned to the mainland as 'the intense heat [...] would prevent his cavalry from undertaking any more plundering expeditions'.[37] Just as he and Amatus lauded the Normans' strategic use of landscape on the mainland, Geoffrey used these examples to underline the qualities of Roger and his companions and how the difficulties they overcame demonstrated their ability to conquer and hold the land.

As noted above, the papal investiture of 1059 did not mean an end to the opposition to Norman rule on the mainland, and likewise, the completion of the conquest of Sicily in 1091 did not lead to a smooth transition to the foundation of the later kingdom. Robert Guiscard's preoccupations on the mainland and his no more than nominal lordship over the island ensured that the counts of Sicily became effectively another independent power in the region.

Robert died in 1085 and was succeeded by Roger Borsa, his son with his second wife Sichelgaita of Salerno. Roger, count of Sicily died in 1101 leaving small boys as heirs, resulting in a period of upheaval and rebellion. It therefore took some years for the man who would become Roger II, king of Sicily to establish himself. Following the death of Roger Borsa's son, William in 1127, Roger became heir to the territories on the mainland. That he managed to unite them was quite some achievement, albeit a short-lived one, as by 1194 Sicily was in the hands of the German emperor. The character of this kingdom, particularly whether it could be described in any meaningful way as Norman, will be discussed in later chapters.

Papal involvement, possibly endorsement, and the fact that there was a religious element to the conquest of Sicily has led some historians to speak of this campaign in terms of a crusade or some form of holy war.[38] In addition, the first crusade, preached in 1095 is close in date to the writing of two of the main histories of the conquest. William of Apulia's chronicle has been dated to between 1096 and 1099 and Geoffrey Malaterra was writing towards the end of that decade, too, so he especially might well have been influenced by some of the rhetoric of crusading ideology. Paul Cheveden has identified certain elements within Malaterra's history in particular that prefigure some of the characteristics of crusade narratives. Roger, at some stage, was rewarded with a papal banner – a mark of favour, as we saw with Pope Alexander's backing of William's invasion and conquest of England. Malaterra also included supernatural or miraculous events in his description of military engagements, for example St George coming to help the Norman army at the battle of Cerami in 1063 or the appearance of signs in the sky.[39] The closest parallel to this story is the appearance of the ghostly army of saints outside the city of Antioch during the crusaders' desperate final attempt to relieve the siege. This event was recorded by the anonymous author of the *Gesta Francorum* who was part of the southern Italian contingent on the first crusade, which might explain the echo.[40] Geoffrey and the author of the *Gesta* are independent sources, but the similarities are striking. Geoffrey also suggests that the pope granted participants absolution, something which is particularly associated with the crusade indulgence by which penance for sins was remitted.[41]

The problem we as historians have with viewing this event as a crusade is the fact that we are reading the sources refracted through our knowledge of the first crusade preached by Pope Urban II in 1095 and culminating in the siege and capture of Jerusalem in 1099. It is possible that there were elements of holy war present in the various accounts. But it is important to note that divine providence and the idea that the working out of God's plan for humanity through human affairs were important parts of most medieval chronicles. We have previously considered that the conquest of England was seen as God's punishment for sinful behaviour. The descriptions of the Normans' migrations to Italy speak of the peninsula as a 'promised land' echoing the Israelites' wanderings during the Exodus.[42] Amatus, writing some years before the crusade was preached in 1095, quoted the Bible extensively and considered that the Normans were successful because God allowed it.[43] Geoffrey Malaterra did include episodes that find resonances in crusade narratives, but he was primarily writing a court history for Count Roger 'in plain and simple words so that it would be readily comprehensible'.[44] He acknowledged the role played by providence, but was more concerned with stressing the qualities and characteristics (desire for land and dominion) of the Normans than providing a discussion of the merits of holy war.[45] William of Apulia, who wrote to describe the deeds of Duke Robert, explicitly mentions the expedition to the Holy Land, commenting that the 'the Gallic race [...] wanted to open the roads to the Holy Sepulchre'.[46] Emily Albu reads this passage as an endorsement of holy war in Sicily.[47] Certainly in the case of Sicily, the Normans' main opponents were the Muslim rulers, but, at times, they were fighting other Christians on the island and depended on Muslim allies for their success. As Metcalfe points out, they were certainly not fighting the Muslims because they were Muslims.[48] It is possible that comparison, in a broad sense, with England might well be helpful here. William's conquest of England cannot be called a crusade, yet he was awarded a papal banner and, from the pope's point of view at least, it was a war fought in the name of the reform movement. To speak of the conquest of southern Italy as a crusade, or even as a proto-crusade, is to view it in the wrong context, or at least to overemphasize factors we see emerging over the events of 1095–9. The story of the conquest of Sicily belongs more in the context of the ambitions of the Hauteville clan than it does a wider Western European narrative of holy war.

THE NORMANS ON CRUSADE

Historians have written a great deal on the subject of why thousands of people from western Latin Christendom heeded Pope Urban's call and undertook the arduous, perilous and, in many cases, fatal journey east to Jerusalem and the Holy Land. Very few would settle for a monocausal explanation to explain such a complex phenomenon. The secular nature of late twentieth- and early twenty-first-century western society has led some scholars to question the piety of those who took the cross. John France proposed that religiosity was less important than a desire for the land, wealth and status that individuals could not achieve within the prevailing western European framework of patronage and lordship.[49] Others, notably Jonathan Riley-Smith, have stressed, through careful analysis of chronicles and charters, that piety and religious fervour were indeed at the heart of many of the decisions to take the cross, among other factors.[50] After all, Jerusalem, although a familiar place in the mental map of western Europe, was many, many miles away through hostile territory. As the crusaders were going with the aim of fighting, they needed to equip themselves and their followers in order to be ready to engage in warfare once they were in Muslim-held regions. The crusade was therefore a very expensive undertaking – its participants had to sell or mortgage land in many cases to finance the expedition – and, if wealth and land were the primary motivators in going, a very risky gamble.[51]

Nevertheless there were tensions between the desire for wealth and piety. These are illustrated very well in the contrasting careers of Bohemond and his nephew, Tancred, while on crusade. Bohemond was Robert Guiscard's son with his first wife Alberada, a woman of Norman descent. Bohemond was effectively disinherited by Robert's marriage to Sichelgaita, a Lombard princess, whose son, Roger Borsa became heir to Robert's lands in Calabria and Apulia. Like others before him, notably his father and uncles, Bohemond needed to carve out his own territory. Prior to the preaching of the crusade in 1095, Robert and Bohemond mounted several campaigns against the Byzantines hoping to expand their territories across the Adriatic Sea. These campaigns ended in failure and it seemed that Norman expansion was destined to stop on the Adriatic coast of Italy.[52] In this context, the call to take the cross might well have come at an opportune moment in Bohemond's career.

Bohemond heard about the call to arms while besieging Amalfi. The account of his taking the cross provided by the author of the *Gesta Francorum* suggests that his actions were deliberate, and perhaps stage-managed. In response to the preaching, Bohemond called for his best cloak, which he then cut up into crosses that he distributed among his retinue. He left the siege, gathered his forces, sailed east and headed towards the Byzantine Empire.[53] The emperor Alexius was anxious about the arrival of all these Franks, as the western sources call the crusaders, in Constantinople and what this might betoken for his position and the security of his lands. According to Anna Comnena's later biography of her imperial father, he was wary of the arrival of the army, especially as it contained southern Italian Normans who had actively campaigned against him. Anna was admittedly writing in the mid-twelfth century and her attitude to the Normans was, on the whole, negative, even though she did admire Bohemond's physique.[54] It is clear, however, that previous Norman activity in the empire did complicate the political picture.[55] Many of the crusade chronicles talk about the oath that Alexius was keen to extract from the leaders of the armies that any land that had formerly belonged to the empire, for example in Syria, was to be held in allegiance to him. In other words, he wanted to limit the scope for the crusaders to set up independent states in territory that had belonged to his predecessors. The author of the *Gesta Francorum* records that Bohemond swore an oath of fealty in return for lands beyond Antioch, as did other leaders. 'But why did such brave and determined knights do a thing like this?' asked the author, knowing that later events showed that Bohemond, if he had indeed sworn the oath, had broken it.[56] It is impossible to know the minds of people who lived in the past, but the crusaders needed the emperor's help in the short term and any oath swearing was surely expedient.

Throughout the march through what is now Turkey and Syria, Bohemond, along with the other Normans like Tancred and Robert Curthose, the eldest son of William the Conqueror and himself then duke of Normandy, acquitted themselves well in various military engagements.[57] Matters came to a head at Antioch, a city that was first besieged by the crusaders before they themselves found them besieged in return by a Muslim relief army. Antioch (the modern city of Antakya) was a well-fortified city, both in terms of man-made fortifications and physical geography, with a citadel situated high on the hills above the river Orontes. The crusade army became bogged down trying to besiege the town and it was only when Bohemond managed to persuade one of the defenders, a man named as Firuz in the *Gesta Francorum*, to lower ladders and let his army in that a plan to capture the city was successfully carried out. Bohemond had told the other leaders of the crusade that he had the means to take the city if they would grant him lordship over it. The crusade leaders all had their eyes on each other as well as the Muslims and were anxious that no one in the army should become too powerful. The question of who would hold Antioch, a key strategic city, was therefore an important one. They initially refused his request. Bohemond persevered with his plan, however, and during the night, Firuz let the army into the fortifications. Once the crusaders had entered the city they in turn were besieged by a Muslim relief force and endured great hardship, eventually fighting their way out after many months of siege, mostly starved, probably half-mad and, according to the sources, with the help of a ghostly army comprising the martial saints and others. It was at this point that Bohemond left the army and did not carry on to Jerusalem. He was by no means the first to do this: some leaders, including Stephen of Blois (married to William the Conqueror's daughter, Adela) had run away from the siege of Antioch and Baldwin count of Boulogne became the ruler of Edessa. In taking the city, Bohemond had what he had been looking for, land and thus the principality of Antioch was founded.

Tancred, by contrast, continued on the march and played a significant role in the capture and siege of Jerusalem. The earliest chronicler of the crusade, the anonymous author of the *Gesta Francorum*, who was probably – and unusually for a chronicler in this period – a lay man, switched from Bohemond's retinue to Tancred's as he deemed the latter, through his intention to fulfil his crusader's vow, a more worthy leader. Tancred by this point was part of Count Raymond of Toulouse's contingent as he had run out of money. We also have a source that specifically records the deeds of Tancred on crusade, written by Ralph of Caen, albeit sometime after the events it narrates.[58] Ralph gives us a picture of Tancred as a pious young nobleman in contrast to the greed of his uncle, Bohemond. He depicts Tancred as a youth who had wrestled with the conflicting demands of Christianity and military endeavour:

Over time, however, his prudent soul raised concerns that caused him anxiety. It seemed that his military life contradicted the Lord's command. The Lord had commanded that after one cheek had been struck the other was to be offered as well. But a secular military life did not even permit the sparing of a relative's blood.[59]

How is it possible, he has Tancred ask, to be a good Christian and a brave knight who kills people? The crusade provided an outlet where one could be both. Historians have spoken of the opportunities the crusade offered to pious laymen who were unsuited to a monastic vocation, but who were anxious about their personal salvation. The crusade allowed these men, in the eyes of the church, to use their martial prowess in God's service. Tancred, at least in Ralph's writing, became the epitome of Christian knighthood. This did not stop him from carrying out atrocious acts of brutality and slaughter during the siege and capture of Jerusalem, but his career does demonstrate the different reasons and responses people could have to crusading. His service was also not without material reward, as he inherited his uncle's territories in Antioch.

The question of Norman participation on crusade raises many questions about identity, not least of which how far the contingents of Robert Curthose, Bohemond and Tancred formed recognizable groups of Normans, rather than just comprising a section of a larger 'Frankish' crusading army, which will be explored in more detail in Chapter 7. Nevertheless, it is pertinent to consider whether Antioch had a Norman character. The work of Alan Murray, who has employed prosopographical methods, that is to say the study of names, to assess how 'Norman' Norman Antioch really was, is helpful here.[60] In so doing he considered characteristics first used by Léon-Robert Ménager to understand how far migration to southern Italy could be considered Norman, rather than associated with other areas of Francia. These include the presence of forenames of Scandinavian origin; Norman toponyms (place names), family names and patronymics; the use of 'Normannus' as a way of describing someone with regard to ethnicity; and finally, whether a particular individual was described as being of Norman origin. For southern Italy, Ménager's study of charter evidence revealed that two-thirds to three-quarters of immigrants to southern Italy came from Normandy in the initial phases of migration.[61] Murray's analysis reveals that the final two characteristics were entirely absent in Antioch: people were not described as Norman or being of Norman origin. In addition, Scandinavian names very rarely occur in the documentary record. By the time of the first crusade it was 200 years since the Vikings had appeared in the Seine valley. Prolonged exposure to Frankish naming patterns, particularly for the southern Italian Normans, whose connection to Normandy must have substantially weakened over the course of the eleventh century, might well have led to the decline in Scandinavian names. The use of toponyms is complicated by the fact that many Norman and French names are similar, so it is hard to pinpoint exactly where someone came from. Murray offers the Sourdeval family as a likely example, which he links to Sourdeval-la-Barre in Manche as opposed to one of the many other places called Sourdeval.[62] We do know that the first four rulers of the principality were all descended from Robert Guiscard. These were Bohemond, Tancred, Roger of Salerno who was the son of Richard of the Principate (a nephew of Robert Guiscard and son of William Iron Arm) and finally Bohemond's son, also called Bohemond, which suggests lineage, rather than ethnicity, was important.

The relative unimportance of ethnicity is also borne out by how Antioch was governed. Although there is some evidence that the household officers were similar to figures found in Norman noble households, Bohemond and Tancred encountered a city with a very ethnically diverse population. In order to rule effectively, the Normans needed to adopt administrative practices that reflected this variation, notably those derived from the Byzantine Empire.[63] The empire was key in understanding the development of the principality. Antioch had formally been part of Byzantium and Alexius and later rulers were keen to ensure that they profited from the activities of the crusaders by returning former provinces to their rule. Indeed, Antioch was forced to accept Byzantine over-lordship in 1137, 1145 and 1158–9. The establishment and administration of this principality has, therefore, to be seen against a background of complex political relationships. This revises earlier work that saw the principality very much as a Norman creation. Haskins, one of the early twentieth-century historians of the Normans, wrote that Antioch had a distinctly Norman character in terms of its institution and rule, but that this identity was short-lived, not surviving beyond the death of Tancred.[64] Douglas, much of whose work about the

Normans' migration focused on military aspects, regarded Antioch as the 'third Norman conquest', completed by Bohemond and Tancred.[65] On this evidence presented above it is hard to follow Douglas here, or even Haskins.

The conquest of southern Italy and Sicily and the foundation of the principality of Antioch took the Normans south and eastwards, further away from the Scandinavian homeland of their ancestors who settled Normandy. If comparisons are to be made between the Normans in one area of Europe and another, then the activities of the Normans in Italy should be compared to the original settlement of Normandy. Here they found a region with tricky enough politics and a fragmented enough society to exploit for their own ends, carving out territories and eventually a new kingdom. In terms of statistics, the Norman migrants numbered fewer than a few thousand in southern Italy and they arrived over a long period of time. As Ménager has shown, between one-third and one-quarter of those involved in the conquest were from Frankish regions other than Normandy.[66] The degree to which either the kingdom of Sicily or principality of Antioch can be considered Norman, therefore, is a moot one. Both Metcalfe and Paul Oldfield have commented on the unhelpfulness of the term. It leads historians into a mode of thinking centred on western European paradigms and runs the risk of privileging the adjective 'Norman' over other identifiers, as well as obscuring continuities with previous structures.[67] We will begin to consider these questions in the chapters that follow, starting with a discussion of society, highlighting the differences in each area of Europe.

4

SOCIETY

Of the aforesaid waste messuages 166 were destroyed on account of the castle.[1]

The victorious duke [Robert Guiscard] went to Troia with a great multitude of knights and foot soldiers. He besieged the city, arranging siege-castles and tents around it. The citizens of Troia took counter measures, though they did not refuse the customary tribute and had even promised to add to it gold and horses from Greece. However, the duke scorned this gesture, for he wanted the highest place in the city upon which he could build a well-fortified citadel from which to control the townspeople.[2]

As these examples from England and southern Italy show, the Normans could and did have a profound impact on the societies they conquered and in which they settled. They stress the often violent nature of Norman interaction with those they encountered. But to speak of 'Norman society' or to suggest that the impact was uniform runs the risk of oversimplifying a very complex topic and masking the differences and variations in experience. The situation that William the Conqueror found in England was not the same as that in southern Italy. England on the eve of 1066 was a relatively united realm, whereas the early Norman settlers in the Mezzogiorno encountered several different traditions, languages and religions. Large-scale economic or agricultural changes also affected these regions in different ways. Society is a vast topic and it is impossible to cover all aspects of social experience. Instead several areas are highlighted for which comparative medieval evidence and lively debate within modern historiography exist: the Normans' use of castles, changes in landholding, the experience of peasants, and the question of marriage alliances as a tool for consolidation of conquest or assimilation.

CASTLES

Castles are associated indelibly in public consciousness with the Normans. They comprise some of the most visible reminders of the Norman presence in Europe and, as such, historians and archaeologists are fortunate in having both the surviving buildings and sites alongside written evidence in order to build up a fuller understanding of the complexities of these structures. Debates have raged fiercely about the exact definition of what a castle was, how it was used and by whom. In 1977 the Royal Archaeological Institute defined a castle as 'the fortified residence of a lord', placing equal weight on defence and habitation. More recently, the work of Charles Coulson and Jean Mesqui among others has focused on the symbolic role of the castle to demonstrate lordship, power and wealth through the ability to command enough resources to build something on such a large scale in the first place.[3] The exact definition of a castle is therefore very hard to pin down. Where do these modern definitions leave siege castles: temporary structures that could be flat-packed, transported to – and then assembled on, a particular site? How do we explain the fact that some, like Castle Rising built in Norfolk in the mid-twelfth century, were not necessarily constructed in the most obviously defensible part of the surrounding landscape, that is the highest patch of ground? The search for definitions means we can lose sight of the fact that castles fulfilled a variety of roles within medieval society. What makes them interesting from a Norman perspective is how they were used in consolidating conquest and what they can tell us about elite society.

Undoubtedly castles had an important role in the military consolidation and administration of the conquest of England following the battle of Hastings in 1066 and the more gradual takeover of territory in southern Italy, particularly by Robert Guiscard and his brother, Roger. In this context, it is important to consider to what extent castles were innovative in the way that the Normans used them. Older scholarship argued that structures known as motte and bailey castles were developed in Normandy and then imported, particularly into England, as an instrument of conquest. Excavation on the continent, however, has shown that mottes (artificial mounds of earth on which sat towers or pallisades) were actually a later development in the duchy.[4] Fortifications, but not castles in the way we know them, existed in both England and Italy prior to the arrival of the Normans. What changed was perhaps their form, number and scale, and the relationship between these buildings and wider society. In Italy, modern historians of the Middle Ages have spoken of a process known as *incastallamento*. This term does not mean that prior to 1,000 people were building structures recognizable as castles all over the landscape; rather it refers to a process by which new units of administration, *castelli*, were founded for the exploitation of agricultural and other resources. They had jurisdictional powers and the settlements were fortified with a hedge or wooden palisade for defensive purposes. For the region of southern Italy, the most famous example is that of the monastery of San Vincenzo al Volturno. This institution used *castelli* as part of a programme of resettlement and economic development. Although this was a phenomenon witnessed across the Italian peninsula there were regional differences and it is possible that the emphasis in the south was as much, if not more, on defence than economic exploitation.[5] In England, a very small number of mottes might pre-date 1066, of which Ewyas Harold in the volatile border region of Herefordshire is the most certain identification. As in Italy, fortifications were more communal in the form of burhs, though there is limited evidence for the fortification of thegns' houses, perhaps the closest parallel to the Norman lord's castle.[6] What certainly differed in both England and Italy was the appearance of fortifications in the form of castles and their systematic use by the Normans. For the twelfth-century chronicler, Orderic Vitalis, they were certainly new and terrifying intrusions on the landscape of his birth in Shropshire and other places: 'the fortifications called castles by the Normans were scarcely known in the English provinces, and so the English – in spite of their courage and love of fighting – could put up only a weak resistance to their enemies.'[7] In southern Italy, rather than continuing the tradition

Fig.15: The motte at Ewyas Harold

of fortifying the settlement, Norman castles are generally found on the edges, separate and commanding.[8] In both cases, regardless of their function either as a military centre or a focus for local administration, these structures were designed to be seen.

On landing at Pevensey in 1066 one of the first things William did, presumably once he had secured the boats, was to fortify the old Roman Saxon shore fort, the remains of which can still be seen today. He also raised a small castle at Hastings, which is depicted on the Bayeux Tapestry. Reading evidence like the tapestry, which is a highly stylized piece of art governed more by artistic conventions than by a desire to provide accurate depictions of eleventh-century life, can be misleading. Archaeological excavation of motte sites, however, supports its evidence in terms of the construction of mounds like the one at Hastings, comprising layers of earth mounted by a wooden palisade.[9] It is possible that William brought materials across from Normandy, but if he did not, then he certainly had the manpower to send foraging parties around the surrounding countryside to gather the necessary materials and force local people to help with its construction. The fortifications at Pevensey and Hastings provided William with a reasonably secure base from which he could sustain his troops by raiding what were Harold Godwineson's ancestral lands, and protect them from any attack launched by the local population. In using castles in this way, he was developing tactics used to good effect in Normandy, for example at the siege of Domfront, where William constructed a number of siege castles to provide cover for foragers and to harry the defenders, who had to make sallies to gather food or water. William's campaigns in the south-west and north in the period of rebellions up to 1070 were also marked by the strategic construction of castles to consolidate his hold on the country.[10]

In southern Italy, scholars have also argued that castles were instruments of conquest, possibly right up to the reign of Roger II (1130–54).[11] The earliest castles were built during the Apulian campaign: at Aversa in *c*. 1030, then at Melfi which had been previously fortified by the Greeks, followed by Squillace built by William Iron Arm in *c*. 1044. These early castles and the later ones built by Robert Guiscard during his conquest of Calabria were probably earth and timber constructions, similar to the campaign castles we find in England in the years immediately following 1066, allowing for differences in construction relating to climate and available building materials. The importance of decent fortifications is underlined by the fact that Robert Guiscard spent a week refortifying Messina after he had taken it during the Sicilian campaign. As this was the main point of disembarkation after crossing the straits of Messina, it was necessary to ensure the Norman forces protected this bridgehead. As the conquest progressed and the Normans took control of towns, they made use of existing city walls, but, importantly, built further castles towards the edges of these towns rather than at the centre. It is possible that this development was designed as a defensive measure against rebellion from the town itself: the Normans could retreat to their stronghold in times of danger. Equally lack of space in existing towns could prevent the imposition of new structures. There might also be pragmatic reasons in terms of space to design the castles according to the ideas the new rulers brought with them. As the campaigns progressed from conquest to consolidation, castles began to take on the character of similar edifices in Normandy and England and were used much in the same way. King Roger II also recognized the importance of castles in consolidating his rule over Sicily and southern Italy. On the mainland, he took control of the tower at Salerno as well as rebuilding castles in Troia and Melfi in 1130. He built a new castle on the outskirts of Bari in 1132/3, which allowed him to control both the town and the surrounding countryside. It also reduced the potential for sieges by the citizens of the town.[12]

So far discussion has centred on the castles as examples of military might and conquest. Flexibility in their design allowed quick construction and provided a means of consolidating territory, but these buildings expressed other concepts relating to the exercise of lordship and administration. The campaign castles built by William, Robert and Roger showed how these men were able to subdue territory, but castles built by lords could be indicative of the weakness of a particular ruler or of the changing relations between neighbouring lords. Normandy provides some instructive examples in this regard.

Changes in the political climate and disputes between neighbouring lords determined to a great extent how castles were both viewed and used. The history of the the castles of Dreux and Tillières-sur-Avre in the Evrecin on the border of Normandy and recorded by William of Jumièges is a case in point. William was particularly well informed about events in this area as his monastery of Jumièges held extensive lands in the region and, although his chronology may be a little crooked in places, we may trust the bare bones of his account. William gives us a record of the disputed territory of the Avre valley contested by Duke Richard II and his neighbour, Count Odo of Blois-Chartres. Odo had married the duke's sister, Matilda in c. 1003 and the territory pertaining to the the castle of Dreux had formed part of her dowry. When she died childless c. 1013–14, Odo refused to return the land to Richard as custom dictated. In retaliation, the duke built a new castle at Tillières from which he could harry his opponent. There followed a period of cross-border raiding by both parties. Richard's actions in fortifying Dreux and then Tillières fit into a broader pattern of lordship on the frontier. In the early eleventh century, the dukes of Normandy began a process of building castles along the edge of their territorial control as a means of consolidating their lands, securing the border and, when circumstances allowed it, the possibility of expansion. These castles became contested sites as the border was not static but dynamic, reflecting the competing interests in the region. If the king of France

Fig.16: The river Avre at Tillières-sur-Avre marking the border between Normandy (left) and France (right)

was in the ascendancy, then, as the later history of Tillières-sur-Avre bears out, the castle was seized and destroyed before a new one was built in its place. The frontier therefore rapidly changed from a demilitarized zone into an area that was openly hostile towards the duke through the construction and destruction of castles.[13] Equally if the duke was powerful, the opposite situation applied.

The death of a ruler and subsequent shift in power proved significant in the way castles were used and understood. According to Orderic Vitalis, when Robert of Bellême was on his way to Rouen to attend William the Conqueror as he lay dying, he received news that the king was dead. Instead of continuing his journey, Robert turned round and rode back to his lands in the south of Normandy to expel the garrisons and fortify his castles in order to capitalize on any power vacuum during the transfer of power from William to his sons.[14] William of Poitiers recounts that during William's minority, the Norman nobles built castles without authorization and held them in spite of the duke. Those people who had been granted holdings, including members of his own family like his uncle,

Fig.17: View from the site of the castle of Tillières-sur-Avre (now occupied by a nineteenth-century house)

William of Arques, fortified their castles against him and instigated rebellion.[15] Some of the southern Italian castles built by Robert Guiscard were destroyed during the disorders following his death. The period of civil war in England following the death of Henry I in 1135 also saw the construction of so-called adulterine castles held outside legitimate patterns of authority. Of course, for the people like Robert of Bellême who built these castles, their activities were legitimate in that they were seeking to secure their lands and perhaps to extend their power in particular localities; they were, in other words, seeking to secure their own interests.

Robert of Bellême's activities lead on to a discussion of the most recent trend in castle studies, and one which has a large bearing on how castles are understood in Norman society: that of the castle as a status symbol reflective of concepts of lordship. Like many terms applied to the Middle Ages, lordship is problematic and slippery. Just as with a castle, its operation was more practical in experience, which is hard to reconstruct, than formally documented in any charter or chronicle. For our purposes, lordship was a means of control and a way of exercising authority over a particular territory or group of people, whether that be on the larger scale of a kingdom or the family and holdings of a small lord like Tancred of Hauteville, and the social bonds that authority created and sustained. These bonds were both horizontal and vertical. How far any given individual – and women could exercise lordship as well as men – was able to exert authority depended on a number of circumstances, including personal charisma, the cooperation of different groups of people and wider political circumstances.

Previous discussion in Chapter 2 considered the imperial symbolism of castles like Colchester, the White Tower and Chepstow. The site and architectural embellishments of these buildings deliberately referred back to the Roman Empire and sought to validate William's hold on the country and that of his leading men. The reuse of Roman sites and building materials might be characterized solely as convenient, but among educated churchmen and lay people, there were individuals who would have read and understood the symbolism quite easily.[16] The idea of the castle as a status symbol, with the primary focus on its visible demonstration of lordship has found its clearest expression in the work of Charles Coulson. For him, the very fact of the castle's existence was designed to secure peace.[17] Coulson and other scholars, notably Robert Liddiard, have shown that castles need not be situated on the most defensible part of a site. What was considered more important was the need to be visible and to make a display of the wealth and power of an individual lord.[18] In southern Italy and Sicily, the Normans initially adopted similar building plans to those in Normandy; after all, that was what they were familiar with. A man like Tancred of Hauteville might not aspire to a substantial stone keep (often a square tower), but his descendants in Italy certainly built castles of this type. What is interesting, though, is how these sites developed over the period of consolidation and into the twelfth century with the foundation of the kingdom of Sicily. Initially, castle building followed the standard square keep plan of a large hall divided from the chamber and chapel by a cross wall, as is seen at Adrano. Gradually buildings became more elaborate as the Normans became more accustomed to and assimilated with the society they had conquered. La Zisa in Palermo, built in 1162, demonstrates Byzantine influences, but also Islamic ones with orchards and water features incorporated into the site of

Fig.18: La Zisa, Palermo, begun in the reign of William I of Sicily

Fig.19: Fountain in the hall at La Zisa, Palermo

the palatial tower.[19] Such influences can be seen in other architectural developments, which will be discussed further in Chapter 6.

Symbolism was not just restricted to the exterior of a castle, but also reflected its key role as a residence and centre of administration and ceremony through its internal arrangements. The interiors of halls and their associated buildings emphasized the importance of these buildings in displaying the power and authority of the people who held them. There are certain elements that most castles generally held in common, regardless of whether they were constructed from wood or stone. During the eleventh century, daily life was largely communal in nature and focused on the hall where the household, from its head down through the servants, would congregate. Archaeological excavations from sites like Grimbosq and Mirville in Normandy have recovered gaming pieces and evidence of benches around the walls demonstrating the communal nature of the hall.[20] Surviving architecture such as the large square keeps like that built at Falaise by Henry I to consolidate his hold on Normandy also contain large halls. Philip Dixon has shown that later keeps in England reflected the lord's power through their internal arrangement, such as the placing of doors and windows so as to illuminate the high seat or force a visitor to step up into the lord's presence, for example at Castle Rising.[21] Most stone keeps had their living quarters on the upper floor. This was partly for defence, but also for light and to demonstrate superiority in a very physical and literal fashion. This was the case in Normandy, England and Wales, and southern Italy.

Such evidence also highlights how the castle also operated as a residence at the heart of the household for the lord and his family. The pages of Orderic's *Ecclesiastial History* give us some important insights into the domestic life of the noble families who had connections with his monastery or its patrons. The veracity of these accounts is less important than the plausibility of Orderic's setting. Many of the monks in his monastery, as well as visitors to it, were well acquainted with the nature of castles and noble households in secular life. Although the details of some of these episodes might derive from literary traditions, Orderic's readers would have recognized the settings and activities therein. For example, he describes Isabella of Conches sitting in the hall of the castle at Conches listening to the knights talking about their dreams. Orderic's choice of words suggests strongly that it was customary for Isabella to do this.[22] In an apocryphal anecdote about the death of Robert son of Giroie, Orderic tells us how he was inadvertently killed when he snatched up a poisoned apple from his wife Adelaide's lap as they sat by the fire on a winter's evening.[23] Other evidence also gives us insights to the life of families within castles and allows us glimpses of otherwise hidden groups of people, in this case children. An account from the 'Discovery and Miracles of St Vulfan' describes the healing of a little girl who fell ill while playing in the courtyard of the castle of Asnebecq. Her mother rushed out to bring her daughter back inside, where she was revived after the mother vowed to light a candle of the same length as the girl to the saint.[24] These stories serve to remind historians that the domestic co-existed with the political. It is in buildings such as castles, where these areas of experience met, that what might otherwise be obscured is allowed to become at least partly visible.

LAND AND SERVICE

During the central Middle Ages, land was held in return for service. As eleventh-century Europe was primarily a warrior society, this service comprised, but not exclusively, military service. The exact details of service are frustratingly vague and the terms historians have used to describe them contested, for example feudalism.[25] There certainly was no such thing as a 'feudal system' in which vertical lines of tenure and lordship were firmly established. Different regions had different customs: what constituted tenure in Normandy was not the same as that in southern Italy, whereas in England the conquest caused a major rupture in the way land was held.

Historians are dependent for their evidence about the conditions of tenure and service on a variety of sources, both documentary and narrative. Charters are, in some respects, especially helpful as they provide a record of the transfer of land from one person or institution to another, but they are rarely explicit in spelling out the details. In Normandy, for example, charters might record transactions, but infrequently mention the kind of services tenants were supposed to provide in return for their land. Emily Tabuteau provides a list of obligations including host service, castle-guard, acting as part of an escort, and so on. One of the clearest expressions is found in a charter that sets out an agreement between the abbot of Mont-Saint-Michel and William Paynel dated to between 1070 and 1081. William held land from the abbey and the tenants on that land owed service including 'forty days of watch and ward' in times of war and the provision of men at arms. Tabuteau notes that this is

the fullest description historians have for military service at this time
and it seemingly owes its existence to the circumstances of William's
marriage, arranged for him by the duke. He held the land as a result
of this union and because he knew nothing about the conditions
of service, he had the agreement drawn up.[26] An early twelfth-
century source also provides us with glimpses into tenure. The *Life*
of Herluin, first abbot of the monastery of Le Bec was written by
Gilbert Crispin between 1109 and 1117. Gilbert was by then abbot
of Westminster, but had previously been a monk at Bec. In describing
Herluin's gradual conversion to the monastic life, Gilbert also
provides information about his service to Count Gilbert of Brionne
in the time of Robert the Magnificent. As well as attendance at the
count's court and military service, Herluin was also expected to act
as a messenger between Gilbert and Duke Robert as required, for
example to bring a law suit:

> Acting over a loss sustained by one of his fellow countrymen, which
> tended towards the man's ruin, Count Gilbert gave Herluin a mission
> to go to Duke Robert of the Normans, for whom anything done about
> this was a matter of importance, and to lay a charge against the person
> arising from the affair.[27]

Gilbert Crispin included this information not because he was
interested in the complexities of feudal tenure, but because Herluin's
subsequent refusal to bring an unjust suit demonstrated his preference
for service of the heavenly lord over fulfilling his obligations to his
earthly superior. What is clear from the fragmentary evidence is that
the exact circumstances of tenure in eleventh-century Normandy
were fluid and flexible.

In England, the conquest resulted in great changes in the pattern
of landholding across the country as land was taken away from
the English nobility and thegns and granted instead to William's
followers.[28] This process is traced in the pages of Domesday Book,
which was the result of a great survey commissioned by William in
1085 in order to determine the resources at his disposal in terms of
land and wealth. As Robin Fleming has shown, William dismantled
the large Anglo-Saxon estates and redistributed land so that the
royal demesne – land controlled directly by the king – was much
bigger than it had been.[29] Under King Edward, the Godwine family

had been the primary landholder with estates larger than those of the king. Killing Harold on the field at Battle in 1066 meant that William not only obtained his crown, but also his land. Golding notes the royal demesne was then twice the size it had been in 1065.[30]

The death of many leading men in 1066 meant that William had land that was immediately available for redistribution to his followers. Some of these men were members of his own family: Odo, bishop of Bayeux was granted land in Kent and Robert, count of Mortain, whose main estates were concentrated in Cornwall, Sussex and Hertfordshire. Other individuals were also well-established in Normandy, but other men like Roger de Mowbray and William de Briouze were of modest origins and owed their advancement to the conquest.[31] It is also important to emphasize that not all the new landholders were Normans. William's army in 1066 comprised men from Brittany, Aquitaine, Maine and Flanders and these too were rewarded, notably Count Alan who held the honour of Richmond in North Yorkshire. There were, however, some English nobles who managed to maintain their estates in the immediate aftermath of the battle, notably Earls Edwin, Morcar and Waltheof, though their land was redistributed following various rebellions and their deaths. In contrast, people of middling rank appear to have stood a better chance of retaining their land after 1066. This group comprised the thegns, or the fighting men of Anglo-Saxon England. Their status was dependent on holding a certain amount of land – five hides at least – as well as the performance of military service. If an individual did not have the requisite amount of land, then he could not be a thegn.[32] While many of the English continued to hold land, it would seem that the conditions on which they held it worsened during the reign of King William.

One of the main debates surrounding how people held land post-conquest is the question of knight service and what that actually means. The debate began with J. H. Round, who argued that William imposed a system of quotas for the provision of fighting men that owed little to the way thegns, who made up the fyrd in Anglo-Saxon England, had been organized and equipped previously.[33] The problem with Round's view is that he was using evidence dating from the twelfth century and projecting it back onto the eleventh. As is the case for Normandy, sources that record military service for England are fragmentary, vague and mostly relate to the provision of armed men from monastic estates. Little evidence exists for how quotas were raised from estates held by lay people. The increase in documents in the twelfth century outlining military service would suggest that this phenomenon was becoming more defined, a process which began in the years following 1066. It is also possible that this development went hand in hand with a similar clarifying of arrangements in Normandy through documents such as the Bayeux Inquest in 1133. The conquest and subsequent need to defend territory on either side of the Channel gradually led to more firm definitions of what that service should be.[34]

The situation faced by the new Norman arrivals in southern Italy was different again. Although Robert Guiscard and his immediate family were perhaps the most prominent among the Norman rulers by the late eleventh century, there were other important figures to consider including Robert of the Principate in Salerno; Count Robert of Loritello, who was becoming increasingly active on the northern edge of Norman activity in the Abbruzi; and Geoffrey of Conversano, whose interests were primarily in southern Apulia and all of whom were Guiscard's nephews. We can also add the kin of Richard I of Capua, the sons of Amicus, the descendants of Gerard of Buonalbergo who were the counts of Ariano, and finally the counts of Boiano. These last two groups had interests in the region around Benevento. Robert Guiscard and his descendants could not, therefore, command the same resources as William the Conqueror, and had significantly more rivals for power. In addition, many Lombard and Greek landholders maintained their positions. As we have already noted, there were many different traditions of law, custom and service. Evidence of any kind of service in return for land is rare and, as Loud states, only really exists from the creation of the kingdom of Sicily in 1130.[35]

PEASANTS

Recent years have witnessed a welcome increase in research relating to the peasants. As is the case with determining landholding patterns and military service, the evidence is vague and subject to uncertainty. The term itself is one of convenience that covers the section of population that worked the land under varying degrees of freedom and unfreedom. Through the exaction of labour services, peasants were forced to work on their lords' castles and other building projects and through these examples historians can get a sense of how society was structured and organized. These developments have been linked to the 'feudal revolution', a term devised particularly by French historians to refer to the changes in the relationship between lords and their tenants that took place around the year 1000. A key theme is the violent and exploitative nature of lordship.[36] The chroniclers had a great deal to say about the unjust nature of these exactions, for example Orderic Vitalis who wrote about the suffering caused to the tenants of his monastery:

> The men of Saint-Evroult [...] were in no way subject to his [Robert of Bellême's] rule [...] He compelled the men of the holy father St Evroult by force to help in the work of his own castles, seizing the possessions of any who defaulted, and even cruelly threatened to destroy the abbey itself.[37]

In the disorders of Robert Curthose's reign as duke, the nuns of La Trinité in Caen also complained that their men had been forced to work on the ducal castles.[38]

The situation of peasants in Normandy prior to the twelfth century, however, is not well understood, in part due to the patchy survival of evidence. Their appearance in the early chronicles is, as Mathieu Arnoux notes, largely symbolic, and at times they appear to be completely absent, as seen in the discussion of the depopulation of the Seine Valley in Chapter 1.[39] Consideration of their situation in Normandy has focused on two key texts: the story of the lost ploughshares in Dudo, and William of Jumièges's account of a rural revolt. Additional material is also included incidentally by later chroniclers or in charters. Dudo included an episode relating to the protection of agricultural tools in his *History of the Normans*.[40] The duke guaranteed that he would reimburse individuals for the loss or theft of their ploughshares. The wife of one particular peasant saw this as an opportunity to make money and hid her husband's tools. The husband claimed compensation from the duke, whereupon the wife restored to him the ploughshares. Horrified at his wife's duplicity, the peasant confessed all to the duke, who had both parties hanged: the wife for stealing the ploughshares and the husband as he knew from previous experience that his wife was a thief. This incident tells us less about the peasants, other than it was considered part of being a good ruler to ensure the land was properly cultivated, and more about how they were viewed (not well) by the chroniclers. Above all, this episode is about the authority of the duke.

Perhaps one of the most famous episodes relating to the Normans' dealings with peasants also relates to the idea that they were used by chroniclers to reflect ideas of lordship. William of Jumièges describes a revolt in 996 against what appeared to be changes in service and conditions:

> Throughout every part of Normandy the peasants unanimously formed many assemblies and decided to live according to their own wishes, such that in respect both of short cuts through the woods and of the traffic of the rivers with no bar of previously established right in their way, they might follow laws of their own.[41]

The most recent assessment of this event is that by Bernard Gowers.[42] He places the revolt in the context of the vestiges of Carolingian assembly politics through which peasants could defend their rights This was not a case of straightforward continuation of tradition but an echo of earlier practices used to try to defend the rural community from negative changes to social conditions. William's emphasis, however, is on how the revolt was supressed – brutally – through the mutilation of its participants by Richard II's uncle, Raoul d'Ivry. It is difficult, therefore, to get beyond a rather limited understanding of the social conditions of the peasantry in early Normandy. The duke had a duty of protection towards them and the peasants owed service to their lords and were supposed to abide by the duke's authority. There was a sense that conditions were changing and not necessarily for the better. Crucially what is absent from the sources is a specific Norman structure that could be exported wholesale to England and southern Italy.

The period during which William the Conqueror and his successor William Rufus established and consolidated Norman rule in England also saw extreme weather, poor harvests and disease, as noted by Golding. Although the conquest was not solely responsible for the dearth, when combined with the devastation wreaked by frequent campaigning, the second half of the eleventh century must have been an especially bad time to be not only a peasant, but also an ordinary householder.[43] The reorganization of land following 1066 changed social relations and the terms on which tenants-in-chief and lesser tenants held land irrevocably and can be traced to a degree in the pages of Domesday Book. As discussed above, the resources available to William in terms of land were much greater than had been the case pre-1066.[44] Changes were not uniform across the country and there was a great deal of regional variation. Individuals who had held land freely now found themselves in a situation of serfdom, in which they were tied to their lord's land through the rents and services that they owed. These included service in the lord's fields, as well as the peasants' own tenements; maintenance and building work on castles, bridges and roads; and various monetary rents and fines. Loss of freedom was particularly marked in the north and east. Rosamond Faith has calculated that in Cambridgeshire, for example, the 900 sokemen or freemen recorded for 1066 fell to just 177 in 1086. In Yorkshire, this category of people was only recorded for the West Riding in 1086.[45]

Domesday Book records the destruction of houses and settlements for the building of castles and other structures associated with the conquerors (as quoted at the beginning of the chapter). The conquest also brought about the reorganization of settlements. The most notorious was the creation of the New Forest in Hampshire as a royal hunting ground. This particularly attracted the ire of the chroniclers due to the number of churches destroyed to make way for the king's deer. We have already noted the destruction of settlements in the north of England during the Harrying of 1069–70. Gradually new settlements were planned and developed. Although the process was not the same as that of *incastallamento* in southern Italy, some of the results were similar. Planned villages and the grouping together of settlements allowed lords to exploit better the economic potential of their land and tenants. Faith cites the example of Ilbert de Lacy, who held extensive estates in the North and Midlands centred on the seat of his lordship at Pontefract in West Yorkshire. The creation of an agricultural unit geared towards providing for the needs of the lordship led to the removal of peasants, their families and plough teams from one area to a more centralized holding.[46] The peasants and their families had as little choice in the matter as their oxen.

In southern Italy and Sicily, economic and agricultural developments were already taking place prior to the arrival of the Normans in the early eleventh century. According to Jean-Marie

Martin, *incastallamento* led to the 'emergence of a seigneurial system which combined land holding and public power'.[47] In other words, the ties between lords and people were becoming more clearly defined. It is crucial to note, however, that the variety of different legal and customary traditions in the Mezzogiorno meant that the Normans faced very different situations in, for example, the Lombard principalities than in Calabria. Statutory labour services were more frequent in northern and western parts of the kingdom in a manner similar, but not identical, to England. In formerly Byzantine areas the Normans held more land directly; in the Lombard principalities land mostly remained in the hands of Lombards. The experiences of the peasants in these areas would accordingly have differed greatly. As Patricia Skinner has pointed out, change relating to the Normans in southern Italy was a much slower process than in England. The reason for this lies in part in the way the takeover of land was achieved. The conquest of England was the planned enterprise of one man; the Norman conquest of Italy was piecemeal, opportunistic and gradual. The early Norman arrivals did not come as conquerors, as 'servants and later allies of ruling dynasties'.[48]

MARRIAGE

In the discussion of castles above, we considered the importance of the castle at Dreux, which had possibly changed ownership due to marriage alliances. It is hard to stress just how important marriage was within eleventh-century aristocratic society. If castles were a way of displaying power and exercising military might when needed, marriage was the means by which families could cement alliances and build political networks. In the longer term, marriage also served as a way to create communities through establishing ties with the native population and assimilating with it.

Evidence about the marriages of the early rulers of Normandy is scarce. The main account is Dudo and on marriage he is not wholly reliable, though how he presents the relationships between the duke and both Frankish and Scandinavian women is interesting in itself. He seems to make a distinction between Frankish wives, who act as a force for legitimizing the settlement of Normandy, and Scandinavian or indigenous concubines whose children actually formed the succession. As part of the negotiations for the treaty of Saint-Clair-sur-Epte, Dudo tells us that Rollo married Gisla, the daughter of the Charles the Simple. As discussed in Chapter 1, there is no other evidence that this marriage took place and it is likely that Dudo borrowed the tale from the career of Godefrid, who did marry a Frankish woman by that name: either way, she was not the mother of William Longsword.[49] However, in suggesting that Rollo had both a 'Danish' and a Frankish wife, Dudo introduces the idea that has been taken up by modern historians, that the Viking settlers practised two forms of marriage: a Christian, Frankish union and Danish marriage, or a form of concubinage. We can see this in the relationships of William Longsword, who married Leyarda of Vermandois, and Richard I, who married Emma, the daughter of Hugh the Great. These were politically significant alliances, yet Dudo makes it clear that any children born to the counts were from their relationships with their 'Scandinavian' concubines: Sprota in the case of William and Gunnor in the case of Richard I. Dudo actually obscures Sprota's Breton origins in order to fit with this narrative. Searle has speculated that this was a calculated policy on the part of the counts of Rouen, that only heirs with a Scandinavian heritage were eligible for designation as heir to their father's land and title. Either the marriages to Frankish women were childless or Dudo very carefully edited out their existence so as to create no problems for the children of these so-called 'Danish' unions.[50] We should perhaps also bear in mind that these distinctions were more clearly drawn in the pages of Dudo's history than was the case at the tenth-century Norman court.

What is interesting here is the case of Gunnor, a particularly long-lived woman, who may even still been alive when the future William II was a baby. Gunnor was therefore a significant figure at court.[51] One of her sons, Richard II, inherited Normandy and another, Robert, became archbishop of Rouen. Her daughters made marriages that furthered the interests of the ducal dynasty: Emma married into the English ruling house; Matilda, as we have seen, married Odo II of Blois-Chartres; and Hadvis married Geoffrey of Rennes in neighbouring Brittany. According to Robert of Torigni, writing over a century later but using reliable sources, her own family went on to make significant marital alliances across Normandy and thus many of the aristocratic families were related to William II by the time he inherited the dukedom.[52] Gunnor came from a Scandinavian family from the west of Normandy and brought to Richard the prospect of the extension of ducal authority and land in the Cotentin and Avranchin. In contrast to William's relationship with Sprota, Richard formally married Gunnor in a Christian ceremony. A later tradition, found in the twelfth-century interpolations in the *Gesta Normannorum ducum* by Robert of Torigni, records that the couple and their children were covered with a cloak in order to make the offspring conceived outside of marriage legitimate.[53] If Richard had plans to make his son, Robert, archbishop of Rouen, then legitimacy was a necessary prerequisite. Also, Richard had children by other women who were also given lands, and thus marriage to Gunnor was a way of marking their children as set apart for the continuation of the dynasty. Richard and Gunnor's marriage was very significant not only in terms of providing heirs, but also in consolidating the hold on the duchy and establishing good relations with neighbouring lords.

Discussion of Norman marriage alliances in England and southern Italy has focused on the degree to which intermarriage took place, that is to say exogamous marriage between one Norman partner (usually male) and a native (usually female), and how far that was an instrument for assimilating a military elite into the society it had conquered. Marriage, like the building of castles or changes in landholding, was a means of consolidating conquest. There has been a great deal of debate surrounding the extent to which intermarriage took place and it would seem that this was a much longer-term development that has hitherto been acknowledged. It is a topic that also highlights the importance of Norman women in the process of conquest and settlement.

Catherine Heygate has studied Norman marriage strategies for eleventh-century southern Italy using chronicle and charter evidence and has come to some interesting conclusions.[54] She has identified 100 marriages or betrothals, from which ethnic origins can be assigned to 70. Of these, only 28 involve one Norman and one Italian: 23 involve marriage between a Norman man and Italian woman, while the remaining five unions involve a woman born to Norman parents. From this quantifiable evidence, Heygate deduces that intermarriage was a gendered phenomenon with the majority of exogamous marriages involving native women. In other words, the statistics highlight the vitally important role women played as intermediaries and as a means of assimilating the newly arrived Normans into the society of southern Italy. This was a development that was recognized as a positive one by writers like Amatus of Montecassino. The figures do not present the whole story though and need fleshing out with discussion of some significant examples from the chronicles. Through cases such as the marriages of Robert Guiscard, it is evident that perhaps attitudes towards marriage, particularly who it was considered suitable to marry, changed. It is interesting to consider when Normans in the peninsula married Norman women and when they chose to make alliances with southern Italian families.

Robert Guiscard's first marriage was to Alberada, aunt of Gerard of Buonalbergo, a woman of Norman heritage.[55] Amatus tells us that Geoffrey offered Alberada to Robert as a means of forming an alliance and of offering his support to Robert's campaigns in Calabria. The strategic potential of this match was underlined by Robert's half-brother Count Drogo's opposition to it. Such a union would give the younger of the sons of Tancred a much better base in southern Italy from which to broaden and increase his power. Later in his career, Robert repudiated Alberada, ostensibly on the grounds of consanguinity, that is to say they were too closely related according to the canons of the Church. As Skinner and others have noted, this argument is somewhat tendentious, given that Robert's second wife was related to two of the women who married his half-brothers.[56] Loud, however, has indicated that Amatus demonstrated that Geoffrey remained loyal to Robert, even after his remarriage, suggesting – though the evidence does not survive to prove the conjecture – that Geoffrey and Robert were related through Tancred of Hauteville's second wife. If this is true, then the marriage between Alberada and Robert can be seen as strengthening already pre-existing Norman ties. Robert's younger brother, Roger, also married women from Normandy. His first wife was Judith, the sister of Robert of Grandmesnil who had been abbot of Orderic's monastery of Saint-Evroult before he was forced into exile by William the Conqueror. His second wife was also a Norman, Eremberga of Mortain. Richard of Aversa, son of Rainulf married Robert and Roger's sister, Fressenda. Heygate's research reveals that where we can assign ethnic origin to marriages that nine unions involved marriages between Norman men and first generation Norman immigrant women. This is not a large number and reflects the gender imbalance in migration. It does, however, indicate that initially some of the Norman migrants preferred to marry women from their homeland. This suggests that either they were not sufficiently powerful enough to attract the attention of the Lombard rulers or, in the early stages of the settlement, alliances between the competing Norman factions were more important than those between Normans and southern Italians.

Whatever the reasoning behind marriage alliances, Robert's actions in marrying Sichelgaita were certainly expedient and timely. Sichelgaita was the daughter of Guaimar of Salerno. This union proved advantageous in many ways, not least of which was the fact that marriage to a Lombard princess in effect provided added legitimacy for the Norman takeover of southern Italy. Guaimar had previously recognized the importance of marriage alliances by marrying two of his nieces to William Iron Arm (the eldest of the sons of Tancred) and William of the Principate, and one of his daughters to Count Drogo (another of Robert's half-brothers). As has been demonstrated by Skinner, Sichelgaita was able to act as an intermediary between her husband's family and her natal family.[57] Although she is largely absent from the documentary material, Amatus indicates she was frequently with her husband during the conquest of Sicily. During the siege of Salerno, on the mainland, Sichelgaita endeavoured to make peace between her husband and her brother, Prince Gisulf, as well as supplying her sister with food. She also influenced his choice of patronage to religious houses. Joanna Drell has also emphasized the importance of lineage here: because Sichelgaita maintained links with her natal family, Robert could use his marriage to justify his position.[58] It is noticeable, that in contrast to the policy of the early rulers of Normandy who favoured children born of Scandinavian marriages, Robert Guiscard was keen to ensure that it was the children from his marriage to Sichelgaita who inherited; Bohemond after all was made illegitimate by the annulment of his mother's union. This status did not prevent him from later marrying Constance, the daughter of Philip I of France during his tour of that country to drum up support for his military activities in the east. By that point, however, he was established in his own right in Antioch.

In contrast to southern Italy, the chroniclers concerned with events in England understood intermarriage as a concept and reflected on it, as Heygate has noted.[59] Orderic Vitalis and William of Malmesbury, both writing in the twelfth century, commented on the importance of Normans and English marrying each other. Both historians were products of mixed marriages themselves, as was Henry of Huntingdon. Previous research on this topic has stressed the importance of intermarriage as a means of cementing Norman control of the country. Searle described the marriage of heiresses to the landless followers of the conqueror as a prerogative of lordship, but recent work by van Houts has suggested that the picture might be more complex.[60] Using prosopographical evidence from documents like Domesday Book and the Durham *Liber vitae*, van Houts demonstrates that for the first decades of the conquest, up to about *c.* 1110, endogamy rather than exogamy was the norm. She also stresses that some of William's soldiers already had Norman wives so were not available to marry English women. Orderic Vitalis, not without monastic disapproval, recorded that some Norman women urged their husbands to return home, otherwise they would find new ones.[61] William was not, however, solely concerned with marrying off English heiresses to his Norman followers. He certainly planned for, or allowed, English survivors of the conquest to marry French wives. Earl Waltheof, eventually executed in 1076 for his part in an unsuccessful revolt, married the conqueror's niece, Judith. Hereward, who had rebelled in East Anglia, married Turfida of Saint-Omer as part of the reconciliation process between himself and the king. Promise of a marriage, which was then unfulfilled, could also breed resentment. Edwin, brother of Morcar, both of whom were earls who survived 1066, was betrothed to William's eldest daughter, Adelaide. That this marriage never took place was suggested by Orderic as a reason for Edwin's discontent and rebellion.[62]

Certainly marriage between Normans and English would be an excellent way of cementing the conquest through the mingling of the two people: the children of mixed marriages could forge a new Anglo-Norman identity and perhaps lessen resistance in future generations to the Norman takeover. That William was concerned to ensure marriage alliances can be seen in a letter from Lanfranc, the first Norman archbishop after the conquest, to Gundulf of Rochester or Geoffrey of Coutances (the addressee is unclear and arguments have been put forward for both men). In the letter, Lanfranc addressed the problem of English women who fled to nunneries after the battle of Hastings 'for fear of the French'.[63] In other words, these women, many of whose menfolk lay dead on the field at Battle or at Stamford Bridge, were fearful for themselves, their property and of being raped or married against their will, so they took refuge in the institutions that convention decreed were not legitimate targets. That William's soldiers did rape English women is attested by the Penitential Ordinance, which conflicts with William of Poitiers's assertion that 'women were safe from the violence which passionate men often inflict'.[64] Once the initial danger had passed, many of these women wanted to leave the confines of the monasteries, but found that because they had adopted the religious habit for safety, this made them nuns in the eyes of some churchmen. Lanfranc made it clear in the letter that if the women could prove that they entered the nunnery through fear, rather than any sense of religious vocation by the testimony of nuns proper, then they might leave and resume their secular lives. He was also careful to state that this was not just his policy, but also the king's. William had a vested interested in marriageable women being available.

Some of these women were politically sensitive: for example Gunhilda, the daughter of king Harold; and Edith, the daughter of King Malcolm Canmore of the Scots and his wife, Margaret, who was the sister of Edgar ætheling. Gunhilda's case is interesting in that the correspondence between her and Anselm of Canterbury suggests that her desire to leave the nunnery at Wilton and marry Count Alan the Red and, when he died, his brother, also called Alan (the Black), was less to do with personal safety and more to do with personal disappointment. It seems that she was at some stage promised the position of abbess in the nunnery and did not get it. Even though William's son, William Rufus was now ruling as king, the potential for political instability that marriage between a surviving member of the house of Godwine and a powerful noble presented warranted close attention.[65]

The case of Edith is significant for a different reason as her suitor was William the Conqueror's youngest son, Henry, who claimed the throne on the death of William Rufus. What was at stake here was an alliance between the Norman holders of the crown and the line of Cerdic, the old English ruling house. Such a marriage would be politically astute, not only from the point of view of linking the descendants of Rollo with those of Alfred the Great, but also because it would build closer relations with England's northern neighbour, Scotland. As recorded by the chronicler, Eadmer, Anselm proved less willing than Lanfranc had been to authorize the removal of Edith from the nunnery of Wilton where her aunt, Christina was abbess and where she had been educated. The sticking point for Anselm was that Edith had been seen wearing the nun's veil. The case had to go before a church court where Edith stated firmly that she had not worn the veil from choice, but because her aunt was fearful of the French and that when her father had visited her at Wilton, he had torn the veil from her head in a rage.[66] Eventually Anselm relented and Henry could marry Edith, who, on her marriage, adopted the French name Matilda, possibly as a mark of respect to Henry's own mother, Matilda of Flanders. This marriage strengthened links between the Norman rulers and the pre-conquest past. It also demonstrates, as did Robert Guiscard's marriage to Sichelgaita, a degree of pragmatism in the Normans' dealings with the Church.

Throughout this chapter discussion has focused on the changes effected by the Normans on the societies they encountered, and some of the practical measures taken to cement their hold on these territories. The picture is not always clear, due to the vaguaries of the evidence. This uncertainty is, in itself, interesting. It underlines that conquest and settlement were not discrete events, but processes that developed over a long period of time. Our sources are not clear, because the people of the eleventh century were still working out either the accommodations between themselves and the Norman settlers or the new structures resulting from conquest. Violence, for example the imposition of castles in existing landscapes or through the seizure of land, went alongside more indirect methods of control through symbolism and marriage alliances. The power of William and his followers in England or of the various Norman lords in Italy might initially be gained through military action, but it had to be maintained through methods that sustained that power on a daily basis. In addition to the themes outlined in this chapter, of vital importance in securing support and bolstering power was the Normans' relationship with the Church, and it is to that we now turn.

5

THE NORMANS AND THE CHURCH

The Church was an integral part of medieval society, not just because of its moral authority, but also due to its close association with secular powers. Popes, bishops and the heads of monasteries were valued as advisers and administrators. They also acted as a powerful corrective for unacceptable behaviour and sought to regulate the worst excesses of a society predicated on violence. The relationship between churchmen and lay rulers was affected by developments in the organization and nature of the institutional Church from the mid-eleventh century onwards, notably changes within the papacy. The number of monasteries founded for men or women was also on the increase and the end of the century witnessed the first crusade, providing the laity with an outlet for military prowess in aid of the Church.

The Normans have a reputation for piety instilled in no small part by their histories. From the time that baptism was set as a prerequisite for the grant of Normandy to Rollo at Saint-Clair-sur-Epte, the rulers enjoyed, for the most part, a close and productive association with the Church in their territories. Cooperation with the Church and papacy after 1066 was essential in consolidating the conquest of England. In Italy, the Normans proved useful allies in Rome's attempts to increase its power at the expense of the Greek rite Christians and in protecting church lands. As we shall see, however, the Normans' piety was often pragmatic and dependent on circumstances. Norman successes in Sicily did not stop Pope Gregory

VII excommunicating Robert Guiscard and Roger, and he certainly thought that William the Conqueror owed more to the papacy in return for the favour granted him by Alexander II. Monasteries could also bolster support where ducal authority was weak, but equally provided a handy source of revenue and lands if the occasion demanded it.

This chapter is divided into three parts that consider what the Normans expected from the Church and what the Church expected in return. It begins with the interaction between the Church and local communities. The role of monasteries and saints' shrines is key here. The second section considers questions of legitimacy and administration: how the Church bolstered the power of Norman rulers and aided in the governance of their territories. Of particular importance here is the relationship with the pope and bishops. If churchmen supported the secular rule of dukes, princes and kings, then those rulers in turn should work to further the Church's interests in their realms and protect its people and institutions. This aspect forms the final part of the chapter. First it is helpful to consider, briefly, the background to some of the changes taking place in the ecclesiastical sphere.

The period from the mid-tenth century onwards witnessed a growing interest in the foundation of monasteries. These institutions housed communities of monks or nuns devoted to contemplation, prayer, learning and manual labour. They provided women with an outlet for spirituality and religious vocation otherwise denied them in the secular clergy with its entirely male priesthood. For much of the period discussed in this book, the predominant form of monasticism was Benedictine, based on the rule written by Benedict of Nursia at the great Italian abbey of Montecassino in the sixth century. The interpretation of that rule in north-western Europe during the Norman period was largely determined by the Burgundian abbey of Cluny, which was to have great influence in the restoration of monasticism in Normandy. It was, after all, a Cluniac monk, William of Volpiano, who came to Fécamp at the behest of Richard II to turn the community from a group of secular canons to a reformed Benedictine house. Cluniac priories were imported into England after the conquest, for example at Castle Acre in Norfolk. Cluniac ideas also influenced the reform of some southern Italy communities, notably Holy Trinity at Cava. The Normans' relationship with religious houses is an interesting one. Their Viking forebears were blamed for destroying the abbeys of Neustria during the period of incursions, while the dukes and their supporters were later lauded by chroniclers for re-establishing monasteries and demonstrating great piety. In England and southern Italy the

Fig.20: West front of Castle Acre priory, Norfolk, twelfth century

Normans were criticized for despoiling monastic lands, while also acting, at least in England, as an impetus for reform. While it is true to say that piety became a characteristic associated with the Normans, at the same time, patronage allowed the Norman rulers to further their family or economic interests. These communities also had a close relationship with ordinary lay people who lived on or around monastic lands and some houses acted as a focus for pilgrimage and devotion to the saints.

The latter half of the eleventh century was the period of papal reform, sometimes called Gregorian reform after Pope Gregory VII. This movement had various aims, for example enforcing clerical celibacy, which often involved attempts to separate priests and their wives by force, and ending the buying and selling of sacred offices such as bishoprics. At the heart of Gregory's agenda was the question of who invested the bishops with both their spiritual and temporal authority and the signs of that authority: the ring and the staff. For the reformers, only the pope could do this; for many rulers in western Europe, the bishops' position as leading secular lords as well as spiritual leaders meant that the king should carry out the investiture. Matters came to a head in the conflict between Gregory and the German emperor Henry IV and their successors, known as the Investiture Contest. This dispute triggered a series of events in which the pope sought to depose the emperor and the emperor sought to elect antipopes who supported his position. These events affected the way the popes, particularly Gregory, saw their position in relation to secular rulers. They also had ramifications for the way Norman rulers sought to control the Church in their lands, particularly in relation to the appointment of bishops.

The Church also operated at a much more local level. The nature of the sources means that much more is known and knowable about the relationship between nobles and their clerical counterparts than the experience of ordinary people and their parish priests or small, local priory. Glimpses into the interaction between the local church and its communities can be seen in accounts of the miracles that happened at a particular saint's shrine or in the pages of chronicles. We must remember, however, that these narratives are always mediated through the churchmen who wrote them and with a clear clerical agenda behind them.

LOCAL COMMUNITIES AND THE CHURCH

Alongside the foundation of monasteries, the importance of saints' cults and associated activities like pilgrimage to medieval society allow us to see how the Church and society operated at a local level. The Church sustained and was, in its turn, supported by the myriad local communities it served throughout Normandy, England and southern Italy. The parish system was in an embryonic state of development and much of our evidence for how the Church functioned on a quotidian basis comes from monastic sources. Monasteries were not only sustained by large grants of land from aristocratic patrons, but also by day-to-day interaction with their local lay society through the tenants who worked in their fields, paid tithes to the houses and also brought gifts at times of importance, as well as pilgrims who might visit their shrines. In return the monasteries provided pastoral care through church services, burial, rudimentary social welfare and access to relics. The monks and nuns within the walls also spent their time in contemplative prayer, an activity that lay people and secular clerics had considerably less time for. Association of a house with saints, either through the physical presence of their relics or dedication of a particular church or religious house, was a means of expressing identity and ensuring protection. The saints could approve or disapprove of behaviour and actions across the social spectrum. Their shrines were sites of healing and intercession as it was believed that holy people acted as an intermediary between the earthly and heavenly worlds. Through examination of hagiographical sources such as saints' lives and *miracula* (the accounts of miracles), as well as the chronicles written in monasteries, we can gain further glimpses into the lives of people otherwise obscured, notably ordinary people in their everyday situations. The sources themselves need to be read with caution. Saints' lives were designed to illustrate the holiness of an individual and provide a model of appropriate Christian behaviour. The miracles served to demonstrate the power of the saint and as a way of attracting further pilgrims, revenue and prestige. Saints' cults, especially those associated with a religious community, also held great importance for the Norman rulers. They needed to be seen as benefactors and supporters of communities in order to have a particular local saint on their side.

Two examples from the *Ecclesiastical History* of Orderic Vitalis demonstrate the link between saints, the Church, community and politics. During the disorder in Normandy under Duke Robert Curthose, his younger brother Henry (future Henry I of England) captured Domfront in *c.* 1092 from Robert of Bellême. Among those captured during these troubles was Ruald, described as from 'the territory of Saint-Evroult' – Orderic's monastery –, in other words, one of its tenants.[1] Finding himself a prisoner in a house in the castle, he called on St Evroult, the monastery's patron, for aid. Ruald was roused from sleep by someone taking him by the hand. This enabled him to have the faith and courage to attempt his escape. The bolt holding the door in place fell to the ground when he took hold of it. On stepping into the garden of the castle, he called on St Evroult again to lead him undetected past the knights in the courtyard. Despite pursuit, Ruald's faith in the saint allowed him to hide without detection and for men ploughing a field to deny having seen him. Orderic states that he heard the tale from Ruald himself and he believed him because of his good character. In reading this story it is clear that events could be presented in a way that showed the patron saint of the monastery protected those who served it.

The sustaining relationship between monastery and community is further illustrated by the experiences of a Breton man by the name of Geoffrey. Previously he had led an ungodly life given over to brigandage and other nefarious practices. Through the influence of Abbot Warin and the good counsels of his wife, he amended his way of life and became devoted to the monks. One year he set off on the feast day of the Holy Innocents to deliver a gift of white bread to the monks. For individuals who had close associations with particular religious houses, important feast days provided ideal opportunities to express their piety. On this occasion the weather was very bad. Heavy snowfall disguised the countryside, making it difficult for Geoffrey, his son and their horse to find their way. They also had to cross a very fast-flowing river, swollen with water from winter storms. Through the intercession of the saint, Geoffrey managed to cross the river while keeping the bread dry. His son was less steadfast in his faith and so got considerably wetter. On arrival at the monastery, Geoffrey recounted his tale to the monks. In this example, we see that spiritual support and counsel were repaid by devotion and gifts that materially supported the community.[2]

These episodes also illustrate one of the key roles played by saints' cults during this period: to provide succour to those in need. Medical care was largely provided by charitable institutions under the oversight of the Church. The second half of the eleventh century witnessed a gradual increase in the foundation of hospitals, including those given over to the care of lepers, a process that accelerated during the twelfth century. This provision was patchy, however, and so for a significant number of people, visiting shrines and invoking the aid of the saints, backed up perhaps by the presence of a medic in a particular community, was essential. Shrines visited by various Normans might have specialist functions; for example, the monastery of Sainte-Catherine-du-Mont in Rouen was visited by women experiencing fertility problems.[3] St Amand, a Merovingian bishop of Rouen, was associated with the cure of people suffering 'demonic possession'. A letter written by Abbess Marsilia of Saint-Amand in Rouen in 1107 to the abbot of Saint-Amand in Flanders described a very moving case of a husband who brought his suicidal wife to the abbey to be looked after by the nuns. She had become disturbed by her neighbour's malicious gossip about her husband and had tried to take her own life. Unfortunately, the woman's despair was so great that the nuns could not prevent her from another suicide attempt, but through their intercession to Amand, she was revived sufficiently to make her confession and so avoid the hellish torments she was convinced were awaiting her.[4]

As well as providing help, the saints could also warn or punish individuals for bad behaviour such as appropriating or pillaging a community's lands, stealing its treasure or harming individuals associated with it. Orderic's account of Ruald's escape demonstrates not only the protection shown to the community, but also disapproval of Henry's actions in imprisoning Ruald in the first place by aiding his escape. Following the conquests of England and southern Italy, local saints also acted to punish people who harmed their communities. Communities in Bury St Edmunds, Durham and Evesham, among others, all provide examples in their hagiographic writings of punitive miracles. A particularly good example comes from the Benedictine monastery at Ely. Following the conquest a very unscrupulous man, Picot, was appointed sheriff of Cambridgeshire. In his role he appropriated land belonging to the monastery, which was under the protection of St Æthelthryth, an Anglo-Saxon princess who became abbess of the community in the seventh century. Picot was warned about his behaviour. He also had a henchman called Gervase, described as 'extremely hostile to St Æthelthryth's people and, as if he had undertaken a special campaign against her, assailed the whole of her property with oppression, whenever he could'.[5] The people appealed to the saint who, in a terrifying dream, appeared to Gervase and accused him of his crimes before stabbing him through the chest with her pastoral staff. S. J. Ridyard suggests that Gervase had suffered a heart attack, but that it suited the monks to present his death in a way that stressed the active intervention of the saint.[6] The fact that Æthelthryth appeared in a way that demonstrated her authority as an abbess was not coincidental, but a very visual and emphatic reminder of her powerful patronage.

Similar examples come from southern Italy, where the Normans were initially regarded as predators and the saints' enemies. The *Dialogues* of Desiderius, abbot of Montecassino, contain a number of miracles showing the saint, in this case Benedict, protecting the monastery. A Norman who robbed the monastery's fishermen of their catch was drowned when a large wave engulfed him. Other groups of Normans were expelled from the land, as foretold by Benedict in visions, as they had pillaged rather than protected it.[7] Another example comes from Holy Trinity, Cava and demonstrates how the saint's actions might help bring about a conversion to a better way of life, even if at first they were unsuccessful. Abbot Peter asked for St Michael's intervention in dealing with a man named Roger who was causing problems for the monastery by abusing its peasants in Cilento. Roger's baby was subsequently killed in a roof fall. He did not, however, amend his behaviour straight away, but instead expelled the peasants and confronted the monks with a group of armed men. Roger's conversion to a better way of life and ceasing persecution of the abbey's tenants ended when Peter and his monks appeared chanting psalms and Roger became a monk himself.[8] Killing babies is not perhaps behaviour we would naturally associate with a saint. Whether or not the Archangel caused the death of the child is not the question, just as the veracity of the visions in the examples discussed above, but the monks could certainly present the sequence of events in such a way that it added to their campaign to bring Roger to heel and serve as a warning to others.

Local religious communities did not just care for the living in times of trouble, but also provided repose for the dead. One of the benefits of founding a monastery or acting as a generous benefactor to an existing house was the expectation that one would be buried within the cloister or church. Sometimes this expectation was formalized with grants made to ensure burial. Many of the Giroire-Grandmesnil clan were buried at the monastery of Saint-Evroult, founded by William Giroie and the Grandmesnil brothers. Robert Giroie, Arnold of Echauffour, Ralph of Montpinçon and Robert of Rhuddlan were all buried in the cloister.[9] Hugh of Grandmesnil and his closest family including his wife, sons and daughters-in-law were all buried in the chapter house.[10] At the abbey of Saint-Pierre-des-Préaux, a house of monks founded in 1035 by Humphrey of Vieilles, several generations of his family, the Beaumonts, were buried within the enclosure, including his sons and grandsons.[11] In England, the Norman settlers founded new religious communities and were buried within them. Robert de Lacy was interred in his Cluniac foundation of Pontefract and Earl Hugh of Chester was buried at St Werburgh's. Sometimes the monuments associated with these graves were very splendid or elaborate. Gundreda, wife of William of Warenne was buried under a black marble slab in the priory at Lewes.[12] The Hauteville clan's foundation of Venosa in southern Italy formed the focus for their burials and family commemorations.[13] As well as the burials themselves, the dead were also commemorated in various documents such as the Winchester *Liber vitae* or through lists that would be placed on the altar at key liturgical feasts.

Burial was not just an effective way of disposing of the dead, but also a means of remembering and commemorating them, as well as ensuring future benefactions and material support for the monastery. Reception of the bodies of benefactors and founders brought the monastic community and its secular supports into much closer relationships. One of the main roles of a house of contemplative monks or nuns was to pray for others and the souls of the departed. Documents such as the Winchester *Liber vitae* acted as a record for the monks of the monastery's dead. The burial of patrons in significant and very visible places within the monastery and cloister served as a reminder to the monks or nuns and also demonstrated that a particular house had connections with powerful secular protectors. If the patron saints of monasteries served as spiritual

Fig.21: The thirteenth-century east range of the cloister at Battle Abbey,
demonstrating the challenges of building on a pronounced slope

protectors, particularly potent ones if the community housed their body, then lay benefactors guaranteed earthly protection.[14]

Religious communities were also sites of memory on a broader scale. An example that is particularly pertinent here was the foundation of Battle Abbey by William the Conqueror. According to the *Chronicle of Battle Abbey*, William promised to found a monastery if God would grant him victory. In the years that followed he commanded the house to be built on the spot where King Harold pitched his standard and was subsequently killed. The *Chronicle*, written in the 1170s, records that the site was deemed unsuitable by the monks as it lacked water and was situated on a very steep slope, so they tried to relocated the monastery. William was furious and demanded the monks follow his original instructions and place the high altar over the spot where Harold died. This the monks did. Even today, one can see the challenges caused by building a monastic house on this site by walking through the ground floor of the east range of the cloister built in the thirteenth century: the rooms gradually increase in height to accommodate the slope. Although the

Chronicle is a late account, written with the considerable benefit of hindsight, earlier traditions also link the foundation of the monastery to thanksgiving for victory. The Peterborough version of the Anglo-Saxon Chronicle notes that the abbey was constructed 'where God granted [William] to conquer England'.[15] Battle Abbey also served as a memorial to the many men who died on the battlefield. Under the Penitential Ordinance of Ermenfrid of Sion, discussed more fully later in this chapter, the foundation of monasteries was set as a means of atoning for the inevitable slaughter of fellow Christians. William's monastery must therefore be seen in the context not only of celebrating and expressing thanks for his victory, but also in commemorating and remembering the dead of both sides.

LEGITIMACY AND ADMINISTRATION

One of the main aspects of the relationship between the Norman rulers and the Church was the ability of the latter to give support and legitimacy to the former's settlement and conquest of various territories. This was not unconditional support, as the rulers had to provide something in return, and the first example is Rollo's settlement of Normandy. Chapter 1 considered the role of conversion in the legitimization of Rollo's possession of the land. His baptism was supposed to mark a change in his behaviour from predator to protector. The sincerity or otherwise of Rollo's conversion has been the subject of debate and, anyway, is impossible to gauge. Dudo's purpose was to demonstrate that the Viking invaders had been accepted into the structures of Frankish society. It was Rollo's successor, William Longsword, who is presented both in the pages of Dudo and later William of Jumièges as undergoing a deeper conversion that involved discussion with both learned churchmen and the foundation of monasteries.

In the *Gesta Normannorum ducum*, William of Jumièges recounts the story of the abbey's refoundation. The monks of Jumièges had fled in the wake of the Viking incursions in the Seine valley, only to return gradually when the situation was more peaceable. While he was out hunting, William Longsword encountered two of the monks gradually clearing the undergrowth, who offered him a simple meal. The duke, conscious of his status perhaps, refused the meal in preference to hunting an enormous wild boar. The animal attacked him and William was brought back to the monastery to recover. During his stay he repented of his refusal of the monks' hospitality and decided to help them rebuild their abbey:

> he sent them agents and had the site cleared of branches and brambles. Thus the church of St Peter, which for some time had been in decay, was skilfully roofed and repaired. And the duke rendered habitable the cloister and all the out-buildings.[16]

William was so impressed by the monks' spirituality that he vowed to become a monk himself and had to be persuaded by the abbot that his proper role in life was to ensure the safety and security of Normandy. A different version of William's desire to enter the religious life is recounted by Dudo, though in the context of a discussion between the abbot and the duke as to what was the path to salvation.[17] Following his assassination at the hands of Arnulf of Flanders' henchmen, William Longsword's followers discovered that he kept a monk's habit locked in a chest, thus demonstrating his piety and devotion to the religious life he was denied.[18]

Fig.22: The abbey of Jumièges in Normandy, showing the surviving Romanesque west front (to left of image)

The inclusion of episodes in chronicles like the foundation of Jumièges was designed to show how far the new rulers had progressed in their Christianity; they also set the tone for demonstrations of piety on the part of later dukes. William of Poitiers in the *Gesta Guillelmi* recorded how the foundation of religious houses under William II rivalled Egypt in terms of the number and holiness of its communities. They were able to flourish as the duke was 'their most faithful protector and constant guardian'.[19] Orderic Vitalis noted that the duke's piety spurred on his nobles also to found communities, stating 'each magnate would have thought himself beneath contempt if he had not supported clerks and monks on his estates for the service of God'.[20] Among these communities was, of course, Orderic's own foundation of Saint-Evroult. By 1087, the year of William the Conqueror's death, there were around forty Benedictine houses in the duchy, including at least seven nunneries. Many of these communities contained members of their founding families devoted to praying for the souls of their benefactors and wider society.

By the time of the conquest and settlement of southern Italy and England, the Normans were firmly established as a Christian people. The papacy, which was seeking to increase its power and influence, therefore had a much greater role to play both in terms of planning (notably England – see Chapter 2) and in recognizing and consolidating conquest (England and southern Italy). At times, the evidence presents various Norman leaders, notably William the Conqueror, Count Richard of Aversa or Robert Guiscard, as particularly favoured; in contrast, letters from the pontificate of Gregory VII reveal some of the tensions between the papal policy and that of the Norman rulers. There was, in the main, a great deal of pragmatism on both sides, and how far either the pope or a duke or king was able to gain an advantage depended to a great extent on the political and social context. The exact nature of the relationship between pope and ruler was a process of continued negotiation through into the twelfth century and beyond.

Recognition for claims to rule and mutual support are evident in the Normans' relationship with the papacy in southern Italy. The popes had watched with alarm as groups of Normans and others had arrived in the region and plundered and pillaged church lands. Amatus of Montecassino is particularly eloquent in this regard and his ambivalent attitude towards the subjects of his history lies in their treatment of the lands of his abbey. As discussed in Chapter 3, the papacy started to take a much greater interest in the struggles between the Normans and rulers in southern Italy in the 1050s under Leo IX, who wanted to promote peace in the region. This initial intervention ended in a notable defeat for the German and papal armies at Civitate in 1053. It was, however, the election of Nicholas II in 1059 that prompted what Cowdrey and, more recently, Loud have termed 'nothing short of a revolution' in the pope's approach to his relationship with the Normans.[21] This was particularly evident through the papal investiture of Robert Guiscard with his territory and the future title of Duke of Sicily. Under the terms of this oath, Robert promised to do nothing that would be prejudicial to the Holy See, to uphold the rights of the papacy and secure its lands, to pay tribute and also to support the election of reform candidates as Nicholas's successors ('I shall, in accordance with the instructions that I am given by the better cardinals, Roman clergy and laymen, assist in the election and ordination of a pope').[22] We must not be misled into thinking that Robert was dependent on the pope for his position. The synod of Melfi certainly helped to legitimize his claims to rule territory in southern Italy and also suggests future plans to invade Sicily, but from the pope's point of view this was also a very pragmatic policy. By this point it was clear that the Normans, particularly the Hauteville brothers and their rivals Richard of Aversa and his descendants in Capua, were not just going to disappear in the unrest between the competing factions. For the pope, accommodation with Robert meant a new ally against other interests, notably the German emperor, and perhaps he also hoped it would keep the rival groups of Normans in check. In return for investiture, Nicholas could rely on military support for the reform faction in Rome against the election of rival candidates.

Nicholas II's pontificate marked a sea change in relations between the southern Italian Normans and the papacy, but the support of his successors was not unconditional or guaranteed. Relations between Robert and Gregory VII, for example, were much more strained. Popes could remove their support for particular rulers in an attempt to correct behaviour seen as contrary to the interests of the Church. Excommunication was the main weapon in the pope's arsenal and it could prove very effective, potentially removing a ruler's legitimacy.

During the investiture conflict with the German emperor Henry IV, Gregory used excommunication as an effective way of releasing his allies in the empire from their oaths of fealty, meaning that rebellion against the emperor was justified. A record of the Lent synod of 1075 records that the pope had already placed Robert Guiscard under anathema and, in addition, excommunicated his nephew, Robert of Loritello.[23] At the centre of this dispute were Norman raids on papal lands following Prince Landulf VI's surrender of Benevento to the pope in 1073. At the same time, Robert Guiscard and other Norman leaders were pushing north into the Abruzzi.[24] The continued expansion of the Norman settlement clashed with Gregory's aim of ensuring the papacy was independent of lay control. Gregory could not afford to alienate the Norman leaders due to his ongoing conflict with Henry IV as he might well need them for military support. In one of the surviving letters from Gregory's pontificate the pope tried to use Arnald, the archbishop of Acerenza to effect a reconciliation, though this was unsuccessful.[25] Eventually Robert and the pope did come to an agreement. In an oath similar to that he had sworn to Nicholas II, Robert reiterated his support. Crucially, however, Gregory was forced to concede that the land the duke had taken, which included Salerno and Amalfi, was lost to papal control for now. Although the Normans despoiled papal lands, they were not challenging the spiritual authority of the pope in quite the same way that Henry IV's defiance over investiture did, though, like William the Conqueror, they were determined to retain some degree of control over the Church in their territory. Gregory needed to be pragmatic and choose which battle to fight. Depriving Robert Guiscard and Roger of their legitimacy to rule would have meant dealing with enemies on two fronts.

Once a territory had been conquered or settled, then it needed to be administered. The institutional side of the Church with all its resources could act as an important bolster to the secular authorities. The benefits to the Church were that it acquired land through the foundation of religious houses and establishment of bishoprics in order to support its activities and also position. This is particularly the case in Normandy and southern Italy where the arrival of the Normans gave impetus to or accelerated the organization of dioceses, the administrative units into which the Church was divided. For the Church in Italy, this was particularly important given that Latin authority in parts of the region was traditionally weak. For the Norman rulers, churchmen provided very able administrators, the expertise for the writing of documents and links with other rulers.

By the time of William II, the Church in Normandy comprised seven dioceses: Rouen, to which, as the archdiocese and seat of the metropolitan bishop, the others – Lisieux, Evreux, Sées, Bayeux, Avranches and Coutances – owed obedience. These units were based on Carolingian divisions. During the Viking incursions and disorders of the tenth century resulting from the struggles between the Carolingian kings and their Capetian challengers, the infrastructure of the dioceses had all but disappeared. Rouen still had an archbishop, but if bishops had been appointed to the dioceses in the west of Normandy, they resided in Rouen. For example, the church of Saint-Lô in the city was so called after the dedication of the diocesan church of Coutances on the Cotentin peninsula. It was not until the 1050s that the new cathedral in Coutances was consecrated and so the bishop could leave Rouen. In Avranches, the cathedral was begun in 1025 during the episcopate of the second bishop appointed after the restoration of the see, Maugis. As for the archbishops themselves, we know from Frankish sources that Archbishop Guy of Rouen was active in the conversion of the Vikings in the Seine valley, but, as discussed in Chapter 1, the activities of Dudo's 'Archbishop Franco' have little basis in fact. Little is known about subsequent archbishops until the appointment of Robert, brother of Richard I, in 989. Robert was very young when he was consecrated and, as a consequence, helped pave the way for the succession of subsequent dukes right the way down to William II. He was also largely responsible for the reorganization of the secular Church in Normandy and the appointment of bishops in the empty dioceses. His was a career, however, that sat firmly in the pre-reform era and that fact colours later sources' interpretations of his character.

Evidence about Robert's activity is confined to the pages of Dudo, the late eleventh-century *Acts of the archbishops of Rouen* and a few surviving charters. This is not unusual for the time, but does make it more difficult for historians to determine the processes by which cathedral churches were re-established and administered. These documents do, however, focus on his activities and allow insights into the role of bishops in ducal Normandy. Bishops had to be good stewards of their cathedrals and build up their endowments. Charter evidence reveals that Robert was active in increasing the patrimony of Rouen. Confirmation of the restitution of land to the cathedral by Robert I demonstrates that the chapter had interests in the Pays de Talou and Pays Bray in Upper Normandy. Crucially it also held land in the west at Falaise and Caen and in the border region of the Norman Vexin.[26] Holding land here was essential for the promotion of ducal interests and the extension of the duke's authority. Robert seems, therefore, to have been an indefatigable administrator and formidable politician. He was also largely responsible for the rebuilding of Rouen cathedral – the choir, transept, lantern tower and crypt were completed under his direction – and other developments in the growing city.[27] Robert was also a patron of the arts.

A close association between bishops and duke was essential for the extension of ducal power across Normandy. A good example is the diocese of Sées, which was very much under the control of the powerful Bellême family. It was gradually brought within the duke's sphere following Roger of Montgomery's marriage to Mabel, the Bellême heiress, and the success of William's campaigns against Geoffrey of Anjou in the 1050s. It was not until after the death of Bishop of Ivo of Bellême that the duke was able to appoint his own man.[28] The same was true for the consolidation of the conquest of England. William recognized that he needed able men in charge of the dioceses. His bishops came from a variety of backgrounds, both monastic and secular, and he seems to have valued equally spiritual authority and administrative ability. Interestingly he did not replace the episcopate wholesale after 1066 and two men who were appointed to bishoprics pre-1066 survived in post for a long time afterwards: the Englishman Wulfstan of Worcester and Giso of Wells, a Lotharingian. However, as Golding notes, no Englishman was appointed after 1066 and so in one fundamental respect, the episcopate at the end of William's reign was very different in character.[29] Had Ealdred of York survived past 1069, he may well have been left in post, though significantly he was replaced by an uncompromising Norman, Thomas of Bayeux. Stigand, tainted as he was by charges of uncanonical election and simony, had to be removed and was replaced by Lanfranc in 1070. William looked for certain qualities in a bishop, notably the ability to perform what could be a very demanding role and a willingness to support his policies in the kingdom.

The physical geography of the episcopate in England was as important to the governance of the Church and the country as it was in Normandy. We discussed above the strategic importance of the lands held by the cathedral at Rouen. Following the conquest in 1066, William moved the seat of some key bishoprics, continuing a process that had started under Edward the Confessor, who moved the see of Crediton in Devon to the nearby larger settlement of Exeter. A charter that probably dates from the early 1070s records William's decision to move the see of Dorchester to Lincoln.[30] Not only was Lincoln more prosperous and an important urban centre, it was also strategically important as the site of a royal castle and defence against any possible invading army from Denmark. The security of William's realm was better served by situating his bishops in areas where the king's authority was perceived to be remote. The relocation of the cathedral from Lichfield to Chester in 1075 also placed a bishop in a potentially volatile area, that of the border between England and Wales.[31]

The diocesan structure of southern Italy is much harder to determine. On the whole dioceses were much smaller and more numerous. In some areas, notably Calabria, the Church looked east to the Byzantine Empire, rather than to Rome, and in Muslim-held Sicily the Latin Church barely existed. In addition, the documentary record for the southern Italian episcopate is much sparser than for north of the Alps. There was not the same tradition of writing narrative histories recalling the deeds of bishops that we see in Normandy and England. According to Norbert Kamp, detailed information exists for only about a tenth of the bishops of this region. What does survive demonstrates far greater continuity in terms of personnel. The Norman takeover of southern Italy did not result in the widespread removal of native prelates in favour of Norman or French appointees. The bishops remained local men. Kamp has, however, argued that the synod of Melfi in 1059 did mark a significant change in that Greek bishops on the mainland were now increasingly replaced with those whose allegiance was to Rome, though this change was geographically limited to lands under Norman control in Apulia. In the Tyrrhenian city states and the Lombard principalities, which were still largely independent from the Normans, the pace of change was much slower.[32]

Once Robert Guiscard and Roger extended their conquests into Calabria and Sicily, bishops in those areas were appointed from monasteries under their patronage, suggesting they had a much greater control in ecclesiastical appointments. This is borne out by the foundation of bishoprics in Sicily recorded by Geoffrey Malaterra, who provides important information about Roger's initial appointments. As he was essentially starting from scratch, the bishops seem to be of more varied backgrounds. Gerland, a Savoyard, was made bishop of Agrigento. Stephen, described as 'an upright man from Rouen', went to Mazara, while Roger, originally from Provence but who had more recently served at Troina, was appointed to Syracuse. After some negotiation and persuasion, Roger appointed Angerius, a monk of Sant'Eufemia, as bishop of Catania.[33] Although Pope Urban II approved the new appointments, the sees remained under Roger's control. Urban's attempt to have a legate – his own direct representative – appointed to oversee the Church in Sicily was unsuccessful.[34]

Monasteries, too, helped the Norman rulers consolidated their power. They might have been made up of communities of contemplative monks or nuns, but the lands they held and administered could act as a powerful tool to spread authority. If the story about William and the abbey of Jumièges was used to stress his piety and to emphasize how far these Scandinavian settlers had progressed in their journey from heathen pirates to Christian princes, then the use of monasteries elsewhere in the duchy reflects a more pragmatic side. Undoubtedly conventional piety governed many of their actions, but the dukes were very much aware of the potential of religious houses to bolster their support in regions far removed from Rouen, to encourage economic growth and to provide opportunities for advancement for ducal relatives. Religious communities also played a vital role in the consolidation of the conquest of England after 1066 and in establishing Norman rule in Italy. They also helped support the ambitions of local lords. Through patronage, which included land, exemption from taxes, and other privileges, these institutions were able to encourage stable settlement and economic growth. They could also exercise justice and a degree of administration in the localities. A good example is the abbey of Mont-Saint-Michel. Successive dukes from William Longsword on took an interest in this community situated off the coast of Normandy and on the border with Brittany. Traditionally the counts of Brittany were the community's main benefactors, but gradually the Normans took over this role. The abbey's networks allowed for a gradual maintenance of ducal authority in the west of the duchy.[35] Other abbeys, like Bernay, were founded on ducal lands, in this case the dower lands of Richard II's wife Judith. Within southern Italy, men like Richard of Aversa, Robert Guiscard and

Fig.23: West front of the abbey of La Trinité in Caen

Roger supported existing communities, notably Montecassino, but also founded new ones such as Venosa and Sant'Eufemia in order to bolster their interests.[36]

We have already noted that a monastery or church's saint could act as a powerful protector of the community and this fact must be recognized when the legitimacy lent by the Church to rulers is discussed. Felice Lifschitz and Samantha Herrick have both discussed the importance of hagiographical writing in the consolidation of ducal authority in Normandy.[37] The adoption of the duchy's ancient episcopal saints, for example Romanus, Vigor, Taurinus and Nicasius, allowed the Normans to present themselves as heirs to their apostolic tradition, demonstrating their transition from raiders to sons of the Church. This was particularly the case in relation to Romanus, patron saint of Rouen, credited with saving the city from the Vikings. In southern Italy, Robert Guiscard also supported local cult centres, notably that of St Matthew at Salerno. According to Amatus, the saint had prophesied the papal defeat at Civitate. In essence, Matthew had lent his support to the Normans in recognition of their possession of the land by divine grant. Robert worked with Bishop Alfanus I to rebuild the cathedral, in the process rediscovering the saint's relics.[38] Such discoveries were often taken as a mark of favour, as the saint would not allow him or herself to be revealed to unworthy people. In England the Norman appointees to abbeys and bishoprics saw value in maintaining the various cults, despite well-known instances of scepticism.[39] The most notable of these examples is perhaps Lanfranc's downgrading of the cult of Ælfeah, martyred by the Vikings under Cnut. He discussed the possible suppression of the cult with Anselm, who persuaded him that Ælfeah was worthy of veneration, and the feast was restored to Canterbury's calendar.[40] Adopting and honouring native saints helped build community and links between the Normans and the people they had conquered.

Patronage of monasteries encouraged the development of authority in other ways, notably through economic growth. The abbeys of Saint-Etienne and La Trinité in Caen serve as excellent examples. The abbeys themselves were an important focus of power and ducal authority in the west of the duchy. The city of Caen is situated on the confluence of the rivers Orne and Odon and was a significant point of communication between Upper and Lower Normandy. The

Fig.24: The abbey of Saint-Etienne in Caen as seen from the castle

ducal capital of Rouen was far removed from territory in the west and so the development of Caen as a new urban centre was vitally important in cementing William's hold on the duchy. As Laurence Jean-Marie has noted, the two abbeys formed 'poles of attraction'. They were founded in two distinct neighbourhoods: La Trinité was situated on the eastern edge of the city on the hill above the rivers, with Saint-Etienne on the opposite side of the town. The ducal castle was located roughly equidistant between them. Although the abbeys were located outside the walls of the city, they functioned as powerful magnets for economic growth. William granted the same privileges to the *bourg* of Saint-Etienne as was the case for his own *bourg* centred on the castle.[41] Closer to the seat of ducal power was the abbey of Montivilliers, whose first abbess was Beatrice, one of Richard I's daughters. Montivilliers is now a suburb of the major port of Le Havre, but in the Middle Ages it was much more significant in terms of its links with fishing, whaling and other industries.[42] The dukes ensured that this abbey was given privileges that allowed it to exploit these resources to the full and contribute to the developing economy. Monasteries in southern Italy, for example Holy Trinity at Cava (founded in *c.* 1020), served a similar purpose. This abbey had close ties to the principality of Salerno, but both the local Lombard population and the Normans continued to support it after the conquest. Its abbots were able to build up and consolidate their patrimony so that by the mid-twelfth century the communities held what amounted to two territorial lordships based on and controlling eight ports.[43]

The economic relationship between the Normans and monasteries in England following 1066 took a somewhat different form. The redistribution of land to William's followers meant that religious houses in Normandy benefitted a great deal from the conquest. La Trinité in Caen, for example, held extensive lands on the other side of the Channel. Norman lords also increasingly founded new houses in England from the reign of William Rufus onwards. However, the way the new rulers treated existing houses caused disquiet, resentment and open rebellion. Monasteries comprised a large community of non-combatants and were vulnerable to attack. It was accepted that armies should not attack or despoil them, but nevertheless it happened. Some communities lost lands, as well as vestments, books and other valuable artefacts necessary for their devotions. In his *Ecclesiastical History*, Orderic recorded that Guitmund, a monk at La Croix Saint-Leufroi, refused to take up an ecclesiastical post in England because he deemed 'all England the spoils of robbery'.[44] This speech was a rhetorical device on the part of Orderic, but the fact that some writers expressed qualms about the Normans' approach to English monasticism reveals unease.

SUPPORT FOR REFORM

The eleventh century witnessed attempts by popes, heads of monasteries and bishops to implement the various tenets of the reform movement, including ideals of clerical celibacy and the freeing of church land and institutions from lay control. A good, pious ruler was expected to uphold these tenets and support the churchmen in his region in their attempts to enforce them, and one of the ways in which the Normans might do this was in their support of church councils or synods. One of the things that the bishops and leading abbots of Normandy, southern Italy and England all had in common was their attendance at church councils. These meetings promulgated the canons of the Church and disseminated decisions from Rome or other key centres to the localities. Fortunately the decrees of many of these councils survive, often copied into other sources such as Orderic's *Ecclesiastical History* or monastic annals. In Normandy and England William was involved in overseeing the discussions. In this respect Normandy differed from the rest of France in which legates, representatives of the pope, presided over councils. This might indicate the thesis put forward by Margaret Gibson that William and Lanfranc were conservative in their understanding of reform.[45] William wished to maintain a higher degree of control over the Church in his territories than, later, Gregory VII would find acceptable. William of Poitiers noted that:

> Whenever at his [William's] command and by his encouragement the prelates, metropolitan and suffragans, assembled to deal with the state of religion of clerks, monks and laymen, he endeavoured not to miss being an arbiter at these synods, so that by his presence he might add zeal to the zealous and circumspection to the provident.[46]

Both William and the English chronicler Eadmer use the king's involvement in synods as evidence of his piety, support for the Church and desire for good governance in all aspects of his realm. For the southern Italian Church, councils were held under the authority of the pope, either when he visited the region, as successive popes did more frequently from the time of Leo IX onwards, or as the influence of the papacy increased, in Rome. Some of the synods held in Normandy and England were presided over by legates in his stead, notably when matters concerned the deposition of bishops or the translation of a bishop from one diocese to another. This was the case at the council of 1070 at which Stigand was deposed, but also at Lisieux in 1054 when Mauger was removed from office.

The material covered by the councils in all three areas encompassed a variety of topics relating to the Church and its role in society. These included preaching the Truce of God, which tried to limit violent conflict, regulations regarding the monastic life, the proper use of church buildings and land, as well as excommunication of those deemed to have offended against the Church in some way. One of the key themes was clerical celibacy. This was an issue that concerned the Church greatly, as it touched on notions of who was considered fit to be a priest. Some individuals in the curia debated whether married priests were proper vessels for the sacraments – a position which came dangerously close to heresy, as it called into question their validity. Under the influence of the reform movement, bishops were charged with separating priests from their families or dismissing them from their positions if they refused to renounce their wives. The canons from various regional synods underline this. William of Apulia noted that the synod of Melfi in 1059 preached chastity and stated that Pope Nicholas 'drove away from those parts all the wives of priests'.[47] The council of Lillebonne in 1080 commanded that 'priests, deacons and sub-deacons, and all canons and deans shall have no wives or kept women'.[48] This policy is also found in the letters between churchmen discussing particular cases. A letter from Archbishop Lanfranc to Archbishop John of Rouen alludes to a riot that happened in Rouen cathedral in 1072 after John had tried to enforce celibacy. Other letters of Lanfranc to bishops in England also deal with this question. He advised Herfast, bishop of Thetford, on the case of a deacon who had been ordained despite his having a wife, telling him to demote the cleric to minor orders until he could remain celibate.[49]

The reform agenda meant that qualities that had been valued in leading churchmen prior to the mid-eleventh century, particularly the degree to which they could overlap the sacred and temporal spheres, were deemed unacceptable in later decades. Three archbishops of Rouen make an interesting comparison in this respect. Robert, son of Duke Richard I, was not only archbishop of Rouen, but also held lands in a secular capacity as count of Evreux and in that role acted as one of the duke's key supporters on the borders of Normandy, as the grants to his cathedral also show. He was an essential figure in the gradual consolidation of ducal authority from the time of Richard I onwards. These activities, alongside his personal life, meant that his reputation has suffered somewhat from a post-reform context. Writers of the late eleventh century criticized him for being too worldly, for being married and having children, and also neglecting spiritual affairs. The anonymous author of the *Acta archiepiscopum Rotomagensis* wrote that although Robert was 'of great piety and honest [...] he was overcome by the weakness of the flesh and had very many sons', though he apparently left his wife at the end of his life.[50] Orderic, in his version of the *Acta*, named his wife as Herleve and listed his sons as Richard, Ralph and William. According to the monk of Saint-Evroult, Robert gave 'abundant alms for the poor' in order to make amends.[51] By the late eleventh century, clerical celibacy was established as the norm by which all churchmen should live. Although the canons on celibacy were difficult to enforce, the monastic tradition of spirituality with its strong emphasis on sexual abstinence was in the ascendant. Robert's successor and nephew, Mauger received a similarly bad press. The *Acta* record that 'it was not the distinction of his merit, but the love of his parents and the support of sycophants' that brought about his appointment.[52] He was also implicated in a rebellion against William II in alliance with William of Arques, one of the duke's other uncles. Figures like Mauger and Robert, who were so obviously far removed from the ideals of the reform movement, but who nonetheless did what they could to promote the interests of the Church and the duke, were deeply ambivalent figures for later writers.

It is interesting to compare the portraits we have of Robert and Mauger with that of the next archbishop, Maurilius, for what it can tell us about how a reform bishop should behave and what qualities he should have. Maurilius's appointment marked a temporary hiatus in the string of prelates related to the ducal family (his successor, John of Ivry, was another ducal relative). An important point to note is that Maurilius came from a monastic background, having spent time in communities at Florence and in Fécamp as well as a spell as a hermit before his elevation to Rouen. Men such as he might well have been considered more reliable in the promotion of the reform agenda, particularly clerical celibacy, though we have to remember that bishops continued to be drawn from the secular clergy as well. In the period 1050 into the early decades of the twelfth century, monasticism was increasingly important in the background of the southern Italy bishops, for example Elias of Bari and Alfanus of Salerno.[53] In England, the first two archbishops of Canterbury following the conquest – Lanfranc and Anselm – had both been monks of Le Bec. The author of the *Acta* noted that Maurilius 'dedicated himself to fasting, sermons and alms giving until the end of his days'.[54] Both Orderic and the *Acta* also stress his completion of the cathedral in Rouen. Although Maurilius's reputation shone brightly among writers of the reform era, it is worth stressing that not all sees became enclaves of reform overnight. Bayeux was in the hands of Odo, William's half-brother, who not only served as the secular earl of Kent following the conquest, but actually fought in battle in 1066.[55]

Reform was also at the heart of the relationship between William the Conqueror and the papacy. We noted that papal support for the invasion of England might well have been dependent on William's help in bringing the Church in England into closer alignment with the reformist programme of the papacy and particularly in ridding the English episcopate of prelates who were deemed problematic. In 1070, the pope sent Ermenfrid of Sion to England as a legate, a representative who could act in his name. While in the country, Ermenfrid deposed some of the English bishops who had otherwise survived the conquest. In contrast to the chronicler John of Worcester's assertion that William 'stripped of their offices many bishops and abbots who had not been condemned for any obvious cause', the numbers removed were small.[56] These included Stigand, whose crimes included holding more than one bishopric at a time, driving a previous archbishop of Canterbury from his see, and receiving his pallium – the mark of archiepiscopal office – from an antipope. The surviving records of synods in Normandy demonstrate that the king did have an interest in these matters. Ermenfrid also issued a document, known as the Penitential Ordinance, that set out the various penances that individuals who had taken part in William's military campaigns should perform. William's campaign may well have been sanctioned by the pope, but it was still war and in line with customs like the Truce of God, restitution had to be made for killing. Ermenfrid was careful to distinguish between the period of war – up to William's coronation on Christmas Day 1066 – and military activity thereafter. If the king's men killed people who were deemed to be unlawfully resisting his authority, then penance was reduced. If, however, their victims were not rebels, the penance was commensurate with that of murder. These penances included the giving of alms and the foundation or benefaction of religious houses and churches.[57]

The fact that the pope should send a legate was, however, very significant as it showed continued support for William's actions and policies in England. From the cooperation of William and the pope via Ermenfrid, it looks as if the relationship between the king and papacy was a close one. The succession of Lanfranc to Canterbury, however, was not unproblematic. On the face of it, Lanfranc's credentials were unimpeachable. He was a monk, an able administrator and close adviser to the king. He had been instrumental in achieving a papal dispensation for William and Matilda's consanguineous marriage and had close connections in the curia. Lanfranc's version of reform differed from that of Alexander's successors. Lanfranc believed that, within the confines of his kingdom, the king was the ultimate authority. This was particularly at odds with Gregory VII (who, prior to his election was an enthusiastic supporter of William's claim to the England throne), who had a much more stark view of the relative power of pope and king. In spiritual matters, he believed, the pope reigned supreme, regardless of the political situation.

A series of letters between Gregory on the one hand and William and Lanfranc on the other still survives. Gregory was anxious that Lanfranc should visit Rome to take part in synods and bring the benefit of his learning to his brother clergy. He wanted William to reinstitute the practice of collecting Peter's Pence, a special tax that English churches collected and sent to Rome, and to swear fealty to the pope. William was more than willing to do the former, but the latter was a sticking point. None of his predecessors had performed such an act of homage and he saw no reason to break with custom. His reply to the pope was succinct: 'I have not consented to pay fealty, nor will I now, because I never promised it. Nor do I find that my predecessors ever paid it to your predecessors.'[58] Lanfranc put forward several excuses why he could not go to Rome, including the fact that the king was unwilling to let him. Certainly the archbishop was a key figure in William's administration and he acted as regent during the king's visits to Normandy. Gregory persevered and reminded both men of their responsibilities as he perceived them. He also wrote to other churchmen asking them to intervene. In reality, though, there was little he could do. Just as his dealings with Robert Guiscard were tempered by the dispute with Henry IV, so too was his relationship with William.

Reform also affected the monasteries in William's newly conquered kingdom. We perhaps can see this most clearly in the imposition of new liturgies and reform practices. Lanfranc, for example, introduced practices based on the customs of the abbey of Le Bec in Normandy and also Cluniac traditions. At Glastonbury in Somerset,

Abbot Thurstan's attempt to impose the liturgy of Fécamp had disastrous consequences in 1083. William of Malmebury provides accounts of the rebellion of the monks against Thurstan in both his *Gesta regum pontificum* and the *Gesta regum Anglorum*. He noted in the former that the Norman abbots 'play the tyrant, rather than the churchman'.[59] In response to the monks' unwillingness to accept the new liturgy, Thurstan ordered soldiers to shoot them in the church. The violence was shocking, leaving 'even the figure of the Crucified bristling with arrows'.[60] Both William and Orderic criticized the level of observance in the English Church prior to the conquest, but certainly William expressed regret that what he saw as the increased support for continental monastic practices came at the expense of the existing institutions:

> Thus the monastic population increased in his [William's] time on both sides of the channel and convents arose with a long history of devotion but new buildings. But at this point I should mention the grumbles of those who said it would have been better to preserve the old foundations in their former state than to rob them to build new ones while they fell into ruins.[61]

He could not fault the piety of the new communities' founders, but he also clearly felt something had been lost.

To sum up the relationship between the Church and society, it is instructive to look at the Benedictine abbeys of Saint-Etienne for men and La Trinité for women in Caen. We have already noted how these institutions functioned as instruments of ducal power in terms of their economic influence, but they also demonstrate the ties between religious foundations and lay society. William and Matilda were both pious individuals and their monastic foundations reflect that piety and the duty of rulers to support and protect the Church and the vulnerable.

The two houses are synonymous with the ducal house and power. They were founded in the years preceding the Norman conquest of England in 1066 and La Trinité was dedicated on the eve of the expedition. The ducal couple's youngest daughter, Cecilia, was given as a child oblate and later became its abbess. Provision was made for supporting those in need. In a charter dated to somewhere between 1066 and Matilda's death in 1083, the couple assigned a portion of the patrimony of La Trinité to the almonry and established a church dedicated to the burial of the poor.[62] Both William and Matilda were buried in the choirs of their respective foundations, the part of the church particularly associated with the religious community. As well as the revenue generated by the institutions, they were also a visual testament to the piety of William and Matilda and their ability to command the necessary resources to build such magnificent structures. Churches in the medieval period were not built in one continuous period, but steadily over a number of building campaigns. La Trinité was constructed over a period of around twenty years between *c.* 1060 and 1080. Usually the east end of the church containing the high altar and thus the focus of Christian devotion in the Eucharist was the first section to be built and dedicated. Eventually, these two abbeys had imposing west fronts, the most visible section to the laity, who would enter the church through the west door. Like many of William's buildings, they were constructed from Caen stone and exhibited many fine Romanesque details in terms of carving. The towers of both abbeys (the spires on the west front of Saint-Etienne are later additions) would have soared over the medieval town. Even today, with the growth of high-rise buildings following the damage of World War II, both churches are visible from the castle. Travellers approaching the city would have seen the work in progress and eventually the splendid churches in all their glory. Further links were made with the conquest of England as Matilda bequeathed her royal regalia, as well as other objects, to the community of La Trinité in a charter probably datable to 1083.[63] The presence of Cecilia in the abbey also provided an important role for her as the spiritual arm of the family. Three of her brothers went on to rule various Anglo-Norman territories and it was expected that her sisters would make advantageous marriages. Cecilia's role as nun and abbess was no less important. She might have been separated from the secular world by virtue of her vocation, but she was still very much part of it, helping to sustain family and community and, in turn, sustained by them. These two abbeys were as much a symbol of ducal authority as the nearby castle. They also show the necessity of temporal and church powers to work in tandem. Without the support of the Church, William the Conqueror would have found the conquest and settlement of England much more difficult. Without the active interventions of men like William or Robert Guiscard, the process of reform and reorganization might have proceeded at a much slower pace.

6

CULTURAL EXCHANGES

This chapter considers the influences and cultures the Normans encountered during their settlement and conquest of different parts of Europe. In so doing it also sets up a consideration of Norman identities and histories discussed in the next chapter. It might not always be possible to discern whether adoption of particular ceremonials, language or art forms was a conscious choice, but what cross-cultural encounters show is both the adaptability of the Normans to new circumstances and sometimes the ways in which those they settled among or conquered responded to or even challenged them. Most of the elements discussed here took place over long periods of time. It is an old adage that the 'Saxons' did not suddenly throw out all their pots, change their names and become Normans on the evening of 14 October 1066. Change at a social and cultural level happened slowly for the most part. It is also important to consider the relationship between the Norman and non-Christian groups, notably Jews and Muslims. This chapter examines these interactions through three key areas: literature and language; objects, art and architecture; and finally, the Normans' relations with Jews and Muslims.

LANGUAGE AND LITERATURE

The Normans came into contact with a wide variety of languages as they settled in various parts of Europe. Rollo and his followers would have spoken a form of Old Norse and, on settling in Normandy, would have needed to get to grips with Latin and the precursors of modern French. Across the Channel, Old English was the language of literature, pastoral care and government prior to 1066, though Latin was used within the Church and in certain circumstances at court. As the Normans gradually moved west and north, they would have also encountered the medieval forms of Cornish, Welsh, Scottish and Irish. The conquest instituted changes in the way language was used, some of which were relatively sudden and some of which were more gradual. In southern Italy and the Holy Land, the Normans had to negotiate various forms of Italian, Greek, Arabic, the ancestors of modern Turkish and so on. In order to govern and go about their daily lives, they would have been highly dependent on native speakers and translators to avoid misunderstandings. A possibly apocryphal story recounted by Orderic Vitalis about William's coronation illustrates this well:

> When Archbishop Ealdred asked the English, and Geoffrey bishop of Coutances asked the Normans, if they would accept William as their king, all of them gladly shouted out with one voice, if not in one language that they would. The armed guard outside, hearing the tumult of the joyful crowd in the harsh accents of a foreign tongue, imagined that some treachery was afoot, and rashly set fire to some of the buildings.[1]

He goes on to say that the English never trusted the Normans after this event. Language mattered.

Within Normandy little information survives to give an indication of how widespread and for how long Old Norse was used and spoken. Dudo's assertion that William Longsword had to send his son, the future Richard I, to Bayeux to learn the language because it was no longer spoken in Rouen has generally been taken as a sign that connections between the Normans and their Scandinavian homeland were very weak from an early point in the duchy's history. Following Searle's argument (discussed in Chapter 1) that Rollo and his men were just one of several groups of Norsemen that settled within Normandy, then it is possible to see William's actions in a different light. Sending his son to the west might well be a way of building alliances and maintaining links. Later events after the death of William bear this out. In the face of Frankish aggression, it was the chief men of Bayeux who came to the rescue of the young Richard.

Other evidence of the influence and use of Old Norse is similarly residual. In terms of linguistic changes, only 145 words from the Scandinavian world survive in the medieval Norman language, as opposed to over 1,000 in English, according to the work of Elisabeth Ridel. These words have a strong maritime and commercial bias, as one might expect from people descended from seafarers.[2] Toponyms and personal names might well have been introduced from England, as discussed in Chapter 1.

Looking at literature might provide additional information, notably sources such as poems. Van Houts argues that the early eleventh-century satirical poem *Morihut*, written in Latin by Warner of Rouen, is actually similar in form to a Scandinavian genre known as the *flyting*. A characteristic of this genre is 'violent invective': the basis of Warner's work is harsh criticism of Morihut's poetic abilities. Such poems are not found outside Scandinavia and British and Irish contexts, so perhaps Warner's work can be seen as a Latin equivalent to this form.[3] Literary contact between Scandinavia and Normandy is attested in later, but no less problematic sources, such as the sagas. Works like the *Heimskringla* of Snorri Sturluson were written in the thirteenth century, long after the events they describe, but based on older oral traditions; nevertheless, many contain earlier material in the form of skaldic poetry. Skalds are likely to have visited Normandy during the eleventh century and almost certainly returned home with tales they then wove into their poems. The Icelander Snorri was certainly aware of the Normans' Viking antecedents as he made reference to the descendants of Rollo (Rolf the Ganger) in an account of Rollo's exile from Norway.[4] If the skalds took stories home with them, then it seems reasonable to suppose that they also brought Scandinavian forms of literature to Rouen and perhaps influenced the poetry circulating round the Norman court such as *Morihut*. Potential Norse literary influences might also be found in other narrative sources, notably the account of Robert the Magnificent's pilgrimage to Jerusalem. Van Houts argues that motifs like the golden shoes on Robert's mule or the use of walnuts for fuel after the Byzantine emperor had banned the selling of firewood are found in the tales of Scandinavians who travelled to the east, notably Harald Hadraada and Sigurd Jerusalem-farer.[5]

The Normans' encounters with Old English need to be seen in a different light. After all, William's invasion was a planned operation with a clear goal: the seizure of the English throne. How language was used can be seen as an indication of how William wanted to rule. Until 1070, writs – one of the primary documents of administration – were still issued in Old English, as they had been in the reign of Edward the Confessor. From that date, writs were issued in Latin.[6] It is tempting to see this as a turning point and a deliberate decision to reduce the importance and power of written Old English by removing it from a privileged place in government. The year 1069 had witnessed two key events: the death of Ealdred, archbishop of York, who had been seen as a mediating influence in the region; and the Harrying of the North, which presented a significant challenge to William's authority. In 1070, Stigand was deposed by the papal legate at the council of Winchester, the same council that promulgated the Penitential Ordinance, designed to exact penance for the bloodshed of the colonization, meaning that both archbishops – Thomas of Bayeux and Lanfranc – were now Norman appointees whose primary language would have been Latin. This is not to say that Old English disappeared. It was still the language of the people and remained so, while Anglo-Norman was the language of the nobility.

We noted in Chapter 2 that the conquest was seen as extremely traumatic and that this led to a break in the writing of histories in England with the exception of the Anglo-Saxon Chronicle. When historical writing resumed in the twelfth century, the language used by Eadmer, William of Malmesbury and Henry of Huntingdon was Latin. As Elaine Treharne has shown, however, Old English continued to be used and copied in manuscripts until the thirteenth century. Through a careful analysis of the survival of Old English in various collections of texts or fragmentary manuscripts, she has shown that a total of eighty-five manuscripts containing Old English survive for the period from between *c.* 1050 x 1060 to 1100. The works contained therein include homilies, saints' lives, law codes, texts relating to science and medicine, pastoral commentaries designed for the spiritual care of the people, literary and biblical works, poetry and romance.[7] The majority of these works come from Canterbury, closely followed by the dioceses of Worcester under Bishop Wulfstan and Exeter under Bishop Leofric, English bishops who survived the conquest. These men needed to protect their sees and ensure the pastoral care of the people, the majority of whom spoke and understood Old English, not Latin and not Anglo-Norman. For many of the rank-and-file monks, Old English would have been their mother tongue. Even in highly luxurious manuscripts, notably Eadwine's psalter from late twelfth-century Canterbury, we can find Old English used to provide glosses or explanations on the psalms.[8] Its use might have disappeared in government, but it continued to be a living language in other areas of life.

In Italy, the Normans were faced with several languages of the Church and government, namely Latin, Greek and Arabic, as well as various vernaculars. Just as Old Norse did not replace the indigenous languages in Normandy, so too did the Normans adapt to the languages of the Mezzogiorno and Sicily in order to rule effectively. Metcalfe has demonstrated that the rulers of Sicily following the conquest by Count Roger, completed in the 1090s, adopted customs from the various traditions and groups on the island.[9] This meant that the language and practice of government owed more to the Fatimid and Byzantine cultures of the southern and eastern Mediterranean than to northern Europe. These changes in administration have been discussed in detail elsewhere.[10] Here we can use the example of the government of what became the kingdom of Sicily under Roger II in 1130. Traditional narratives state that the Normans took over Muslim administrative practices from the completion of the conquest to the fall of the kingdom to the German emperor at the end of the twelfth century.[11] As Jeremy Johns has pointed out, this does not take into account a very real break in practice after the death of Count Roger. He died while both his sons were still children and to compound the situation, the elder, Simon, died while still a child, which meant Roger's widow had a long regency for her other son, the second Roger. During this period there was an increase in the number of immigrants from Latin traditions not conversant with the methods of administration in the island. In addition, no Muslim lords formed part of Count Roger's close circle. The Normans were heavily dependent on Greek administrators from the east of Sicily and Calabria. Arabic was dropped as a language of governance and Greek became dominant. It was only after the coronation of Roger II that Arabic came into use again with the formation of the royal dīwān, a body concerned with financial administration.[12]

The reasons for this are interesting and not straightforward. On the face of it, the reuse of Arabic might be explained by the fact that the beneficiaries of documents or their scribes were Arabic speakers, but this does not account for the Arabic documents concerning monasteries where the language used would have been Greek or Latin.[13] Initially Arabic was used alongside Greek, but eventually it became the dominant language, before it was itself supplanted by Latin in the reigns following that of Roger. Johns suggests that the reason does not only lie in expedience, but also in experiments with Islamic court styles and titles within the dīwān. In this, rather than looking east to Byzantium, Roger's court, particularly influenced by the admiral George of Antioch, was looking south to the Fatimid caliphate. Roger was referred to with an Arabic variant of his name – Rujār – and his dynastic title al-malik al muʿaẓẓam, which means 'the glorified king'. Added to these were epithets emphasizing the quality of kingship, the territories he ruled over and titles that referred to the relationship between the king and the Church ('defender of the pope', 'protector of the Christian community').[14] These last two underline the fact that Roger was, fundamentally, a Christian ruler, so why adopt such a style that can be seen elsewhere, for example in his art, coinage and objects? It seems Johns's argument, that this was a means by which Norman rule could be made acceptable to a Muslim society, particularly in the west of the island, is persuasive.[15] It also has implications for our ideas of what might constitute being 'Norman', considered in the next chapter.

Arabic was also vitally important as a language of intellectual endeavour within the court. Roger II was a great patron of learning and scholarship and one figure stands out in particular: Muḥammad ibn ʿAbd Allāh al-Idrīsī, an Arabic scholar commonly known as al-Idrīsī and who died somewhere between 1164 and 1175. Roger commissioned him to produce a geographical description of the world and of his kingdom, which is known in the west as *The Book of Roger*.[16] As well as the written account al-Idrīsī also produced a series of maps to accompany the text. As Metcalfe has noted, this work was completed at the same time the Arabic scribes of the dīwān 'were defining provinces with outer boundaries and internal estates'.[17] It shows a concern on the part of Roger to know as much as he could about his kingdom and to employ the best people available to help him in this endeavour. It was a powerful act of royal patronage.

The use of Latin, Greek and Arabic on the island has led historians to characterize this society as trilingual. Certainly evidence such as the trilingual psalter now kept in the British Library as MS Harley 5786 supports such a view. This book preserves ecclesiastical rites in all three languages and was designed for use in the royal chapel in Palermo.[18] The idea of a trilingual society follows the description of the people of Palermo in a poem by Peter of Eboli in a panegyric for emperor Henry VI who conquered Sicily in the 1190s. This work also contains a famous illustration of the scribes in the last of the Hauteville line, Tancred's royal chancery. They are depicted drawing up documents: one in Latin, one in Greek and one in Arabic. Their ethnicity is distinguished by distinctive forms of dress, facial hair and other markers like turbans for the Muslims and beards for the Greeks.[19] It is necessary, however, to sound a note of caution. Such evidence of patronage and seeming cooperation, stemming as it does from the royal court, can present a misleading picture of tolerance and cooperation that masked elements of coercion and naked power.

OBJECTS, ART AND ARCHITECTURE

One of the key questions historians of the Normans face is how much the activities of this people affected material aspects of society. Can we identify any visual changes stemming from the activity of the Normans? What connections existed between the different parts of Europe settled or conquered by these people? Key to this is how contact with England and southern Italy might affect Normandy and what influences can be detected there?

In relation to England, a key debate is how far events of 1066 and subsequent years marked a fundamental rupture in English society. As noted in earlier chapters, Domesday Book records the level of dispossession as land was taken away from the English survivors and reallocated to William's followers. Some of the estates themselves might have remained intact, but the new landlords were from across the Channel. Conditions for the peasantry declined with changes in the way they held land and paid rent to their lords. This much can be gleaned from the administrative and economic sources, but what of day-to-day life? How was that affected by the arrival of a new king and ruling aristocracy?

In this respect, recent work in archaeology can help us a great deal to understand how society changed and affected the way that people went about their daily business. Ben Jervis has analysed pottery assemblages from Southampton to show how the design, use and disposal of cooking vessels changed post-conquest and how these practices actively changed or modified individual or group identity.[20] According to Domesday Book, the land of Oda of Winchester, Eskil the priest, Ketil, Fugel, Tosti, the sons of Alric Gering and Cypping had all passed to Ralph de Mortimer by 1086; Bernard Pauncevolt held three houses previously belonging to Godwine. Other people claiming revenues from the town included the abbess of Wherwell, abbots of Norman monasteries, Norman bishops, prominent men like Hugh de Grandmesnil of the family that founded the monastery in which Orderic was a monk, the count of Evreux and the count of Mortain. Altogether, 65 Frenchman and 31 Englishmen were settled in the town.[21] In these circumstances, we might expect to see a gradual sharing of methods and utensils as people encountered unfamiliar ways of doing things.

Jervis's study reveals a stark contrast between the western and eastern sections of the town. In the east the pottery assemblages reveal continuity with pre-conquest practices. For example, pottery was disposed of in middens (rubbish heaps) and the resulting compost used as fertilizer in gardens. These gardens were used by the inhabitants to generate a surplus to go towards paying off taxes. In terms of use before deposition, the ceramic evidence shows that people in this part of Southampton continued to use Saxon flint-tempered wares as cooking vessels, which, according to the soot deposits found on the pots, were placed in or close to the embers of the fire. The western side of the town, which was closer to the waterfront, possibly had a greater concentration of merchants and 'French' poeple settled before the conquest. Here we find a higher preponderance of scratch-marked wares, which show evidence of suspension of the pots above the fire. It would seem that this new technique was introduced through merchants whose houses would have been located closer to the port areas. Gradually, by the thirteenth century, the practice of cooking by suspending vessels above the fire seemed to become widespread.

What can this tell us about how everyday life changed in the wake of the Norman takeover? This is not simply a process of a dominant immigrant group imposing foreign customs on the indigenous population of Southampton, even though the Domesday evidence indicates significant changes in property holding and land ownership; rather it shows a process of negotiation on the part of the people doing the cooking. Those cooks who were used to suspending their pots had to come to terms with vessels designed to be placed in the embers, while English cooks possibly employed in

Fig.25: Late twelfth-century merchant's house in Southampton on Porters Lane not far from the quay (known erroneously as 'Canute's Palace')

Norman households need to learn new techniques of cooking over the fire. For both groups the conquest marked a degree of disruption and negotiation in their daily working lives. These methods also affected what food was eaten. Cooking above a fire means that food, for example the meat from younger animals, can be cooked more slowly. For Normans and other settlers from France, this marked continuity, but for the English, the adoption of these new ways might have been part of a process of coming to terms with their new situation and managing the resultant social relationships. For those who were unable or unwilling to adopt these new customs, the pottery evidence reveals how the conquest might have changed the economic circumstances of households forced to raise a surplus to pay taxes.[22]

Zooarchaeology, the study of animal bones, can also reveal fascinating insights into post-conquest life. Naomi Sykes has pointed out that the new Norman settlers did not impose a new French way of doing things wholesale across England, but that changes, possibly reflecting wider developments in Europe, did occur.[23] Notable among these changes was the increase in pig bones found at elite sites after 1066. Although the levels did not reach the same heights as those in corresponding sites in northern Europe, as England was less suitable for intensive pig farming, this evidence suggests the importation of new dietary preferences with the Normans. Animal bone assemblages also reveal changes related to elite hunting practices. The appearance of heron and pea fowl in the zooarchaeological record might relate to changes in falconry with the introduction of new prey. In addition, it is possible to detect an increase in the hunting of red deer and a corresponding decrease in hunting roe deer linked to a shift from enclosed parks to hunting in more open ground. The post-conquest period also saw the introduction of fallow deer to England and ritual butchery practices associated with this species, though not, it appears, from northern France. Sykes suggests that fallow deer might have been imported from Sicily, though far more work needs to be done here to prove this hypothesis. Changes such as these are also to a degree reflected in language used for animals and joints of meat. When a pig, sheep or cow is browsing or rootling in its field, then we know it by words derived from Old English; once that animal is cooked and served up at table then it becomes the French pork, mutton or beef.

Cultural links between Normandy and England had, however, flourished, prior to 1066. It would be wrong to think of the England of the first half of the eleventh century and earlier as separated from the continent. The late Saxon state was very much part of wider North Sea and continental networks, whereas Wales and Scotland had extensive links across the Irish Sea. King Æthelstan (d. 939) had fostered links with the ruling houses of Francia and Germany and Æthelred, as we know, married Emma of Normandy. A number of Edward the Confessor's bishops had continental origins and the English Church was well aware of developments happening across the Channel. Within monasteries themselves, monks and nuns travelled between communities, not only on business, but also to carry manuscripts for copying or, after the conquest, with mortuary rolls through which the dead were remembered. Letters also travelled backwards and forwards. After he became archbishop of Canterbury in 1093, Anselm did not forget the monks who had been under his care at Le Bec and sent letters of spiritual direction back to the community.[24] The cross-Channel exchange of objects and artistic influences was also very much a part of this dynamic, whether as a result of cooperation or coercion.

English monasteries and cathedrals were key centres of production for luxury manuscripts and needlework, goods that were highly prized by the Normans. Monastic scriptoria, the institutions that produced books, thrived on the exchange of texts and sometimes personnel. This process was essential in order to develop learning by expanding the holdings of various monastic libraries. Books would be sent to another community for copying. In this way work was disseminated and artistic and intellectual influences spread. Several manuscripts exist in which the text was written in an area of France before being sent back across the Channel for illumination in England, for example the Boulogne Gospels.[25] A mid-eleventh-century copy of the treatises of three church fathers, Jerome, Augustine and Ambrose was made at Mont-Saint-Michel. The miniatures within it show distinct Anglo-Saxon influences and certainly by this time texts from England were circulating in Normandy which the scribes could copy.[26]

Books were also sent as gifts. A good example here is the *Sacramentarium* of Robert of Jumièges. A sacramentary contains prayers that the priest alone recited during the Mass. The thirteen full-page illuminations with rich use of colour and attention to the drapery and style of the figures is characteristic of what art historians call the Winchester school. It was a style much favoured for high-status liturgical manuscripts. Robert gave the *Sacramentarium* to his monastery of Jumièges during his tenure as bishop of London 1044–50.[27] After the conquest, the new Norman prelates brought books across the Channel to their new abbeys and cathedrals in England. Bishop Obsern of Exeter was possibly responsible for the acquisition by that cathedral of a copy of Jerome's commentary on Isaiah. This book had probably been made in Jumièges during the late eleventh century and was decorated by Hugh Pictor, who included a little self-portrait – a rare survival from this period.[28] This manuscript, in contrast to the full-page biblical scenes in the Sacramentary, has the highly decorated initials that became popular after the conquest. Throughout the eleventh century these manuscripts were not only important as a means of strengthening links between communities but also for training personnel in various artistic traditions and the development of new ideas.

One of the most famous artefacts of the Norman period is the Bayeux Tapestry. Actually an embroidery in wool on linen, the work measures around 70 metres in length, although the last portion is missing. The tapestry documents the events leading up to and including the battle of Hastings, beginning with Edward the Confessor addressing Harold before he ventured to Normandy. It depicts, among other things, the infamous occasion on which Harold swore his oath to William on sacred relics, the death and funeral of Edward the Confessor in his new church at Westminster, and Halley's Comet foretelling disaster for the English kingdom. The concluding scenes of the tapestry no longer survive, but in all likelihood showed the coronation of William at Westminster, Christmas 1066. There are many debates surrounding the patronage of the tapestry, for example who it was made for and why. Legend has it that Queen Matilda made it herself to document her husband's victory. Carola Hicks favours the idea that Queen Edith, Edward's widow, commissioned it as an act of remembrance.[29] George Beech proposes that William himself was the patron and that it was embroidered at the monastery of Saint-Saumur de Florent.[30] Despite these theories, it is widely accepted that the Bayeux Tapestry was commissioned by William's half-brother, Odo, who was bishop of Bayeux and earl of Kent, and was completed at the monastery of St Augustine in Canterbury.

Fig.26: St Augustine's Abbey, Canterbury, looking across the site of the church with the cathedral in the background

The extent to which Odo's patronage extended to the design and content is also debated and raises interesting questions for the nature of English input to the finished article. As well as visual depictions of the events leading up to the battle of Hastings, the tapestry also contains captions identifying events and people. These are in Latin, but analysis of the text has revealed English elements in the spelling and use of certain words, for example *ceastra* used to describe the castle at Hastings. The motifs used in the embroidery also derive from those found in manuscripts produced at St Augustine's abbey in Canterbury. Elizabeth Pastan and Stephen White, while accepting the role of Odo in commissioning this work, have argued for the agency of the monks in incorporating elements of memorialization of figures associated with the monastery, notably Wadard and Vital who are mentioned in other texts associated with the abbey. English figures also appear both on the tapestry and in written sources. The Martyrology – a list of dead associated with the community – includes King Harold and 'many of our brothers' who fell at Hastings.[31] That the tapestry could simultaneously recount the Norman victory but

Fig.27: The castle at Hastings showing Old English influence in the spelling of 'ceastra': detail of the Bayeux Tapestry – eleventh century (with special permission from the city of Bayeux)

also commemorate the passing of the English kingdom and so, perhaps, come to terms with that loss, is a persuasive argument.

Objects and manuscripts also circulated between Normandy and southern Italy and Sicily. Orderic Vitalis, for example, had access to Geoffrey Malaterra's *Deeds of Count Roger*. Amatus of Montecassino described how the first Normans employed as mercenaries returned to their homeland with many exotic gifts including 'citrus fruits, almonds, preserved nuts, purple cloth, and instruments of iron adorned with gold [horse harnesses]' in the hope of encouraging others to make the same journey.[32] Certainly the Normans would have been sent back with something, if not the actual goods described by Amatus. Orderic provides information about the types of goods that circulated between Normandy and southern Italy in discussing the links between Saint-Evroult and the monks who fled with Roger of Grandmesnil into exile. William Giroie, a founder of the monastery, visited Apulia and collected gold, precious vestments and liturgical vessels for the monks. These gifts were unfortunately stolen after he died on the return journey. Later, the monk Arnold of Tilleul also make the journey to bring back treasure to his monastery.[33] Such items served as a connection between the community and their brethren and lay associates who had journeyed to Italy.[34] We can imagine such precious objects being

Fig.28: Durham cathedral: work on the site began during the reign of
William Rufus

Fig.29: The north transept of Winchester cathedral, eleventh century

displayed to visiting dignitaries to demonstrate the prestige of the monastery and piety of its founders. Perhaps the vestments were used on special occasions, their richness combining with the candlelight in the monastery's church to sparkle and glow.

Cross-Channel and ultramontane links are perhaps most visible today in the surviving architecture created by the Normans. The eleventh century saw the growth of the style of building known as the Romanesque, often typified by solid pillars, rounded arches and geometric designs. Although this has been termed a pan-European phenomenon, it is essential to remember that different regions used and built this style in different ways. In England it has become particularly associated with the Normans due to the scale on which they built following the conquest. Great cathedrals like Winchester and Durham were of a size and volume unknown in Normandy. To what extent the Normans accelerated a process already developing is a significant point. Edward the Confessor's new abbey church at Westminster testifies to the existence of the Romanesque in England prior to 1066. The building no longer survives, having been rebuilt by Henry III in the mid-thirteenth century. It does, however, appear on the Bayeux Tapestry, albeit in a stylized form, and it seems that

Fig.30: Edward the Confessor's church at Westminster Abbey: detail of the Bayeux Tapestry – eleventh century (with special permission from the city of Bayeux)

it was planned very much along the lines of Romanesque churches in Normandy with grand nave arcades and elevations. Conquest and events such as fires, as at the cathedral church of Christ Church Canterbury or York Minster, presented opportunities to build in this new and imposing style. This continued to be the dominant form of architecture through to the late twelfth century.

The creation of the Sicilian Kingdom in 1130 led to some very interesting developments in terms of art and architecture in conjunction with the court of King Roger and later monarchs. Buildings associated with the Normans include the Capella Palatina in Palermo, the cathedrals of Monreale and Cefalù and the church of Santa Maria dell' Ammiraglio (later known as La Martorana). These buildings also contained elaborate and detailed mosaics that provide information about how the Norman rulers were represented.

The church of Santa Maria dell' Ammiraglio was founded by the admiral George of Antioch in 1143 and contains a mosaic depicting the coronation of Roger II. Roger is shown wearing the Byzantine imperial ceremonial robes as Christ places the crown on his head. He also has longish hair and the beard associated with the Greeks. This is most definitely not one of the close-cropped, clean-shaven men of the north as seen on the Bayeux Tapestry. As Houben notes, there is

Fig.31: The cathedral at Cefalù begun in the reign of Roger II

Fig.32: Roger II crowned by Christ in the church of La Martorana, twelfth century

Fig.33: Ceiling of the Capella Palatina in Palermo

no evidence that Roger II actually wore such garments and he never assumed the title 'emperor'. Instead this perhaps is an example of how one of Roger's subjects – his admiral George – fitted him into already existing conceptions of what it meant to be a ruler in this part of the medieval world.[35] It seems a safe assumption that Roger was happy to be portrayed in his way.

Perhaps the most famous site associated with the Normans in the south is the Capella Palatina in Palermo, the royal chapel associated with Roger II's palace. This building typically has been read as an amalgam of the different influences on Roger's court style: Latin, Byzantine, Greek and Muslim. The wonderful mosaics are influenced to some degree by Byzantine iconography. The ground plan might echo the design of churches in the north with its nave and side aisles, and the magnificent wooden stalactite ceiling demonstrates high-quality Islamic work. When considered alongside the trilingual psalter described in the previous section, the use of Greek in official documents, and the continued employment of administrators with an Islamic background, it is tempting to see the chapel as an embodiment of a multicultural kingdom. But that is to think in modern terms rather than medieval ones and, as Metcalfe has noted, it is very difficult to construct a coherent narrative along the lines of tolerant cooperation.[36] What Roger's chapel does show is the influences on how he wanted his rule to be seen.

If the different components of the chapel are taken together it is possible to see how this might work: first, the mosaics. The central dome of the chapel depicts Christ Pantocrator, which is a Greek theological motif similar, though not equivalent, to the western depiction of Christ in majesty. The other mosaics in the choir represent episodes from the life of Christ, angels, prophets, the four evangelists (Matthew, Mark, Luke and John) and various saints. The inscriptions associated with the depictions are in Greek. The mosaics in the nave show scenes from the Old Testament with stories of Saints Peter and Paul, busts of other saints and holy women with accompanying Latin texts, and they date from the reign of Roger's successor, William I. In contrast, the inscriptions on the ceiling are in Kufic script with the ceiling itself decorated with figures and activities associated with leisure. The inscriptions refer to qualities associated with government and the projection of good kingship: health, good fortune, power and prosperity. In the ceiling are also

Fig.34: Apse of the Capella Palatina in Palermo showing the mosaic of Christ
Pantocrator *c.* 1140

depictions of a seated ruler in Islamic dress identified as Roger. To understand the meaning of such features it is necessary to consider the function of the building. As the royal chapel it served a liturgical function where the king and his household could attend worship, the king sitting in his balcony above the sanctuary. Its other function was as a reception hall, notably the nave. Here the king would stand on a platform ready to receive his guests or petitions, drawing on Fatimid and Byzantine customs.[37]

As noted above, the mosaics in the nave date from the reign of Roger's successor, William. These additions had a notably more Christian aspect that speaks to the wider marginalization of Muslims on the island. In terms of reading the significance of the building, it is tempting to see Roger's designs as embracing elements of rule present on the island on which to base his new kingdom. The Christian elements, which were always present – and Roger saw himself very much as a Christian ruler – became more prominent in the visual representations of his successors at the expense of the Sicilian Muslims.

JEWS AND MUSLIMS

With a concentration on the importance of the Church to medieval society, it is easy to lose sight of the fact that medieval Europe was not monolithically Christian. In fact it was not monolithically subservient to the Church of Rome. Normans encountered Jews and Muslims and both the latter groups had thriving communities before and during Norman rule. William the Conqueror is credited with settling the Jews in medieval England, but the nature of medieval society meant that Jewish and Muslim traders, travellers and scholars would have visited more northern climes regardless. In southern Italy, Jewish and Islamic communities were perhaps more fully established given the proximity to the Mediterranean basin and the Middle East.

The history of the Jews anywhere in medieval Europe is punctuated by breaks, persecutions, expulsions, tensions and sometimes uneasy tolerance. This was the case in Normandy where Jewish communities settled from the late tenth century onwards, particularly in Rouen.[38] The origin, size and development of this community is a matter of some debate. It is clear from archaeology and written evidence that it was located in the north-western corner of the original Gallo-Roman city walls, and as such was situated close to the ducal centres of power. Although Norman Golb has suggested a Jewish presence in the city stretching back to the Roman period, it is more likely that it was established in the late tenth and eleventh centuries.[39] The growth of Rouen's Jewish quarter met an abrupt halt in 1096. We are perhaps more familiar with the horrific massacres of the Jews in the Rhineland, but the departure of the crusaders from Normandy resulted in the massacre of Rouen's Jews. This event was recorded by Guibert of Nogent in his autobiography. He tells us that the Jews were given a choice of forcible conversion to Christianity or death. There were elements within the crusading armies that saw the Jews very much as the enemies of God at home and this, combined with the absence of political control, might well have contributed to the event. It is worth noting, however, that this was the only such violent outbreak in northern France in the 1090s and so possibly reflects the wider disorder in Normandy during Robert Curthose's tenure as duke, rather than crusading fervour.

Following the events of 1096, the Jewish community quickly recovered. The twelfth century saw the construction of various significant buildings essential to the practice of Jewish religious and cultural life. The community also had its own cemetery on the *Mons Judeorum* close to what is now the city's railway station.[40] Many of the buildings on the south side of the rue aux Juifs survived until Rouen was substantially rebuilt in the nineteenth century, though the construction of the Palais de Justice in the late Middle Ages destroyed buildings on the north side. In 1976, archaeological excavations under the Palais de Justice revealed the remains of a building identified as a yeshiva, a Jewish centre of education. Although the building is similar in plan to a house, features such as shelves, lamps and a large room that might have served as a communal study suggest an educative function.[41] The remains of other well-constructed stone buildings, identified as houses, have also been recovered. The site of Rouen's synagogue remains uncertain as it no longer survives. Bernard Blumenkranz originally identified the yeshiva as the synagogue, though this attribution is not widely accepted.[42] The identification of a firm location is hampered also by the patchy written record. Potential sites are not labelled as the synagogue on maps and plans until the eighteenth century.[43] Even without a firm site for the Jewish religious centre, the solid, high-quality Romanesque remains, along with the intellectual and financial activities that developed throughout the twelfth century, are testament to the visibility and vibrancy of the Jewish community in the heart of Normandy.

The early history of the Jews in England is vague. Far more is known about the development of the community from the late twelfth century until its expulsion in 1290. This is because administrative documents, like the Pipe Rolls and Fine Rolls, began to be kept and survive in greater numbers. In contrast no specific Jewish settlements are mentioned in Domesday Book at all.[44] William of Malmesbury, writing in the early twelfth century, records that it was William the Conqueror who transferred the Jews from Rouen to London. Further Rouennais Jews arrived in England after the 1090 revolt, part of the wider disorder in Normandy under Robert Curthose, and as a result of the 1096 massacre. Gradually other communities were established in key urban and mercantile centres, for example Oxford by 1141 and Winchester by 1148, as well as other places such as Cambridge, Norwich, Lincoln and York. In all likelihood the Jews were encouraged to settle due to the financial services they could provide, not only in terms of loans to the chief magnates of the realm, but also as a source of revenue to the crown through fines, loans and items recorded as 'gifts' in the documents, which almost certainly mask an element of coercion.[45] In order to protect them, the Jews and their possessions were regarded as the property of the king. This protection was not always effective, as massacres of the communities in 1189 and 1190 demonstrate. The most infamous example was the events at York on 17 March 1190: the Jews were killed even though they had sheltered in the castle.

As in Rouen, the Jews in England established intellectual and cultural traditions. One of the leading members of the community in London was Rabbi Josce, whose family continued to play a significant role up to 1236. For example, they built the synagogue at the back of their house in London's Jewish quarter.[46] Ritual baths or mikva'ot have also been discovered in London and Bristol, though the identification of the Bristol mikveh is uncertain.[47] Perhaps the most famous monuments associated with the Jewish community are the houses in Norwich and Lincoln. Like the examples in

Fig.35: Clifford's Tower in York, built in the thirteenth century after the wooden castle was deliberately burned down in 1190, killing the Jewish community sheltering inside

Rouen, however, these buildings are similar in style to those of their Christian neighbours and so can only be identified as Jewish through information found in charters.[48] The community also had its own burial ground. Until 1177 the Jews had to make what could have been a difficult journey to London to bury their dead. After that date, cemeteries were established elsewhere, for example York. Excavations here reveal neat graves on a distinctive alignment that have not subsequently been recut for later burials.[49] This is in keeping with Jewish traditions that prohibit the disturbance of the dead.

In common with the experience of Jews in other parts of Europe, the late twelfth and thirteenth centuries proved to be a difficult and violent time for the communities in England and Normandy. Accusations of ritual child murder without supporting evidence, most notably the case of William of Norwich; the continued crusader expeditions to the Middle East; and political change, for example, the loss of Normandy in 1204, all contributed to more hostile attitudes on the part of the state and some local communities. For the period under consideration here, the Jews were nonetheless a significant part of Norman society.

In southern Italy and Sicily the Normans encountered Muslims in greater numbers. In terms of the initial conquest of Sicily, some Muslims were allied with the Normans and it is important to bear in mind the fractured nature of politics in this region: for example, the Byzantines were enemies of both Normans and Muslims. Ibn Thumna saw the Normans as handy allies in the civil war he had been waging on the island. Other groups of Muslims feared the Normans, as can be seen in the pages of the chronicles: Geoffrey and Amatus record how the Norman soldiers were accused of rape and other crimes. In contrast to England and Normandy where the Jews were encouraged to settle by kings and dukes, Muslims on the whole experienced the Normans as conquerors. In Chapter 3 we noted that the tendency to view the Sicilian campaigns as a crusade is anachronistic, which is supported by the fact that, with some exceptions like the main mosque in Palermo, few mosques were converted into churches. In the initial years of Norman rule on the island, administrative arrangements were initially based on the form of rule practised prior to the conquest. As Metcalfe has noted, authority over the different groups on the island – Muslim and Jewish – was based on the fact that the non-Christians were taxed on the basis of their religion. A similar situation had existed previously under the dhimmī system whereby Christians and Jews paid tribute to the Islamic rulers.[50] Muslims once again played a significant role in government from 1130.

This is not to say that everyone settled down and lived in a multicultural state of easy tolerance. Conquest brought land redistribution and the forced settlement of families. Following Roger's death, his widow Adelaide, ruling as regent for her young sons, encouraged settlement from the Italian mainland, particularly from Lombardy in the north where she came from. At the same time, some educated and wealthy Muslims emigrated to North Africa and Spain from Palermo and other large urban centres. Many more were, however, unable and perhaps unwilling to migrate in large numbers.[51] Even in the court of Roger II, a man regarded as being tolerant of the Muslims, violence was not far beneath the surface. Muslim administrators rose to prominence, especially the palace eunuchs, but if the political situation demanded, the king could and did remove them. Towards the end of his reign he executed Philip of al-Mahdiya, his leading minister.[52] After Roger's death, the Muslims faced pogroms under his successor William I. The population continued to decline through emigration and what Oldfield terms 'indirect cultural pressure to convert'.[53] Further acts of violence and Muslim rebellions followed. It was the end of Norman rule and the advent of the Hohenstaufen dynasty that was the final blow to the presence of Muslims on the island. After a series of rebellions, the emperor Frederic II deported them to Lucera on the mainland in the 1220s and 1230s.

As we have seen in the last three chapters, the Normans changed and were changed by the societies in which they settled. This naturally had implications for how they saw themselves, how historians wrote about them and what being Norman meant, if anything. It might seem strange to discuss this at the end, but we can only make sense of the debates surrounding identity if they are placed in the context of wider developments.

7

NORMAN HISTORIES, NORMAN IDENTITIES

Throughout this book we have used the word 'Norman' as both a noun and an adjective, as if there were something quantifiable and identifiable as 'Norman', the very essence of someone or something that comprised a Norman. This concept is usually referred to as *Normannitas* in modern historical writing. In books that seek to provide an overview, the tendency is emphasized: for example Marjorie Chibnall's book *The Normans* is part of a series called 'The Peoples of Europe'. Earlier histories like D. C. Douglas's *The Norman Achievement* and *The Norman Fate* set this group apart as defining a period. More recent histories that treat the Normans as their topic, rather than an event such as the conquest of England or settlement of southern Italy, are somewhat scaled back in their ambition. David Crouch's book is subtitled *The History of a Dynasty* focusing on the Normans in Normandy and England, whereas the most recent work to consider the Normans comparatively is François Neveux's *Brief History*, a title less ambitious in terms of the claims it makes for the Normans themselves, if not the difficulty of writing a concise history of nearly three centuries of past events in very diverse geographical areas.[1] As we have seen throughout this book, the experiences of the 'Normans' differed greatly depending on circumstance. Any attempt to discuss a Norman identity or what it meant to be a Norman has to be set against that context.

Some historians, notably R. H. C. Davis, have gone so far as to argue that Norman identity, or at least the idea of shared characteristics, was a 'myth', an invention of the chroniclers, specifically Orderic Vitalis writing in the twelfth century. For Davis, the Normans could not be a distinct people because they did not have a shared racial origin or a unique language, and the chroniclers emphasized actions rather than anything that could be categorized as innately Norman.[2] This view has largely been discredited in an article by Graham Loud. By looking at the eleventh-century writers from Dudo onwards, it is clear that the Normans had a strong idea of themselves as a distinct people.[3] How long this identity or consciousness lasted is a matter of some debate. Writing in the early part of the twentieth century, Haskins focused on assimilation as a key characteristic.[4] Followed to its logical end point, this meant that the Norman 'success' was to disappear from history, a point echoed by Cassandra Potts in 1995 and Robert Bartlett in a BBC documentary on the Normans.[5] Encounters with other societies have led historians like Hugh Thomas and literary scholars such as Laura Ashe to point to the development of a specific English identity at the expense of anything solidly Norman.[6] Emily Albu by contrast suggests the Normans deliberately rejected any idea of *Normannitas* due to unease with its violent and brutal nature made manifest in stories of treachery and betrayal.[7] All these, of course, are modern interpretations drawing on various ethnicity paradigms to try to make sense of a complex issue.

To illustrate some of the difficulties surrounding discussion of identity in a pan-European context, it is instructive to consider Ibn al-Athir's description of Roger II of Sicily. The king

> followed the way of the Muslim rulers with mounted companions, chamberlains, arms-bearers, body-guards and others of that kind. Thus he broke with the custom of the Franks, who were not acquainted with such things. He founded a court of complaints, dīwān-al-Muẓālim, to which those [Muslims] who had been unjustly treated brought grievances and [the king] would give them justice, even against his own son. He treated Muslims with respect, took them as his companions, and kept the Franks off them, so that they loved him.[8]

Roger is talked about in modern historical writing as founding the *Norman* kingdom of Sicily. The main qualifications for this description stem from his descent from the island's conqueror, his father Roger, and from Tancred of Hauteville, his grandfather. Roger II was therefore a second-generation immigrant and not that far removed from the Hauteville origins. Yet here he is described as breaking 'with the custom of the Franks'. Ibn al-Althir uses the term 'Franks', common in Arabic usage for western Europeans, rather than Norman, a term which had little meaning in the Mediterranean by the late twelfth century. At the same time that Roger was abandoning Frankish customs and adopting practices based on the Fatimid court, the grandchildren of William the Conqueror – Empress Matilda and King Stephen – were engaged in a bloody and protracted civil war for the English crown. One of the many battles fought was the battle of the Standard in 1138 between Stephen and his Anglo-Norman allies and the forces of King David of Scotland in support of Matilda. A verse account of this event was written by Aelred, abbot of the Cistercian abbey of Rievaulx, who included a lengthy battle speech in which Stephen's forces were exhorted to emulate the deeds of their famous ancestors:

> Why should we despair of victory when victory has been given our people by the Most High as if it were our due? Did not our ancestors invade the largest part of Gaul with few soldiers and erase its very name along with the people? How many times did they scatter the army of the Franks? How many times did a few Celts, Angevins and Aquitanians bring back a victory over many? Indeed we and our fathers in a short time mastered this island, which once the most victorious Julius [Caesar] could hardly take [...] We have seen, seen with our own eyes the king of France and his whole army turn their backs to us and all the finest barons of his realm, captured by us, some to be ransomed, some to be handed over in chains, some to be condemned to prison. Who subdued Apulia, Sicily, Calabria if not your Normans?[9]

Here are two roughly contemporaneous accounts of people we might term Normans that show a wide gulf in the way their activities and behaviour might be portrayed and that underline the difficulties modern historians have in using the term to refer to a wide variety of experiences. For example, historians have persisted, as we have done in this book, in referring to the kingdom of Sicily as 'Norman', though both Metcalfe and Oldfield have sounded notes of caution against so doing.[10] On the one hand Roger abandoned much of what could be identified as Frankish while the descendants of the Normans in England were making direct links between themselves and those they viewed as compatriots in Italy. Clearly the term Norman is problematic and needs greater explanation if we are to understand the long tradition of historical writing about these groups of people. To do so, it is necessary to go back to the sources and think about this topic from the point of view of how the medieval authors saw identity or how they determined what a Norman was. We will look at several key aspects: connections to Scandinavia; the significance of Normandy itself and characteristics, actions, behaviours and lineage (family connections). It is also important to consider whether ideas of what it meant to be Norman covered all groups in society or if it was more restricted.

THE IMPORTANCE OF SCANDINAVIA

As we know from various early sources, Rollo and his war band settled in the Seine valley from somewhere in Scandinavia.[11] To what extent then was a conscious connection to Scandinavia a part of Norman identity? The Scandinavian antecedents form a large part of Dudo's book 1 in which he talks about the predations of the ruler Hasting. A crucial part of their background is that the ancestors of Rollo were pagan. Rollo himself, as the *Planctus* of William Longsword states, was not born a Christian and the sincerity of his later conversion has been questioned.[12] As we have seen, chroniclers took pains to stress the baptism and Christianization of Rollo's followers as part of their settlement of the Seine valley. This is perhaps best reflected in Rollo's dream with which this book began and its interpretation by a Christian prisoner. Rollo was washed in a 'spring of sweet-smelling water' that cleansed him from 'leprosy and the itch' – the contagion of sin.[13] Dudo was also keen to place Rollo's Scandinavian connections within a classical context. He associated the nascent Normans with Antenor of Troy, claiming for them a background that placed them on a par with the Franks. He also played fast and loose with geography, relocating the classical province of Dacia to Denmark. By so doing he gave the Scandinavian people a place and a past that was recognizable to the educated elite that formed part of his audience. He also made it acceptable.[14]

After Dudo, later chroniclers were more uneasy with claiming a past for the Normans that connected them so closely with pagans. William of Jumièges cut out a great deal of Dudo's earlier sections, preferring to present a more biblical past. As Johnson points out, he also only used the word 'Norman', which Dudo employed to describe the followers of the duke, once Rollo's conversion had been agreed.[15] Yet William also shows that the Normans continued to have strong political links with Scandinavia well into the reign of Richard II. His account of the troubles surrounding the castles of Dreux and Tillières-sur-Avre on the southern border of Normandy, later retold by Wace, illustrates this very well and suggests that the dukes had no qualms about calling on Viking allies to counter threats from their Frankish neighbours.

Groups of Scandinavians had come to the aid of the Normans during the problems following William Longsword's death (discussed in Chapter 1), but in 1013–14 Richard II called on his North Sea allies to help him in his dispute with Count Odo of Blois regarding the castle of Dreux. These allies are described as 'two kings of lands overseas'. The kings were named by William as Olaf of the Norsemen (identified with the Norwegian king who was later canonized) and Lacman of the Swedes (a mis-identification). The appearance of Viking leaders in Francia frightened King Robert sufficiently that he called a meeting to agree to a truce between Richard and Odo. Following these events, William of Jumièges records that Olaf was then counselled in the Christian faith and baptized by Archbishop Robert and returned to Norway.[16]

In its eleventh-century context, this event must have been considered quite shocking. The second decade of that century was, after all, a time of renewed Viking raiding, leading up to the invasion of England by Swein Forkbeard and Cnut in 1013. The Danes had been permitted to sell booty in Normandy and receive aid under a treaty agreed between Richard and Swein at a time when the duke's sister, Emma was married to Æthelred, king of England, the target of much of the Vikings' activity.[17] Here, then, was a Christian duke making an alliance with heathens to force his overlord to engineer a peace between him and his Christian neighbour. Although there is no doubt that Richard II was Christian, his dealings with the Vikings show a pragmatism in his politics and also the continued importance of links with Scandinavia. The Normans were certainly no longer

Vikings in the sense of sea raiders, but we should hesitate to think of them as Franks. It is significant that Wace included this account in his twelfth-century verse chronicle stressing the pagan nature of Olaf and Lacman.[18] This is important as Wace was writing for a court audience and suggests that alliance between the ancestors of his patron Henry II and Viking heathens was not considered a source of embarrassment to the Angevin king, but perhaps marked instead a degree of independence or autonomy from the Frankish king.

The eleventh-century southern Italian chronicles make no mention of Scandinavia as a place of origin, nor, as Johnson has shown, do they draw on origin myths from the classical world to locate the Normans, as did Dudo. This is hardly surprising as it was the 1080s by the time the earliest writer, Amatus, was working on his chronicle and so getting on for 200 years since Rollo and his band had left their homeland. The Viking antecedents of the Normans in Italy were very much in the distant past, long out of the living memory of Amatus, Geoffrey Malaterra and William of Apulia's informants.[19] In contrast, elements of twelfth-century English historical writing do refer back to Scandinavia, particularly in the sense of calling on the deeds of ancestors. Henry of Huntingdon put a long speech into the mouth of William the Conqueror as an exhortation to his troops at the battle of Hastings. Henry had the duke refer back to the deeds of Rollo and his victories over the French before exclaiming:

> Let any Englishmen whom our Danish and Norwegian ancestors have conquered in a hundred battles, come forth and prove that the nation of Rou, from his time until now, have ever been routed in the field, and I will withdraw in defeat.[20]

Not only was William's speech claiming a direct link to Rollo, but also a wider kinship with Danes and Norwegians who had harried, raided and conquered England in the past. It certainly demonstrates that for some audiences in twelfth-century England the Normans were not that far removed from the Vikings and, indeed, Henry regarded them as just another group in the long line that had invaded the country. In Normandy, poems such as Stephen of Rouen's *Draco Normannicus* and an anonymous poem in praise of Rouen, both written in the mid-twelfth century, use Scandinavian antecedents as a way of marking the Normans out as distinct from the Franks.[21]

THE SIGNIFICANCE OF NORMANDY

We now turn to association with a particular territory: in other words, was a Norman someone who came from or who had a strong association with Normandy? By using the motif of a dream, Dudo cast Rollo and his followers in many ways as a chosen people seeking a promised land. Through Rollo's conversion and settlement, the Frankish church would be restored and 'the walls of the devastated cities' rebuilt. His people would settle the land and make it fertile. Certainly Dudo depicted Normandy as a land most desirable in terms of its resources and potential:

> [It] is full of good trees, is intersected by rivers stocked with various sorts of fish; it teems with game, is not unfamiliar with vines, bears fruit in soil worked by the plough, is hemmed in on one side by a sea which will afford an abundant wealth of different commodities, and on the other by the outflow of waters carrying all sorts of goods by ship [...] if it were occupied by a dense population it would be mightily fertile and very rich.[22]

The idea of a carefully defined territory is given further expression in the specifics of the negotiations between Rollo and Charles the Simple, though Dudo is wildly extravagant in the land he claims for the Normans. Later Orderic was to emphasize the desirability of Normandy and its heartland around Rouen in particular through a speech he placed into the mouth of Henry I following the capture of the leader of the 1090 revolt against Robert Curthose, Conan, son of Gilbert Pilatus.

> Regard, Conan, the beauty of the country you tried to subordinate. See to the south before your eyes lies a delightful park, wooded and well-stocked with beasts of the chase. See how the river Seine, full of fishes, laps the wall of Rouen and daily brings in ships laden with merchandise of many kinds. See on the other side the fair and populous city, with its ramparts and churches and town buildings, which has rightly been the capital of all Normandy from the earliest days.[23]

Here Orderic was demonstrating the productivity of the land – Normandy – in order to demonstrate the illegitimacy of Conan's actions. Conan's punishment was to be thrown from the window of the tower and his body dragged through the streets he tried to seize.

Rouen, as Orderic shows, was at the heart of this land. For much of the tenth century, the counts' territory did not extend much beyond this part of the region. If enemies were to seize Rouen then Normandy would be lost. This link is brilliantly illustrated by the events surrounding an assault on Rouen in 946 by Louis IV, the Frankish king, and his allies Otto I, the German emperor and Arnulf of Flanders. Writing later, Wace stressed the importance of Rouen's location by having the leaders of the siege acknowledge that they would have to cut off access to the Seine to stand a chance of taking the city. Accounts of this assault also exist in Dudo and William of Jumièges.[24] During the siege, Otto's nephew made an attack on the bridge into the city where he was killed. Neither of these early accounts name his opponent, but Wace states it was Richard I himself 'who emerged from the town on an iron-grey horse, fully armed and brandishing his sword'. Wace goes on to write that 'many people looked at his skilful display' and noted that 'in his hand the land was well placed'.[25] This last comment is interesting, especially if we place it in the context of Wace's audience. He was, after all, writing for Henry II and there is a didactic message here. Henry would need to defend his territories across the Channel in a display of martial prowess that would guarantee the safety of its people. Normandy was the patrimony of the kings of England and their ancestor, Richard I provided an example of how to defend it.[26] The conclusion to Orderic's account of Conan's rebellion also underlines the need for guardianship of the land. That chapter ends with a lament about the disasters 'that overwhelmed proud Normandy' resulting from the weak leadership of Robert. The Normans here were strongly associated with their territory.

Normandy was also significant for other writers. We noted how the southern Italian chronicles had little interest in Scandinavia as a place of origin for the Normans. They did, however, have an understanding that someone who came from Normandy might be described as a Norman or have connections with others so described. Chapter 3 discussed the process of exile as a means by which people migrated to Normandy. As exile need not be permanent, there was always the chance people might return, so this meant a continued interest in Normandy as a place. Amatus describes it as a 'plain filled with woods and fruit trees', which, indeed, Normandy still is. Geoffrey goes further and provides a more detailed geographical description:

Rollo took note of the pleasantness of this region and chose it to embrace
with his love over the others through which he had passed. Normandy
is most abundant in rivers filled with fish and forests filled with game; it
is most suitable for falconry. It is fertile with wheat and other types of
grain, abundant in sheep, and nourishes many cattle.[27]

Again Normandy is shown as a land that is desirable and seems
to echo Dudo, whom Geoffrey had read. He also described the
boundaries of Normandy and the terms under which it was settled
under Rollo. For both Amatus and Geoffrey the idea of a land that
was desirable translated into a southern Italian context, linking
Robert Guiscard and the other Norman leaders closer to their new
territory.[28]

In an anonymous twelfth-century poem about Rouen, the subject
of land is a prominent theme. Like Dudo, William of Jumièges and
Wace's description of the assault and siege of the city in 946, Rouen
is made to stand for Normandy as a whole, and more than that,
it is the centre of all land conquered or settled by the Normans:
Brittany, England, Scotland and France all are in some way subject
to Normandy. What is interesting, though, is long after the southern
Italian Normans had lost any sense of an identity rooted in a
northern homeland, the poem also claims a direct link between the
city and Roger II of Sicily:

Sprung from you of famous Norman blood,
Rules Roger victorious, wise and wealthy
You mighty Roger, you greatest glory amongst kings;
You conquered Italy and Sicily and Africa.[29]

Not long after the kingdom of Sicily was modelling its administration
on practices from the Fatimid court and Muslim writers were
extolling his kingship, a writer in Rouen was claiming Roger as one
of the illustrious Normans, one of its sons. Although Normandy was
unimportant for the southern Italians by this time, for some writers
in the Anglo-Norman realm, the southern Italian Normans were
still part of the story in which all were connected to Normandy as
embodied by the city of Rouen and descent from Rollo.

A defined territory was undoubtedly important for the chroniclers
of the Normans. It is perhaps this factor that led Nick Webber to
characterize a Norman as anyone who was born in Normandy.[30]

This is somewhat reductive and we need to take into account whether everyone who fell under Norman rule was described or thought of as a 'Norman'. One aspect of Norman identity was military ability. This is something that not everyone was capable of or indeed allowed to develop. Peasants, priests, monks, nuns and lay women were not combatants, so did definitions of Norman have a class and gender element?

NORMAN CHARACTER AND BEHAVIOUR

The third category to consider is that of characteristics and behaviour: in other words, did people considered to be Normans act in certain ways that bound them together?[31] One of the most famous expressions of the Norman character is found in Orderic's *Ecclesiastical History* in two passages. He described them as 'an untamed race, and unless they are held in check by a firm ruler they are all too ready to do wrong'. He continued: 'they were from the first a cruel and warlike people', they have 'natural ferocity and a love of fighting for its own sake' and are 'innately warlike and bold'.[32] This echoes similar sentiments found in Amatus of Montecassino, who wrote of the Normans: 'like the ancient warriors they desired to have all people under their rule and dominion. They took up arms, breaking the bond of peace and created a great army of foot-soldiers and horsemen.'[33] Geoffrey Malaterra described them as 'avid for profit and domination' and possessing *strenuitas*, defined by Metcalfe as 'ruthless determination'.[34] These are not pictures of the type of people medieval rulers would necessarily want in the vicinity of their county or duchy and Orderic did say that Normandy's neighbours had reason to fear.

Given that conquest requires the exercise of violence to enforce it, military activities figure largely in the pages of the chronicles. In Chapter 2 we noted the importance of the landscape in William of Poitiers's accounts of Duke William's campaigning in Normandy and Maine prior to 1066. Poitiers also stressed William's capabilities through his comparison of the duke with Julius Caesar, much to the detriment of the illustrious Roman. Amatus and Geoffrey were both aware of the Normans' military reputation and Amatus even included a brief account of the battle of Hastings in his history.

Further afield, the Byzantine writer, Anna Comnena, who composed a biography of her father the emperor Alexius, gave an account of Bohemond's campaigns in the Balkans. She acknowledged his skill as a commander in avoiding a trap laid by her father for the Norman cavalry.[35] As the primary role of the Normans in the Mediterranean was that of mercenaries, it is perhaps unsurprising that their military activities drew attention. Crucially, however, it was their success that merited them being written down.

Another aspect of the Normans' warlike nature that finds expression in the chronicles is their ability to deploy a cunning ruse to good effect. The use of feigned flights at Hastings and elsewhere are good examples. This is, however, a theme that stretches back to Dudo. The Normans' ancestor Alstignus/Hasting sought to conquer Rome by means of pretending he was dead and being smuggled into the city in a coffin. Having leapt out, catching the defenders unaware and sacking the city, Hasting and his men realized they were not in Rome at all, but a city called Luna.[36] This was a good trick, but in the wrong place. While raiding along the river Seine, Rollo and his men had to counter an attack from the Franks. Dudo states that in order to protect themselves and their ships, they dug an encampment. By leaving a gap in the bank, they lured their enemies into the enclosure, whereupon those who had been hiding under their shields to disguise their numbers rose up and routed the Franks.[37] Certainly the Normans adopted tactics like ambushes or lightning cavalry skirmishes. Interestingly, Hasting's ruse finds an echo in the pages of Anna Comnena, who provided an elaborate and detailed description of Bohemond's successful attempts to avoid Alexius. Bohemond spread a rumour he was dead and then hid himself in a coffin, complete with a decomposing cockerel for added veracity, and sailed to Corfu.[38] Anna might well have invented this story – it is from an independent tradition to Dudo – but it serves to underline the reputation that leading commanders had for tactical nous. They were not just good at fighting; they were smart too.

If participation in warfare was an essential part of being Norman, it is necessary to consider whether non-combatants were always excluded from that definition. There were occasions in the chronicles when, if we follow Dudo's definition of the word Norman as meaning followers of the duke, this extended to more than just an aristocratic military elite. Following the assassination of William Longsword,

Richard was detained at Louis IV's court when the Frankish king visited Rouen. According to Dudo, this was regarded as a breach of faith by the citizens, who, along with people from the suburbs, searched the streets to find their duke. Calm was only restored when Louis presented the boy Richard to the people, so demonstrating that he was safe. Here Dudo made a very clear link between place, ruler and all the people, not just the military elite. These sentiments are echoed in Wace's description of the events during the siege of 946. Richard I led the counter-attack that resulted in the death of Otto's nephew. In this case he was not only supported by his troops, but also 'villeins and the peasants [...] and the squires [who] followed their lords with pikes'.[39] If the word Norman could be used to describe the followers of the duke, then surely at these key moments of crisis all these people were acting as such, even if they were not described explicitly as Norman.

At the level of the aristocracy, women could, to some extent, act like warriors, certainly in defence of their husband's lands. Again, they might not specifically be referred to as Normans, but the way they conducted themselves might find praise in the chronicles. Orderic provides us with a couple of examples here. He described Isabel of Conches in the following manner: 'she rode armed as a knight among the knights; and she showed no less courage among the knights in hauberks and sergeants-at-arms than did the maid Camilla.'[40] The reference to Camilla is a classical allusion to the ally of Turnus, king of the Rutuli, who appears in book 21 of Virgil's *Aeneid*. Orderic also wrote about Isabel's presence in the hall at the castle of Conches with her husband's knights and the comfort they gained from that. The wider context for this episode is the disorder in Normandy during Robert Curthose's rule in the 1090s. Isabel had apparently drawn her husband into a dispute between herself and Hawise, countess of Evreux. Instead of criticizing her as we might expect – Orderic could be scathing about women who transgressed their roles – he praised her spirit and character, possibly because no serious harm was done. A later example from *c*. 1124–25 concerns Sibyl, wife of Robert Bordet, who had gone to fight in Spain. Robert had taken the city of Tarragona before leaving for Normandy to gather more troops. He left Sibyl in charge of the castle where:

She kept sleepless watch; every night she put on a hauberk like a soldier and carrying a rod in her hand mounted onto the battlements, patrolled the circuit of the walls, kept the guards on the alert and encouraged everyone with good counsel to be on the alert for the enemies stratagems.[41]

In this way Sibyl was not acting any differently from military commanders counselling their troops, such as William the Conqueror on the eve of Hastings.

If non-combatants could behave as Normans, equally aristocratic men might act in ways that called that status into question. In common with other parts of western Europe, the Normans had certain expectations of the way people should conduct themselves, including adult elite men, and these tied in with ideas of masculinity and good lordship. One of those expectations is that an adult man would have his own household and be able to reward his followers. An episode from Orderic's *Ecclesiastical History* regarding Robert Curthose is instructive here. Robert had a difficult relationship with his father, believing that William did not permit him sufficient independence or authority.[42] This also stoked up rivalry with his brothers, William (Rufus) and Henry. While Robert was staying at the house of Roger Cauchois in L'Aigle, William and Henry, his younger brothers, arrived and 'began to play dice in the upper gallery, as soldiers do', before pouring slops and urine on Robert and his followers in the hall below. Robert's friends were understandably outraged:

Just look at the way your brothers had climbed up above your head and are defiling you and us with filth to your shame. Don't you see what this means? Even a blind man could. Unless you punish this insult without delay it will be all over with you: you will never be able to hold up your head again.[43]

Robert Curthose was the anti-hero of Orderic's narrative precisely because of his weak rule. A lack of strength from the duke left monasteries like Orderic's at the mercy of rapacious lords.[44] We can think back to his unflattering portrait of the Normans as a people difficult to govern in light of these tribulations.

Prowess, or its opposite, in battle was also a crucial marker in determining membership of a wider group. Battle speeches have been discussed above, with various writers referring back to the deeds of the Norman ancestors in encouraging them to great deeds. Examples of failure in battle, by contrast, can be found in the crusade narratives. Ralph of Caen, attached to the crusader contingent led by Bohemond and Tancred, described the desertion by three Normans from the army during the siege of Antioch. William, Albert and Ivo, who were brothers and part of the Grandmesnil clan, fled:

> Alas and shame, it was Normandy who sent forth the brothers. Everywhere the Normans had victory and were the glory of the world. This people were victorious over the English, the Sicilians, the Greeks, the Campanians and Apulians. The people of Maine, Calabria, Africa and Japix served them. Oh that shame should come from such a lineage.[45]

Desertion was not behaviour becoming to anyone who claimed kinship with the Normans.[46] This idea of kinship and lineage is also picked up on later by Ralph. Following the capture of Jerusalem in 1099 and the sack of the temple, Tancred had incurred the wrath of Arnulf of Choques, by this time the spiritual leader of the crusade. Previously Tancred had been presented as a pious knight, the epitome of the crusader ideal. Now he was being criticized for behaviour that was deemed unacceptable and – what is interesting – with direct reference to his lineage, notably his connections to his great uncle, Robert Guiscard. Instead of praise for the person who succeeded in conquering Apulia, Arnulf focused on Guiscard's cunning and treachery:

> For who threw his comrade from the walls while in the midst of an embrace and kisses? Surely it was Guiscard. And who pretended to be dead, while still alive, and had himself carried to Montecassino to be buried while still in good health? Again Guiscard. Who, in order to make peace with his nephew first acted warmly but soon acted very coldly? Guiscard again.[47]

Nevertheless, even Robert Guiscard stopped short of sacking holy places and despoiling the church. Tancred had crossed a boundary. His response was to accuse Arnulf of envy as his family had never produced a leader to equal Robert. The importance of this episodes lies in the very real ambivalence some writers felt towards their subjects. The Normans were capable of great deeds, but they were also flawed human beings.

This chapter shows that any concept of Norman identity is hard to pin down and, indeed, it is not desirable to do so. As historical writing about the Normans spanned over two centuries, and vernacular continuations of the *Gesta Normannorum ducum* continued to be written in the thirteenth century, it would be very surprising indeed if associations with the word Norman stayed the same. Each writer was working in a specific context and for different reasons. If Orderic's work is tinged by the troubles that afflicted his monastery, then others like William of Poitiers or Dudo had a far more celebratory tone. The answers to the questions 'who were the Normans?' or 'what makes a Norman?' must lie in greater consideration of the changing nature of medieval society over the course of the tenth to the thirteenth centuries in terms of its political, social and cultural contexts. As their relations with different groups of people, be they Franks, English, Lombard, Greek or Muslim altered over time, so did perceptions of the Normans. One might be tempted to say that what made a Norman was not words, but deeds, their conquests, the very fact that they were successful enough to commission works of history. To that extent Norman identities were an interpretation by the literate churchmen who produced many of the histories. It is impossible to know what people thought about themselves as individuals and it may be the case that they did not consciously think about who they were on a daily basis, but events might cause them to take stock, examine their position more carefully and express a shared identity. In other words, the Normans were Normans when they were called to be. At times of crisis or other significant moments, writers brought to mind the deeds of their ancestors and the characteristics associated with them. We might not go so far as Marjorie Chibnall and say that the Normans 'were the product, not of blood, but of history',[48] but the telling of that history was absolutely essential, both to their conception of themselves, and also our understanding of how their society created its past.

Further Reading

SOURCES

Many of the key sources are available in translation. A good anthology to start with is *The Normans in Europe*, ed. E. van Houts (Manchester: Manchester University Press, 2000). An older anthology of sources, which contains some of the Norman charters in translation, is R. Allen Brown, *The Norman Conquest of England: Sources and Documents* (Woodbridge: Boydell, 1984). *English Historical Documents, vol. 1: c. 500–1042*, ed. D. Whitelock (London: Eyre and Spottiswoode, 1955; 2nd edn Eyre Methuen, 1979) and *English Historical Documents, vol. 2: 1042–1189*, ed. D. C. Douglas (London: Eyre and Spottiswoode, 1953; 2nd edn Eyre Methuen, 1981) are useful for sources relating to England.

For the early history of Normandy see Dudo of Saint-Quentin, *History of the Normans*, trans. E. Christiansen (Woodbridge: Boydell, 1998); *The Annals of Flodoard of Reims 919–966*, ed. and trans. S. Fanning and B. S. Bachrach (Toronto: University of Toronto Press, 2011). Later Norman narrative sources include William of Poitiers, *The Gesta Guillelmi*, ed. and trans. R. H. C. Davis and M. Chibnall (Oxford: Clarendon Press, 1998); *The Gesta Normannorum of William of Jumièges, Orderic Vitalis and Robert of Torigni*, ed. and trans. E. van Houts, 2 vols (Oxford: Clarendon Press, 1992–5); *The Carmen de Hastingae Proelio of Guy Bishop of Amiens*, ed. and trans. F. Barlow (Oxford: Clarendon Press, 1999); Orderic Vitalis, *The Ecclesiastical History*, ed. and trans. M. Chibnall, 6 vols (Oxford: Clarendon, 1969–80); *A History of the Norman People: Wace's Roman de Rou*, trans. G. Burgess with notes by G. Burgess

Leonie V. Hicks

and E. van Houts (Woodbridge: Boydell, 2004). A translation of the *Life* of Herluin is provided in S. Vaughn, *The Abbey of Bec and the Anglo-Norman State, 1034–1136* (Woodbridge: Boydell, 1981).

The Anglo-Saxon Chronicle has been translated by M. Swanton (London: Dent, 1996). The twelfth-century chroniclers based in England include William of Malmesbury, who wrote the *Gesta regum Anglorum*, ed. and trans. R. A. B. Mynors, R. M Thomson and M. Winterbottom, 2 vols (Oxford: Clarendon Press, 1998–99) and *Gesta pontificum Anglorum*, ed. and trans. M. Winterbottom and R. M. Thomson, 2 vols (Oxford: Clarendon Press, 2007); Eadmer, *History of Recent Events in England*, trans. G. Bosanquet (London: Cresset Press, 1964); Henry of Huntingdon, *Historia Anglorum*, ed. and trans. D. Greenway (Oxford: Clarendon Press, 1996).

Two of the main eleventh-century chronicles for southern Italy also available in published translations: Amatus of Montecassino, *History of the Normans*, trans. P. N. Dunbar, rev. G. A. Loud (Woodbridge: Boydell, 2004); Geoffrey Malaterra, *The Deeds of Count Roger of Calabria and Sicily and of his Brother Duke Robert Guiscard*, trans. K. B. Wolf (Ann Arbor: University of Michigan Press, 2005). A translation by G. A. Loud of William of Apulia's *The Deeds of Robert Guiscard* is available at http://www.leeds.ac.uk/arts/downloads/file/1049/the_deeds_of_robert_guiscard_by_william_of_apulia. Sources relating to the kingdom of Sicily are published in *The History of the Tyrants of Sicily by Hugo Falcanuds 1154–69*, trans. G. A. Loud and T. Wiedemann (Manchester: Manchester University Press, 1998) and *Roger II and the Creation of the Kingdom of Sicily*, trans. G. A. Loud (Manchester: Manchester University Press, 2012). The key chronicles for the Normans on Crusade are *The Gesta Francorum*, ed. and trans. R. Hill (Oxford: Clarendon Press, 1962) and *The Gesta Tancredi of Ralph of Caen: A History of the Normans on the First Crusade*, trans. B. S. Bachrach and D. S. Bachrach (Aldershot: Ashgate, 2005).

Editions of charters and other documentary sources include *Regsta Regum Anglo-Normannorum: the Acta of William I (1066–1087)*, ed. D. Bates (Oxford: Clarendon Press, 1998). Domesday Book is most readily available in the Penguin translation by A. Williams (London, 2002) and online courtesy of the University of Hull at http://opendomesday.org/, which includes images of the original document. The Archives départementales de Seine-Maritime in Rouen have digitized many of the original ducal charters and cartularies in their holdings http://www.archivesdepartementales76. net/rechercher/archives-en-ligne/. The letters of both Lanfranc and Anselm are published in modern translations: *The Letters of Lanfranc Archbishop of Canterbury*, ed. and trans. H. Clover and M. Gibson (Oxford: Clarendon Press, 1979); *The Letters of Saint Anselm of Canterbury*, trans. W. Fröhlich, 3 vols (Kalamazoo, MI: Cistercian Publications, 1990–4). Many of the letters of Gregory VII are published as *The Register of Pope Gregory VII 1073–1085*, trans. H. Cowdrey (Oxford: Oxford University Press, 2002). The English Episcopal Acta project continues to produce editions of the charters of English bishops.

GENERAL HISTORIES

The following list is not exhaustive, but is intended to give a flavour and overview of many general histories of the Normans written over the past hundred years. R. A. Brown, *The Normans* (Woodbridge: Boydell, 1984); M. Chibnall, *The Normans* (Oxford: Blackwell, 2000); D. Crouch, *The Normans: A History of a Dynasty* (London: Continuum, 2002); D. C. Douglas, *The Norman Achievement, 1050–1100* (London: Eyre and Spottiswoode, 1969) and *The Norman Fate, 1100–1154* (London: Eyre Methuen, 1976); C. H. Haskins, *The Normans in European History* (New York: Houghton Mifflin, 1915; repr. Ungar, 1966); F. Neveux, *A Brief History of the Normans: The Conquests that Changed the Face of Europe*, trans. H. Curtis (London: Robinson, 2008).

CHAPTER 1: ROLLO AND THE SETTLEMENT OF NORMANDY

D. Bates, *Normandy Before 1066* (London: Longman, 1982) is currently the most accessible introduction to the early history of Normandy in English in print, but it should be read along side E. Searle, *Predatory Kinship and the Creation of Norman Power, 840–1066* (Berkeley, 1988) and M. Hagger, 'Confrontation and Unification: Approaches to the Political History of Normandy, 911–1035', *History Compass* 11 (2013) pp. 429–42. Hagger will provide a more comprehensive account of the development of ducal Normandy in *Normandy under the Normans, 911–1154* (Boydell, forthcoming). P. Bauduin, *La première Normandie (Xe–XIe siècles). Sur les frontières de la haute Normandie: identité et construction d'une principauté* (Caen: Presses Universitaires de Caen, 2004) is also essential. The articles in volume 3 of *The New Cambridge Medieval History*, ed. T. Reuter (Cambridge: Cambridge University Press, 1999) provide the wider tenth-century context. For Frankish politics see J. Dunbabin, *France in the Making, 843–1180* (Oxford: Oxford University Press, 1985).

CHAPTER 2: WILLIAM OF NORMANDY AND THE CONQUEST OF ENGLAND

The best general introduction to the Norman Conquest of England is Brian Golding, *Conquest and Colonisation: The Normans in Britain, 1066–1100*, 2nd edn (Basingstoke: Palgrave, 2013). For looking at the effect of the conquest from an English perspective see Ann Williams, *The English and the Norman Conquest* (Woodbridge: Boydell, 1995). There are several modern biographies of William, the earliest of which is D. C. Douglas, *William the Conqueror: The Norman Impact upon England*, rev. edn (New Haven: Yale University Press, 1999). David Bates is currently writing a new biography, but in the meantime see *William the Conqueror* (Stroud: Tempus, 1989) and most recently Mark Hagger, *William: King and Conqueror* (London: I.B.Tauris, 2012). For the battle itself see M. K. Lawson, *The Battle of Hastings, 1066* (Stroud: Tempus, 2007) and *The Battle of Hastings: Sources and Interpretations*, ed. Stephen Morillo (Woodbridge: Boydell, 1996), which contains source extracts and reprints of scholarly articles. For William in Normandy see David Bates, *Normandy Before 1066*, Eleanor Searle, *Predatory Kinship*, and the work of Mark Hagger cited above.

CHAPTER 3: NORMANS IN THE MEDITERRANEAN: THE HAUTEVILLE CLAN AND OTHERS

The fullest English-language account of the conquest of southern Italy and Sicily is G. A. Loud, *The Age of Robert Guiscard* (Harlow: Longman, 2000). Many of his articles and essays relating to

Norman activity in the Mezzogiorno are collected together in G. A.
Loud, *Conquerors and Churchmen in Norman Italy* (Aldershot:
Ashgate, 1999). An interesting French collection is *Les Normands
en Méditerranée dans le sillage des Tancrède*, ed. Pierre Bouet and
François Neveux (Caen: Presses universitaires de Caen, 1994). For
Sicily in more detail see A. Metcalfe, *Muslims and Christians in
Norman Sicily: Arabic Speakers and the End of Islam* (London:
Routledge 2003); *The Muslims of Medieval Italy* (Edinburgh:
Edinburgh University Press, 2009). Good introductions to the
first crusade in general are J. Riley-Smith, *The First Crusade and
the Idea of Crusading* (London: Athlone, 1986; 2nd edn, London:
Continuum, 2009); C. Tyreman, *God's War: A New History of the
Crusades* (London: Allen Lane, 2006). A recent collection of essays
dealing with the Norman experience of crusading is *Crusading and
Pilgrimage in the Norman World*, ed. K. Hurlock and P. Oldfield
(Woodbridge: Boydell, 2005). See also N. Hodgson, 'Reinventing
Normans as Crusaders? Ralph of Caen's *Gesta Tancredi*', *Anglo-
Norman Studies* 30 (2008), pp. 117–32. For Antioch in particular
see T. Asbridge, *The Norman Principality of Antioch* (Woodbridge:
Boydell 2000) and the work of Alan Murray cited in the notes for
this chapter.

CHAPTER 4: SOCIETY

Good overviews of 'Norman' society include the essays *The Society
of Norman Italy*, ed. G. A. Loud and A. Metcalfe (Leiden: Brill,
2002), particularly those by Martin, Skinner and Drell. *Italy in the
Central Middle Ages*, ed. D. Abulafia (Oxford: Oxford University
Press, 2004) is also useful for placing developments in southern Italy
in a wider context. For England see M. Chibnall, *Anglo-Norman
England* (Oxford: Blackwell, 1986); Williams, *The English and the
Norman Conquest* and *The World before Domesday: the English
Aristocracy 900–1066* (London: Continuum, 2008); the essays in *A
Social History of England, 900–1200*, ed. J. Crick and E. van Houts
(Cambridge: Cambridge University Press, 2011). For Normandy see
*Law and Government in Medieval England and Normandy: Essays in
Honour of Sir James Holt* (Cambridge: Cambridge University Press,
1994), ed. G. Garnett and J. Hudson; E. Z. Tabuteau, *Transfers of*

Property in Eleventh-Century Norman Law (Chapel Hill: University of North Carolina Press, 1998). The essays in the section entitled 'History, Family and Women' in E. van Houts, *History and Family Traditions in England and the Continent, 1000–1200* (Aldershot: Ashgate, 1999) are also useful.

There is a huge amount of scholarship on medieval castles, though very little up-to-date work that considers them in a European perspective. An excellent overview is O. Creighton, *Early European Castles: Aristocracy and Authority AD 800–1200* (London: Duckworth, 2012) and the recent historiographical developments are discussed in R. Liddiard, *Castles in Context: Power, Symbolism and Landscape, 1066 to 1500* (Macclesfield: Windgather, 2005). C. Coulson, *Castles in Medieval Society: Fortresses in England, France and Ireland in the Central Middle Ages* (Oxford: Oxford University Press, 2003) is a very detailed study. J. Mesqui, *Châteaux et enceintes de la France médiévale: de la défense à la résidence*, 2 vols (Paris: Picard, 1991–3) is essential for France. Key works for Italy are R. Licinio, *Castelli medievali Puglia e Basilicata: dai normanni a Federico II e Carlo I d'Angiò* (Bari: Dedalo, 1994); F. Maurici, *Castelli Medievali in Sicilia: dai bizantini ai normanni* (Palermo: Sellerio, 1992). A brief summary in English of the evolution of the castle in southern Italy can be found in C. Gravett, *Norman Stone Castles (2): Europe 950–1204* (Oxford: Osprey, 2004). The Castle Studies Group based in the UK publishes an annual journal. Useful French journals include *Archéologie médiévale* and *Annales de Normandie*: the work of M. de Boüard, A.-M. Flambard Héricher, A. Renoux and J. Yver therein is particularly important.

Key works for changes in tenure, service and peasants are S. Reynolds, *Fiefs and Vassals: The Medieval Evidence Reinterpreted* (Oxford: Oxford University Press, 1994), which proved very controversial on its publication. For England see R. Fleming, *Kings and Lords in Conquest England* (Cambridge: Cambridge University Press, 1991); R. Faith, *The English Peasantry and the Growth of Lordship* (London: Leicester University Press, 1997), and for Normandy see the work of Tabuteau. Good summaries are provided in Golding, *Conquest and Colonisation*. For Normandy the recent work of M. Arnoux and for Italy P. Skinner, both cited in the notes, are essential. The literature on Domesday Book is vast. F. W. Maitland, *Domesday Book and Beyond: Three Essays in the Early History of England* (1897, various reprints) is still immensely valuable. See also the essays edited by James Holt for the novocentenary of Domesday book, *Domesday Studies* (Woodbridge: Boydell, 1987) and the Alecto edition. The work of David Roffe is controversial: *Decoding Domesday* (Woodbridge: Boydell, 2007) and *Domesday: The Inquest and the Book* (Oxford: Oxford University Press, 2000). The best recent study is S. Harvey, *Domesday: Book of Judgement* (Oxford: Oxford University Press, 2014).

There is no comparative study of marriage in the Norman areas of Europe. See the work of Drell, Heygate, Searle, Skinner and van Houts cited in the notes. In addition see P. Stafford, *Queens, Concubines and Dowagers: The King's Wife in the Early Middle Ages* (London: Batsford 1983; new edn Leicester University Press, 1998) and *Queen Emma and Queen Edith: Queenship and Women's Power in Eleventh-Century England* (Oxford: Blackwell Press, 1997).

CHAPTER 5: THE NORMANS AND THE CHURCH

The literature and sources for the Church in the eleventh century are vast. Many useful primary sources can be found in the section on sources above, with documents relating to the reform movement and investiture contest in B. Tierney, *The Crisis of Church and State, 1050–1300*, 2nd edn (Toronto: University of Toronto Press, 1988). Important documents relating to the southern Italian church can be found in translation in many of Graham Loud's articles and books. Chronicles, in the main written by churchmen, are invaluable and have been cited elsewhere in this book. In addition, see Eadmer, *The Life of St Anselm of Canterbury*, ed. and trans. R. W. Southern (Oxford: Clarendon, 1962).

For background and context to the development of the papacy as an institution see C. Morris, *Papal Monarchy: The Western Church from 1050–1250* (Oxford: Clarendon Press, 1989); I. S. Robinson, *The Papacy, 1073–1198* (Cambridge: Cambridge University Press, 1990). For Normandy, the work of Richard Allen is essential and many of his articles, including editions of some charters and the *Acta Archiepiscopum Rotomagensis*, can be found in the open access journal *Tabularia*, accessible at http://www.unicaen.fr/mrsh/craham/

revue/tabularia/. Along with Grégory Combalbert, he is preparing editions of Norman bishops' charters along the lines of the English Episcopal Acta. Veronique Gazeau has produced an extensive study of the careers of the Benedictine abbots of Normandy: *Normannia Monastica*, 2 vols (Caen: Publications du CRAHM, 2007). For Italy, the work of Graham Loud is the best introduction: see in particular *The Church in Norman Italy* (Cambridge: Cambridge University Press, 2007) and the collections of articles published as *Conquerors and Churchmen* and *Montecassino and Benevento in the Middle Ages* (Aldershot: Ashgate, 2000), along with H. E .J. Cowdrey, *The Age of Abbot Desiderius: Montecassino, the Papacy, and the Normans in the Eleventh and Early Twelfth Century* (Oxford: Clarendon Press, 1983). A very good introduction to the structures of the English Church is F. Barlow, *The English Church, 1066–1154* (London: Longman, 1979). For monasticism see J. Burton, *Monastic and Religious Orders in Britain 1000–1300* (Cambridge: Cambridge University Press, 1994). See also C. Harper-Bill, 'The Anglo-Norman Church', in *A Companion to the Anglo-Norman World*, ed. C. Harper-Bill and E. van Houts (Woodbridge: Boydell, 2002), pp. 165–90.

For the Church and its relationship with wider society, including pilgrimage, see L. V. Hicks, *The Religious Life in Normandy, c. 1050–1300* (Woodbridge: Boydell, 2007); P. Oldfield, *Sanctity and Pilgrimage in Medieval Southern Italy, 1000–1200* (Cambridge: Cambridge University Press, 2014); E. Cownie, *Religious Patronage in Anglo-Norman England, 1066–1135* (Woodbridge: Boydell, 1998); C. Potts, *Monastic Revival and Regional Identity in Early Normandy* (Woodbridge: Boydell, 1997); Vaughn, *Abbey of Bec*.

CHAPTER 6: CULTURAL EXCHANGES

This is an emerging area in Norman studies. The most recent collection of essays relating to this topic is *Norman Tradition and Transcultural Heritage: Exchange of Cultures in the 'Norman' Peripheries of Medieval Europe*, ed. S. Burkhardt and T. Foerster (Farnham: Ashgate, 2013), though this focuses primarily on textual traditions. For considering the material culture associated with the Normans, exhibition catalogues are very useful, for example:

I Normanni: popolo d'Europa, 1030–1200, ed. Mario D'Onofrio, 2nd edn (Venice: Marsilio, 1994); *English Romanesque Art, 1066–1200*, ed. G. Zarnecki, J. Holt and T. Holland (London: Arts Council of Great Britain, 1984). Many Norman architectural sites are open to the public in Normandy, the United Kingdom and Sicily.

For Jews and Muslins see *Jews in Medieval Britain: Historical, Literary and Archaeological Perspectives*, ed. P. Skinner (Woodbridge: Boydell, 2003); Metcalfe, *Muslims of Medieval Italy*; and the survey by E. Brenner and L. V. Hicks, 'The Jews of Rouen in the Eleventh to the Thirteenth Centuries', in *Society and Culture in Medieval Rouen, 911–1300* (Turnhout: Brepols, 2013), pp. 369–82.

CHAPTER 7: NORMAN HISTORIES, NORMAN IDENTITIES

To follow through the debate on Norman identity, it is useful to start with R. H. C. Davis, *The Norman Myth* (London: Thames & Hudson, 1976) and then move on to the critiques of his argument, notably G. Loud, 'The *gens Normannorum* – Myth or Reality', *Anglo-Norman Studies* 4 (1982), pp. 13–34; and for a different view, C. Potts, '*Atque unum ex diversis gentibus populum effecit*: Historical Tradition and the Norman Identity', *Anglo-Norman Studies*, 18 (1996), pp. 139–52. The most recent and innovative work on Norman identities is by Ewan Johnson – see the notes to this chapter. H. Thomas, *The English and the Normans: Ethnic Hostility, Assimilation, and Identity, 1066–c.1220* (Oxford: Oxford University Press, 2003) should also be consulted. Ambiguity and ambivalence about Norman identity are analysed by E. Albu, *The Normans in their Histories: Propaganda, Myth and Subversion* (Woodbridge: Boydell, 2001) and P. A. Hayward, 'The Importance of Being Ambiguous: Innuendo and Legerdemain in William of Malmesbury's *Gesta Regum* and *Gesta Pontificum Anglorum*', *Anglo-Norman Studies* 33 (2011), pp. 75–102. For the Normans, history and community see L. Shopkow, *History and Community: Norman Historical Writing in the Eleventh and Twelfth Centuries* (Washington DC: Catholic University of America Press, 1997).

Notes

Introduction

1 Dudo of Saint Quentin, *History of the Normans*, trans. E. Christiansen (Woodbridge: Boydell, 1998), pp. 29–30.

2 *The Normans in Europe*, ed. and trans. E. van Houts (Manchester: Manchester University Press, 2000), no. 14.

3 Ed. and trans. E. van Houts, 2 vols (Oxford: Clarendon Press, 1992–95).

4 William of Poitiers, *The Gesta Guillelmi*, ed. and trans. R. H. C. Davis and M. Chibnall (Oxford: Clarendon Press, 1998), p. xvi.

5 Orderic Vitalis, *The Ecclesiastical History*, ed. and trans. M. Chibnall, 6 vols (Oxford: Clarendon Press, 1969–80), vol. 2, pp. 184–5; 258–61.

6 Amatus of Montecassino, *The History of the Normans*, trans. P. N. Dunbar and G. A. Loud (Woodbridge: Boydell, 2004). 'Introduction', p. 1.

7 K. B. Wolf provides a brief summary of Geoffrey's origins in *Making History: The Normans and their Historians in Eleventh-Century Italy* (Philadelphia: University of Pennsylvania Press, 1995), pp. 143–4. Among other historians G. A. Loud, *The Age of Robert Guiscard: Southern Italy and the Norman Conquest* (Harlow: Longman, 2000), p. 82 argues that he was a Norman. M.-A. Lucas-Avenel, 'Le récit de Geoffroi Malaterra ou la légitimation de Roger, grand compte de Sicile', *Anglo-Norman Studies* 34 (2012), pp. 169–92 argues for Frankish origins.

8 Geoffrey Malaterra, *The Deeds of Count Roger of Calabria and Sicily and of his Brother Duke Robert Guiscard*, trans. K. B. Wolf (Ann Arbor: University of Michigan Press, 2005).

9 Wolf, *Making History*, pp. 123–5.

10 A translation by G. A. Loud of William of Apulia's *The Deeds of Robert Guiscard* is available at http://www.leeds.ac.uk/arts/downloads/file/1049/the_deeds_of_robert_guiscard_by_william_of_apulia. Line numbers in this volume refer to the Latin edition *Gesta Roberti Wiscardi*, ed. M. Mathieu (Palermo: Istituto siciliano di studi bizantini e neoellenici,

1961), also available online at http://www.intratext.com/IXT/LAT0871/_
INDEX.HTM.

11 The Anglo-Saxon Chronicles began as the court annals of Alfred the Great
in the late ninth century. *The Anglo-Saxon Chronicle*, trans. M. Swanton
(London: Dent, 1996)

12 For Orderic's background see Orderic, *Ecclesiastical History*, vol. 1,
'Introduction'.

13 The works that concern us here are *Gesta regum Anglorum*, ed. and trans.
R. A. B. Mynors, R. M. Thomson and M. Winterbottom, 2 vols (Oxford:
Clarendon Press, 1998) and *Gesta pontificum Anglorum*, ed. and trans.
M. Winterbottom and R. M. Thomson, 2 vols (Oxford, Clarendon Press,
2007).

14 Henry of Huntingdon, *Historia Anglorum*, ed. and trans. D. Greenway
(Oxford: Clarendon Press, 1996).

15 M. Aurell, *The Plantagenet Empire, 1154–1224* (Harlow: Longman,
2007), p. 138; C. Urbanski, *Writing History for the King: Henry II and
the Politics of Vernacular Historiography* (Ithaca: Cornell University
Press, 2013), Ch. 3. Wace's history is published as *A History of the
Norman People: Wace's Roman de Rou*, trans. G. Burgess with notes by
G. Burgess and E. van Houts (Woodbridge: Boydell, 2004).

Chapter 1: Rollo and the Settlement of Normandy

1 Dudo, *History of the Normans*, pp. 48–49.

2 S. Reynolds, *Fiefs and Vassals: the Medieval Evidence Reinterpreted*
(Oxford: Oxford University Press, 1994), pp. 121, 126, 136–8, 140.
For a concise summary of the debate surrounding whether Rollo's
actions on the Epte constituted an act of homage, see M. Hagger,
'Confrontation and Unification: Approaches to the Political History
of Normandy, 911–1035', *History Compass* 11 (2013), pp. 429–42
(pp. 435–6).

3 S. Coviaux, 'Baptême et conversion des chefs scandinaves du IXe au XIe
siècle', in *Les fondations scandinaves en Occident et les débuts du duché
de Normandie*, ed. P. Bauduin (Caen: Publications du CRAHM, 2005),
pp. 67–80.

4 E. Searle, 'Frankish Rivalries and Norse Warriors', *Anglo-Norman Studies*
8 (1984), pp. 198–213 and further developed in *Predatory Kinship and
the Creation of Norman Power, 840–1066* (Berkeley: University of
California Press, 1988). For historical opinion on Dudo see D. Bates,
Normandy Before 1066 (London: Longman 1982), pp. xii–xiii, though
Bates and the profession as a whole have reconsidered Dudo in the light
of Searle's work. See also L. Shopkow, *History and Community: Norman
Historical Writing in the Eleventh and Twelfth Centuries* (Washington
DC: Catholic University of America Press, 1997), esp. pp. 68–79; E. Albu,
The Normans in their Histories: Propaganda, Myth and Subversion
(Woodbridge: Boydell, 2001), Ch. 1.

5   Viking, Norsemen and Northmen are taken as terms of convenience in this book and are thus used as synonyms.

6   J. Dunbabin, *France in the Making 843–1180* (Oxford: Oxford University Press, 1985), pp. 44–100.

7   *The Annals of St-Bertin: Ninth-Century Historys, vol. 1*, trans. J. L. Nelson (Manchester: Manchester University Press 1992), *s.a.* 841, p. 50.

8   *Annals of St-Bertin*, trans. Nelson, *s.a.* 845 p. 60.

9   Ibid., *s.a.* 841, p. 51.

10 *Normans in Europe*, ed. van Houts, no. 5 (Norman annals); Dudo, *History of the Normans*, p. 35.

11 *Normans in Europe*, ed. van Houts, no. 1 (905 grant to Ernustus), no. 2 (906 concerning the transfer of the relics and community of Saint-Marcouf from the west of Normandy to Corbény), no. 3 (918 grant to Saint-Germain).

12 *Normans in Europe*, ed. van Houts, no. 3.

13 For discussion see Reynolds, *Fiefs and Vassals*, pp. 121, 126, 136–8, 140.

14 Flodoard, *Historia Remenensis ecclesiae*, ed. M. Stratmann, (Hannover: Hahn, 1998), p. 407.

15 S. Coupland, 'The Vikings in Francia and Anglo-Saxon England to 911', *The New Cambridge Medieval History, II: c. 700–c.900*, ed. R. McKitterick (Cambridge: Cambridge University Press, 1995), pp. 190–201 (p. 197).

16 *The Annals of Flodoard of Reims*, ed. and trans. S. Fanning and B. S. Bachrach (Toronto: University of Toronto Press, 2011), p. 23.

17 Hagger, 'Confrontation and Unification'.

18 Flodoard, *Historia Remenensis ecclesiae*, p. 407. For discussion see J. L. Nelson, 'Normandy's Early History since *Normandy Before 1066*', in *Normandy and its Neighbours, 900–1250: Essays for David Bates*, ed. D. Crouch and K. Thompson (Turnhout: Brepols, 2011), pp. 3–15 (pp. 5–7).

19 Dudo, *History of the Normans*, p. 15.

20 E. Johnson, 'Origin Myths and the Construction of Medieval Identities: Norman Chronicles 1000–1100', in *Texts and Identities in the Middle Ages*, ed. R. Corradini, and others (Vienna: Österreichischen Akademie der Wissenschaften, 2006), pp. 153–64 (p. 155). See also S. Reynolds, 'Medieval *Origines gentium* and the Community of the Realm', *History*, 68 (1983), pp. 375–90; M. Coumert, 'Les récits d'origine et la tradition historiographique normande', in *L'Historiographie médiévale normande et ses sources antiques (Xe-XIIe siècles)*, ed. P. Bauduin and M.-A. Lucas-Avenel (Caen: Centre Michel de Boüard – CRAHAM, 2014), pp. 137–54.

21 Albu, *The Normans in their Histories*, pp. 7–46; L. Shopkow, 'The Carolingian World of Dudo of Saint Quentin', *Haskins Society Journal* 15 (1989), pp. 19–37; E. Searle, 'Fact and Pattern in Heroic History: Dudo of St Quentin', *Viator*, 15 (1984), pp. 119–37.

22 G. Koziol, *Begging Pardon and Favour: Ritual and Political Order in Early Medieval France* (Ithaca: Cornell University Press, 1992), pp. 149–50.

23 There is some debate as to whether Rollo sacrificed Christian captives after his conversion, based on D. C. Douglas's reading of Adémar of Chabannes' Chronicle ('Rollo of Normandy, *English Historical Review*,

57 (1942), pp. 417–36 (pp. 433–4)), though Adémar wrote that he beheaded them before he was made a Christian: *Normans in Europe*, ed. van Houts, no. 11. Douglas's reading is incorrect.

24   D. Crouch, *The Normans: the History of a Dynasty* (London: Continuum, 2002), p. 321 n. 14.

25   Nelson, 'Normandy's Early History', pp. 10–11. For the dynastic importance of Dudo's account see Crouch, *The Normans*, p. 292.

26   F. Lifshitz, 'Dudo's Historical Narrative and the Norman Succession of 996', *Journal of Medieval History* 20 (1994), pp. 101–20.

27   J. Le Maho, 'The Fate of the Ports of the Lower Seine Valley at the End of the Ninth Century' in *Markets in Early Medieval Europe: Trading and 'Productive' Sites 650–850*, ed. T. Pestell and K. Ulmschneider (Macclesfield: Windgather, 2003), pp. 234–47.

28   J. Le Maho, 'Le groupe épiscopal de Rouen du IVe au Xe siècle', in *Medieval Art, Architecture, and Archaeology at Rouen*, ed. Jenny Stratford (Leeds: Maney, 1993), pp. 20–30 (pp. 27–30); 'Les fouilles de la cathédrale de Rouen de 1985 à 1993: esquisse d'un premier bilan', *Archéologie médiévale* 24 (1994), pp. 1–49 (pp. 28–31) and 'The Fate of the Ports', pp. 238, 240.

29   L. Mazet-Harhoff, 'The Incursions of the Vikings into the Natural and Cultural Landscape of Upper Normandy', in *Viking Trade and Settlement in Continental Western Europe*, ed. I. Skibsted Klaesøe (Copenhagen: Museum Tusculanum Press, 2010), pp. 81–122 (p. 92).

30   A. Nissen-Jaubet, 'Some Aspects of Viking Research in France', *Acta Archaeologia*, 71 (2000), pp. 159–69; 'Implantations scandinaves et traces matérielles en Normandie: que pouvons-nous attendre?', in *Les fondations scandinaves en Occident et les débuts du duché de Normandie*, ed. P. Bauduin (Caen: Publications du CRAHM, 2005), pp. 209–23. See also D. Hadley, *The Vikings in England: Settlement, Society and Culture* (Manchester: Manchester University Press, 2006), esp. p. 273 for place names.

31   For the settlement of the Vikings in England see Hadley, *The Vikings in England*.

32   P. Bauduin, 'Chefs normands et élites franques, fin IXe-dé-but Xe siècle', in *Les fondations scandinaves en Occident et les débuts du duché de Normandie*, ed. P. Bauduin (Caen: Publications du CRAHM, 2005), pp. 181–94. *La première Normandie (Xe–XIe siècles. Sur les frontières de la haute Normandie: identité et construction d'une principauté* (Caen: Presses Universitaires de Caen, 2004), pp. 99–101.

33   F. Lifshitz, *The Conquest of Pious Neustria: Historiographic Disccourse and Saintly Relics 684–1090* (Toronto: Pontifical Institute of Medieval Studies, 1995), p. 121, and 'La Normandie carolingienne, essai sur la continuité avec utilisation de sources négligés', *Annales de Normandie*, 48 (1998), pp. 505–24.

34   J. C. Moesgaard, 'A Survey of Coin Production and Currency in Normandy, 864–945', in *Silver Economy in the Viking Age*, ed. J. Graham-Campbell and G. Williams (Walnut Creek, CA: Left Coast Press, 2004), pp. 99–121 (pp. 102–9).

35 Le Maho, 'Le groupe épiscopal de Rouen'; B. Gauthiez, 'The Urban Development of Rouen, 989–1345', in *Society and Culture in Medieval Rouen, 911–c.1300*, ed. L. V. Hicks and E. Brenner (Turnhout: Brepols, 2013), pp. 17–64.

36 Dudo, *History of the Normans*, pp. 64–8. For discussion see Searle, *Predatory Kinship*, pp. 73–5.

37 Dudo, *History of the Normans*, pp. 82–4.

38 *Normans in Europe*, ed. van Houts, no. 9. Images from the manuscripts of the *Planctus* can be viewed on Rob Helmerich's website http://vlib.iue.it/carrie/documents/planctus/planctus/index.html.

39 Searle, *Predatory Kinship*. p. 58; Lifshitz, 'Dudo's Historical Narrative and the Norman Succession of 996'. For the borders of Normandy see Bauduin, *La première Normandie*.

40 E. van Houts, 'The *Planctus* on the Death of William Longsword (943) as a Source for Tenth-Century Culture in Normandy and Aquitaine', *Anglo-Norman Studies* 36 (2014), pp. 1–22 (p. 2).

41 Dudo, *History of the Normans*, pp. 100–18. For relations between Richard and Louis as played out in Rouen, see L. V. Hicks, 'Through the City Streets: Movement and Space in Rouen as seen by the Norman Chroniclers', in *Society and Culture in Medieval Normandy*, ed. Hicks and Brenner, pp. 125–49 (pp. 128–34).

42 *Annals of Flodoard*, pp. 37–8.

43 Dudo, *History of the Normans*, pp. 127–32.

44 Bauduin, *La première Normandie*.

45 For the most recent summary see Bauduin, *La première Normandie*, pp. 26–33, but also Bates, *Normandy before 1066*, pp. 2–43; Searle, *Predatory Kinship*, pp. 1–11.

46 D. Bates, 'West Francia: the Northern Principalities', in *The New Cambridge Medieval History, III: c.–900–c.1024*, ed. T. Reuter (Cambridge: Cambridge University Press, 1999), pp. 398–419 (p. 404).

47 Moesgaard, 'Coin Production and Currency in Normandy'.

48 J. Dunbabin, 'West Francia: the Kingdom', in *The New Cambridge Medieval History, III: c.900–c.1204*, ed. T. Reuter (Cambridge: Cambridge University Press, 1999), pp. 372–97.

49 Dudo, *History of the Normans*, pp. 167–73.

50 Searle, *Predatory Kinship*, p. 124.

51 A. Renoux, 'Fouilles sur le site du château ducal de Fécamp (Xe-XIIe siècle', *Anglo-Norman Studies* 4 (1982), pp. 133–52 (pp. 142–4).

Chapter 2: William of Normandy and the Conquest of England

1 The most recent biography of William is that by M. Hagger, *William: King and Conqueror* (London: I.B.Tauris, 2012). For contrasting views see D. Bates, *William the Conqueror* (Stroud: Tempus, 1989) and D. C. Douglas, *William the Conqueror: the Norman Impact upon England*, rev. edn (New Haven: Yale University Press, 1999).

2   Wace, *Roman de Rou*, p. 123. William's mother was actually the daughter of an undertaker with connections to the ducal court and was called Herleva. See E. van Houts, 'The Origins of Herleva, Mother of William the Conqueror', *English Historical Review* 101 (1986), pp. 399–404.

3   *Gesta Normannorum ducum*, vol. 2, pp. 124–5

4   Orderic, *Ecclesiastical History*, vol. 4, pp. 106–7

5   *Regesta regum Anglo-Normannorum: the Acta of William I (1066–1087)*, ed. D. Bates (Oxford: Clarendon Press, 1998), no. 232 and discussed in D. Bates, *The Normans and Empire* (Oxford: Oxford University Press, 2013), p. 67.

6   William of Malmesbury, *Gesta regum*, vol. 1, p. 509.

7   For the problems and processes of ducal succession see G. Garnett, '"Ducal" Succession in Early Normandy', in *Law and Government in Medieval England and Normandy: Essays in Honour of Sir James Holt*, ed. G. Garnett and J. Hudson (Cambridge: Cambridge University Press, 1994), pp. 80–111.

8   See for example J. Yver, 'Les chateâux forts en Normandie jusqu'au milieu du XIIe siècle', *Bulletin de la Société des Antiquaires de Normandie* 53 (1955), 28–121; Bauduin, *La première Normandie*, passim.

9   Douglas, *William the Conqueror*, pp. 53–80.

10 D. Bates, 'The Conqueror's Adolescence', *Anglo-Norman Studies* 25 (2003), pp. 1–18; M. Hagger 'How the West was Won: the Norman Dukes and the Cotentin, c. 987–1087', *Journal of Medieval History* 38 (2012), pp. 20–55.

11 For vicomtes see M. Hagger, 'The Norman Vicomte, c. 1035–1135: What did he do?', *Anglo-Norman Studies*, 29 (2007), pp. 65–83.

12 Bauduin, *La première Normandie*, pp. 178–85; *Gesta Normannorum ducum*, vol. 2, pp. 22–9, 100–3.

13 Bates, 'Conqueror's Adolescence', p. 3.

14 Searle, *Predatory Kinship*, pp. 156, 198.

15 Hagger, 'How the West was Won', pp. 37–40.

16 For a discussion of the accounts see L. V. Hicks, 'Coming and Going: the Use of Outdoor Space in Norman and Anglo-Norman Chronicles', *Anglo-Norman Studies* 32 (2010), pp. 40–56 (pp. 49–52).

17 William of Poitiers, *Gesta Guillelmi*, pp. 24–5; L. V. Hicks, 'The Concept of the Frontier in Norman Chronicles: A Comparative Approach', in *Norman Expansion: Connections, Continuities, and Contrasts*, ed. K. Stringer and A. Jotischky (Farnham: Ashgate, 2013), pp. 143–64 (pp. 153–4).

18 For the Truce of God see D. Barthélemy, 'The Peace of God and Bishops at War in the Gallic Lands from the Late Tenth to the Early Twelfth Century', *Anglo-Norman Studies* 32 (2010) pp. 1–24. For Normandy in particular, M. de Boüard, 'Sur les origines de la trêve de Dieu en Normandie', *Annales de Normandie* 9 (1958), pp. 169–89; Bates, *Normandy before 1066*, pp. 163–4.

19 William of Poitiers, *Gesta Guillelmi*, pp. 80–1, 96–7.

20 G. Fellows-Jensen, 'Les relations entre la Normandie et les colonies

Scandinaves', in *Les fondations scandinaves en Occident et les débuts du duché de Normandie*, ed. P. Bauduin (Caen: Publications de CRAHM, 2005), pp. 225–39.

21 *English Historical Documents: vol. 1 500–1042*, ed. Dorothy Whitelock, 2nd edn (London: Eyre Methuen, 1979), no. 230. See also L. Abrams, 'England, Normandy and Scandinavia' in *A Companion to the Anglo-Norman World*, ed. C. Harper-Bill and E. van Houts (Woodbridge: Boydell, 2002), pp. 43–62, (p. 45).

22 Æthelred's invasion was recorded by William of Jumièges in the *Gesta Normannorum ducum*, vol. 2, pp. 10–15.

23 Rodolfus Glaber, *Historiarum libri quinque*, ed. J. France (Oxford: Clarendon Press, 1989), pp. 54–7. See also S. Keynes, 'The Æthelings in Normandy', *Anglo-Norman Studies* 13 (1991), pp. 173–205 (p. 182). Rodolfus Glaber was writing in Burgundy in *c*. 1030.

24 M. Fauroux, *Recueil des actes des ducs de Normandie (911–1066)*, MSAN, 36 (Caen: Caron, 1961), nos 69 and 76.

25 *Gesta Normannorum ducumm*, vol. 2, pp. 76–7; E. van Houts, 'The Political Relations between Normandy and England According to the *Gesta Normannorum Ducum*', in E. van Houts, *History and Family Traditions in England and on the Continent* (Aldershot: Ashgate, 1999), essay v. See also Keynes, 'The Æthelings in Normandy'.

26 For the Godwine family see F. Barlow, *The Godwins: The Rise and Fall of a Noble Dynasty* (Harlow: Longman, 2002); E. Mason, *The House of Godwine: The History of a Dynasty* (London: Hambledon, 2004).

27 C. P. Lewis, 'The Normans in England', *Anglo-Norman Studies* 17 (1994), pp. 123–44.

28 E. van Houts, 'Edward and Normandy', in *Edward the Confessor: the Man and the Legend*, ed. R. Mortimer (Woodbridge: Boydell, 2007), pp. 63–76; Hagger, *William*, p. 34.

29 For detailed discussion on late Saxon succession see A. Williams, 'Some Notes and Considerations on Problems Connected with the English Royal Succession, 860–1066', *Anglo-Norman Studies* 1 (1979), pp. 144–67.

30 *Anglo-Saxon Chronicle*, trans. Swanton, D version, p. 176.

31 *The Life of King Edward who Rests at Westminster*, ed. F. Barlow, 2nd edn (Oxford: Clarendon Press, 1992), p. 123.

32 This argument is explained fully in G. Garnett, *Conquered England: Kingship, Succession, and Tenure, 1066–1166* (Oxford: Oxford University Press, 2007), Ch. 1. An introduction to the argument can be found in G. Garnett, *The Norman Conquest: A Very Short Introduction* (Oxford: Oxford University Press, 2009), Chs 1 and 2.

33 S. Vaughn discusses the possibility that Alexander II was a student of Lanfranc's at the abbey of Bec, though this is by no means conclusive: *Anselm of Canterbury and Robert of Meulan: the Innocence of the Dove and the Wisdom of the Serpent* (Berkeley, University of California Press, 1987), p. 33.

34 *English Historical Documents, vol. 2: 1042–1189*, ed. D. C. Douglas, 2nd edn (London: Eyre Methuen, 1981), no. 99.

35 S. Baxter, 'Edward the Confessor and the Succession Question', in *Edward the Confessor: the Man and the Legend*, ed. R. Mortimer (Woodbridge: Boydell, 2007), pp. 77–118; B. Golding, *Conquest and Colonisation: the Normans in Britain, 1066-1100*, 2nd edn (Basingstoke: Palgrave, 2013), pp. 15–24.

36 Baxter, 'Edward the Confessor', p. 92.

37 Ibid., pp. 91–2.

38 William of Poitiers, *Gesta Guillelmi*, pp. 100–1.

39 J. Gillingham, 'William the Bastard at War', in *Studies in Medieval History Presented to R. Allen Brown*, ed. C. Harper-Bill et al. (Woodbridge: Boydell, 1989), pp. 141–58 (p. 141).

40 For preparation see C. Gilmor, 'Naval Logistics of the Cross-Channel Operation, 1066', *Anglo-Norman Studies* 7 (1985), pp. 105–31.

41 E. van Houts, 'The Ship List of William the Conqueror', *Anglo-Norman Studies* 10 (1988), pp. 159–83.

42 Not all historians accept this. See C. Morton, 'Pope Alexander II and the Norman Conquest', *Latomus* 34 (1975), pp. 362–82.

43 To provide another account here seems redundant, but my editor insists that no book on the Normans is complete without a description of archers, trumpets, feigned flights and arrows in eyes.

44 Several of these papers are reprinted in *The Battle of Hastings*, ed. S. Morillo (Woodbridge: Boydell, 1996), including R. Glover, 'English Warfare in 1066', pp. 173–88; B. Bachrach, 'The Feigned Retreat at Hastings', pp. 189–93; R. A. Brown, 'The Battle of Hastings', pp. 194–218; S. Morillo, 'Hastings: an Unusual Battle', pp. 219–27. The most recent and detailed account is M. K. Lawson, *The Battle of Hastings 1066* (Stroud: Tempus, 2003).

45 Orderic, *Ecclesiastical History*, vol. 2, pp. 172–3; *Anglo-Saxon Chronicle*, trans. Swanton, D version. p. 199.

46 M. Bintley, *Trees in the Religions of Early Medieval England* (Woodbridge: Boydell, 2015), p. 78.

47 William of Poitiers, *Gesta Guillelmi*, p. 128–9.

48 Quote from Henry of Huntingdon: *Normans in Europe*, ed. van Houts, no. 45. See also William of Malmesbury, *Gesta regum*, vol. 1, pp. 454–5.

49 *The Carmen de Hastingae Proelio of Guy Bishop of Amiens*, ed. and trans. F. Barlow (Oxford: Clarendon Press, 1999), pp. 32–3.

50 William of Malmesbury, *Gesta regum*, vol. 1, pp. 456–7.

51 M. Foys, 'Pulling the Arrow Out: The Legend of Harold's Death and the Bayeux Tapestry', in *The Bayeux Tapestry: New Interpretations*, ed. M. Foys, K. Overby and D. Terkla (Woodbridge: Boydell, 2009), pp. 158–75.

52 William of Poitiers, *Gesta Guillelmi*, pp. 128–9; William of Malmesbury, *Gesta regum*, vol. 1, pp. 454–5; *Carmen*, pp. 24–5; Wace, *History of the Normans*, p. 181.

53 Eadmer, *History of Recent Events in England*, trans. G. Bosanquet (London: Cresset Press, 1964), p. 9.

54 *The Letters of Lanfranc, Archbishop of Canterbury*, ed. and trans. H. Clover and M. Gibson (Oxford: Clarendon Press, 1979), no. 53.

55 *Carmen*, pp. 34–5.
56 *Anglo-Saxon Chronicle*, trans. Swanton, D version, p. 200.
57 E. van Houts, *Memory and Gender in Medieval Europe 900–1200* (Basingstoke: Macmillan, 1999), p. 129.
58 William of Malmesbury, *Gesta regum*, vol. 1, pp. 452–5, 456–61.
59 Orderic, *Ecclesiastical History*, vol. 2, pp. 232–3, 266–7.
60 E. van Houts, 'The Norman Conquest through European Eyes', *English Historical Review*, 110 (1995), pp. 832–53.
61 *Normans in Europe*, ed. van Houts, no. 38.
62 Cited in van Houts, 'The Norman Conquest', p. 837.
63 See discussion in van Houts, 'The Norman Conquest', pp. 835–6.
64 Bates, *Normans and Empire*, p. 2 notes that Haskins was almost certainly the first to use the term.
65 J. Le Patourel, *The Norman Empire* (Oxford: Clarendon Press, 1976), pp. 89–117.
66 N. J. Sykes, *The Norman Conquest: A Zooarchaeological Perspective* (Oxford: Archaeopress, 2007), p. 1; M. Sartore, 'Eleventh- and Twelfth-Century Similarities in the Norman Influence, Contact and "Conquests" of Sicily, Southern Italy and England', *Al-Masaq* 25 (2013), pp. 184–203.
67 D. Bates, 'Normandy and England After 1066', *English Historical Review* 104 (1989), pp. 851–80.
68 Orderic, *Ecclesiastical History*, vol. 2, pp. 232–3.
69 William of Malmesbury, *Gesta regum*, vol. 1, pp. 462–5. See also his *Gesta pontificum*, vol. 1, pp. 324–5.
70 D. M. Palliser, 'Domesday Book and the "Harrying of the North"', *Northern History* 29 (1993), pp. 1–23.
71 Thomas of Marlborough, *History of the Abbey of Evesham*, ed. and trans. J. Sayers and L. Watkiss (Oxford: Clarendon Press, 2003), pp. 166–7.
72 A. Williams, *The English and the Norman Conquest* (Woodbridge: Boydell, 1995), p. 38.
73 Bates, *Normans and Empire*, p. 4
74 H. E. J. Cowdrey, 'The Anglo-Norman Laudes Regiae', *Viator* 12 (1981), pp. 37–78; M. Hare, 'Kings, Crowns and Festivals: the Origins of Gloucester as a Royal Ceremonial Centre', *Transactions of the Bristol and Gloucester Archaeological Society* 115 (1997), pp. 41–78; J. Nelson, 'The Rites of the Conqueror', *Anglo-Norman Studies* 4 (1982), pp. 117–32.
75 Orderic, *Ecclesiastical History*, vol. 2, pp. 234–5.
76 E. van Houts, 'Rouen as Another Rome in the Twelfth Century', in *Society and Culture in Medieval Rouen, 911–1300*, ed. L. V. Hicks and E. Brenner (Turnhout: Brepols, 2013), pp. 101–24.
77 *Chepstow Castle: Its History and Buildings*, ed. R. Turner and A. Johnson (Almeley: Logaston, 2006).

Chapter 3: Normans in the Mediterranean: The Hauteville Clan and Others

1   Amatus, *History of the Normans*, p. 46.
2   William of Malmesbury, *Gesta regum*, vol. 1 pp. 484–5.
3   R. Bartlett, *The Making of Europe: Conquest, Colonization and Cultural Change* (London: Penguin, 1994), Ch. 2.
4   Malaterra, *Deeds of Count Roger*, p. 52.
5   H. Houben, *Roger II of Sicliy: A Ruler between East and West*, trans. G. A. Loud and D. Milburn (Cambridge: Cambridge University Press, 2002), p. 4.
6   For the composition of migrants to southern Italy see G. A. Loud, 'How "Norman" was the Norman Conquest of Southern Italy', in G. A. Loud, *Conquerors and Churchmen in Norman Italy* (Aldershot: Ashgate, 1999), essay II; L.-R. Ménager, 'Pesanteur et etiologie de la colonisation Normande de l'Italie' and 'Inventaire des familles normandes et franques émigrées en Italie méridionale et en Sicilie, XIe-XIIe siècles', in *Roberto il Guiscardo e il suo tempo: Relazioni e communicazioni nelle prime-giornate normanno-sveve*, Bari, 28–29 maggio 1973 (Rome: Il centro di ricerca, 1975), pp. 203–30, 259–390; repr. in Léon-Robert Ménager, *Hommes et institutions de l'Italie Normande* (London: Variorum Reprints, 1981), essays iv and v.
7   The Lombards were one of the many groups of people who carved out new territories in the former Roman Empire. The Lombard principalities of the south were, however, independent from the Lombard kingdom in the north.
8   B. M. Kreuz, *Before the Normans: Southern Italy in the Ninth and Tenth Centuries* (Philadelphia: University of Pennsylvania Press, 1991); G. A. Loud, *The Age of Robert Guiscard: Southern Italy and the Norman Conquest* (Harlow: Longman, 2000), pp. 12–59. See also P. Skinner, 'The Tyrrhenian Coastal Cities Under the Normans', in *The Society of Norman Italy*, ed. G. A. Loud and A. Metcalfe (Leiden: Brill, 2002), pp. 75–96.
9   Amatus, *History of the Normans*, p. 50.
10   William of Apulia, *Gesta Roberti Wiscardi*, book I, lines 11–54.
11   In contrast J. France, 'The Occasion of the Coming of the Normans to Southern Italy', *Journal of Medieval History* 17 (1991), pp. 185–205 argues that the 1017 campaign marks the first appearance of the Normans in Italy.
12   Loud, *The Age of Robert Guiscard*, p. 65.
13   See the papers in *Culte et pèlerinages à Saint Michel en Occident: les trois monts dédiés à l'archange*, ed. P. Bouet, G. Otranto and A. Vauchez (Rome: Ecole française de Rome, 2003).
14   Malaterra, *Deeds of Count Roger*, p. 54.
15   *Normans in Europe*, ed. van Houts, no. 69. See also E. Joranson, 'The Inception of the Career of the Normans in Italy – Legend and History', *Speculum* 23 (1948), pp. 353–96 for the importance of papal involvement in Norman activity in southern Italy.
16   Orderic, *Ecclesiastical History*, vol. 5, pp. 156–9.

17 E. Johnson, 'The Process of Exile into Southern Italy', in *Exile in the Middle Ages*, ed. L. Napran and E. van Houts (Turnhout, 2004), pp. 29–38 (p. 32).
18 Orderic, *Ecclesiastical History*, vol. 5, pp. 158–9.
19 Johnson, 'Exile', p. 38.
20 Amatus, *History of the Normans*, p. 60 and n. 66 for discussion of Rainulf's identity.
21 Loud, *Age of Robert Guiscard*, p. 77.
22 Malterra, *Deeds of Count Roger*, p. 55; Loud, *Age of Robert Guiscard*, p. 77.
23 Amatus, *History of the Normans*, pp. 76–7. As Loud highlights in n. 52, it is impossible to identify all the individual Normans.
24 Malaterra, *Deeds of Count Roger*, p. 59.
25 Discussed in L.V. Hicks, 'Journeys and Landscapes of Conquest: Normans Travelling to and in Southern Italy and Sicily', in *Journeying Along Medieval Routes*, ed. A. L. Gascogine, L. V. Hicks and M. O'Doherty (Turnhout: Brepols, 2016) pp. 115–42.
26 Amatus, *History of the Normans*, p. 83.
27 'The Life of Pope Leo IX', in *The Papal Reform of the Eleventh Century: Lives of Pope Leo IX and Gregory VII*, trans. I. S. Robinson (Manchester: Manchester University Press, 2004), p. 141.
28 Loud, *Age of Robert Guiscard*, p. 118.
29 For accounts of the battle see Amatus, *History of the Normans*, pp. 100–1; Malaterra, *Deeds of Count Roger* pp. 61–2; William of Apulia, *Gesta Roberti Wiscardi*, book II. 'The Life of Pope Leo', trans. Robinson, pp. 149–50 provides a different slant in which the pope voluntarily accompanied the Normans to Benevento.
30 Loud, *Age of Robert Guiscard*, p. 130–45.
31 For Sicily before the Normans and the initial stages of the conquest see A. Metcalfe, *Muslims and Christians in Norman Sicily: Arabic Speakers and the End of Islam* (London: Routledge, 2003), pp. 1–29; Loud, *Age of Robert Guiscard*, pp. 146–85.
32 Malaterra, *Deeds of Court Roger*, p. 85. See also Loud, *Age of Robert Guiscard*, p. 146.
33 Metcalfe, *Muslims and Christians in Norman Sicily*, pp. 25–6.
34 Loud, *Age of Robert Guiscard*, p. 149.
35 Malaterra, *Deeds of Count Roger*, pp. 102–4.
36 Ibid., p. 114. For Normans and farting as humour in the twelfth century see Hagger, *William: King and Conqueror*, p. 61 (Roger I farts in response to bad counsel as recounted by Ibn al-Athir) and p. 147 (Daniel Beccles counsels against 'farting for fun' in the lord's hall).
37 Malaterra, *Deeds of Count Roger*, p. 112.
38 Loud, *Age of Robert Guiscard*, pp. 163–5.
39 Malaterra, *Deeds of Count Roger*, pp. 109–10.
40 *Gesta Francorum*, p. 69.
41 P. Chevedden, '"A Crusade from the First": the Norman Conquest of Islamic Sicily, 1060–91', *Al-Masāq* 22 (2010), pp. 191–225.

42 Bouet, 'Les normands: le nouveau peuple élu', in *Les normands en Méditerranée dans le sillage des Tancrède*, ed. Pierre Bouet and François Neveux (Caen, 1994), pp. 239–52.

43 Loud, 'Introduction', in Amatus, *History of the Normans*, pp. 24–6.

44 Malaterra, *Deeds of Count Roger*, p. 42.

45 See Woolf, 'Introduction', in Malaterra, *Deeds of Count Roger* and also *Making History*, pp. 143–61.

46 William of Apulia, *Gesta Roberti Wiscardi*, book III, lines 100–5.

47 Albu, *The Normans in their Histories*, p. 131.

48 A. Metcalfe, *The Muslims of Medieval Italy* (Edinburgh, 2009), p. 88.

49 J. France, 'Patronage and the Appeal of the First Crusade', in *The First Crusade: Origins and Impact*, ed. J. Philips (Manchester: Manchester University Press, 1997), pp. 5–20.

50 J. Riley-Smith, *The First Crusaders* (Cambridge: Cambridge University Press, 1997), chs 3–4.

51 J. Riley-Smith, *What were the Crusades?* 4th edn (Basingstoke: Palgrave Macmillan, 2009), pp. 72–3.

52 William of Apulia provides the fullest account: *Gesta Roberti Wiscardi*, books IV and V.

53 Ralph of Caen, *Gesta Francorum*, p. 7.

54 Anna Comnena, *The Alexiad*, trans. E. R. A. Sewter (London: Penguin, 1969), p. 319. Anna refers to the crusaders as 'Kelts'. The war with the Normans is described in books IV–VI and the description of Bohemond is at p. 422.

55 For the Normans in Byzantium see W. McQueen, 'Relations between Normans and Byzantium, 1071–1112', *Byzantion* 56 (1986), pp. 427–76.

56 Ralph of Cear, *Gesta Francorum*, p. 12.

57 For Robert Curthose see W. M. Aird, *Robert Curthose: Duke of Normandy (c.1050–1134)* (Woodbridge: Boydell, 2008), pp. 153–90.

58 For Ralph of Caen and the character of the Norman crusaders see N. Hodgson, 'Reinventing Normans as Crusaders? Ralph of Caen's *Gesta Tancredi*', *Anglo-Norman Studies* 30 (2008), pp. 117–32.

59 Ralph of Caen, *Gesta Tancredi*, p. 22.

60 A. Murray, 'How Norman was the Principality of Antioch? Prolegomena to a study of the Origins of the Nobility of a Crusader State', in *Family Trees and the Roots of Politics: the Prosopography of Britain and France, from the Tenth to the Twelfth Century*, ed. K. S. B. Keats-Rohan (Woodbridge: Boydell, 1997), pp. 349–59.

61 Ménager, 'Inventaire des familles normandes et franques émigrées'.

62 Murray, 'How Norman was the Principality of Antioch', p. 356.

63 T. S. Asbridge, *The Creation of the Norman Principality of Antioch* (Woodbridge: Boydell, 2000), pp. 181–94; M. Bennett, 'The Normans in the Mediterranean', in *A Companion to the Anglo-Norman World*, ed. C. Harper-Bill and E. van Houts (Woodbridge: Boydell, 2002), pp. 87–102 (pp. 93–6).

64 C. H. Haskins, *The Normans in European History* (New York: Houghton Mifflin, 1915; repr. Ungar, 1966), pp. 215–16.

65 D. C. Douglas, *The Norman Fate 1100–1154* (London: Eyre Methuen, 1976), p. 172
66 See note 6.
67 Metcalfe, *Muslims of Medieval Italy*, p. 89; P. Oldfield, 'Problems and Patterns of Medieval Migration: the Case of Southern Italy', in *Journeying Along Medieval Routes in Europe and the Middle East*, ed. A. L. Gascoigne, L. V. Hicks and M. O'Doherty (Turnhout: Brepols, 2016) pp. 89–113.

Chapter 4: Society

1 *English Historical Documents*, vol. 2, no. 211; http://opendomesday.org/place/SK9771/lincoln/ (accessed 31 October 2015).
2 Amatus, *History of the Normans*, p. 135.
3 C. Coulson, *Castles in Medieval Society: Fortresses in England, France and Ireland in the Central Middle Ages* (Oxford: Oxford University Press, 2003); J. Mesqui, *Châteaux et enceintes de la France médiévale: de la défense à la résidence*, 2 vols (Paris: Picard, 1991–3). Contrast this with earlier work in which the emphasis is on defence by R. A. Brown, *English Castles*, 3rd edn (London: Batsford, 1976).
4 R. Higham and P. Barker, *Timber Castles*, 2nd edn (London: Batsford, 2004), p. 103.
5 Kreuz, *Before the Normans*, pp. 134–5; D. Osheim, 'Rural Italy', in *Italy in the Central Middle Ages, 1000–1300*, ed. D. Abulafia (Oxford: Oxford University Press, 2004), pp. 161–82 (pp. 161–7).
6 Ann Williams, 'A Bell-House and a Burh-Geat: Lordly Residences in England before the Conquest', in *Medieval Knighthood, IV*, ed. C. Harper-Bill and R. Harvey (Woodbridge: Boydell, 1992), pp. 221–40.
7 Orderic, *Ecclesiastical History*, vol. 2, pp. 218–19.
8 Some castles in both England and Normandy were also located on the edge of (e.g. Falaise) or outside settlements (e.g. Stafford), but this practice seems to be more widespread in southern Italy.
9 A.-M. Flambard Héricher, 'Archaeology and the Bayeux Tapestry', in *The Bayeux Tapestry: Embroidering the Facts of History*, ed. P. Bouet et al. (Caen: Presses Universitaires de Caen, 2004), pp. 261–87 (pp. 264–6).
10 As described by William of Poitiers, *Gesta Guillelmi*, pp. 24–5 for Domfront and Orderic Vitalis, *Ecclesiastical History*, vol. 2, pp. 218–19 for the march north.
11 For castles in southern Italy and Sicily see H. Bresc, 'Les normands, constructeurs de châteaux', in *Les normands en Méditerranée dans le sillage des Tancrède*, ed. P. Bouet and F. Neveux (Caen: Presses Universitaires de Caen, 1994), pp. 63–75; R. Licinio, *Castelli Medievali. Puglia e Basilicata: dai normanni a Federico II e Carlo I d'Angiò* (Bari: Dedalo, 1994); F. Maurici, *Castelli Medievali in Sicilia: dai bizantini ai normanni* (Palermo: Sellerio, 1992).

12 Houben, *Roger II of Sicily*, pp. 155–6. For detailed discussion of Bari see Licinio, *Castelli Medievali*, Ch. 2.

13 *Gesta Normannorum ducum*, vol. 2, pp. 22–9. For discussion see Bauduin, *La première Normandie*, pp. 175–85; Hicks, 'The Concept of the Frontier in Norman Chronicles', pp. 149–52.

14 Orderic, *Ecclesiastical History*, vol. 4, pp. 112–13.

15 William of Poitiers, *Gesta Guillelmi*, pp. 34–5.

16 A. Wheatley, *The Idea of the Castle in Medieval England* (Woodbridge: Boydell, 2004), pp. 34–5.

17 C. Coulson, 'Peaceable Power in English Castles', *Anglo-Norman Studies*, 23 (2001), pp. 69–96.

18 R. Liddiard, 'Castle Rising, Norfolk: A "Landscape of Lordship"', *Anglo-Norman Studies*, 22 (2000), pp. 169–86.

19 R. di Liberto, 'Norman Palermo: Architecture between the 11th and 12th Century', in *A Companion to Medieval Palermo: The History of a Mediterranean City from 600 to 1500*, ed. A. Nef (Leiden: Brill, 2013), pp. 139–94 (pp. 161–3).

20 J. Decaëns, 'La Motte d'Olivet à Grimbosq (Calvados), résidence seigneuriale du XI siècle', *Archéologie médiévale*, 9 (1979), pp. 167–201; J. Le Maho, 'Note sur l'histoire d'un habitation seigneurial des XIe et XIIe siècles en Normandie: Mirville', *Anglo-Norman Studies*, 7 (1985), pp. 214–23.

21 P. Dixon, 'Design in Castle Building: The Controlling of Access to the Lord', *Château Gaillard* 18 (1998), pp. 47–56 (p. 48).

22 Orderic, *Ecclesiastical History*, vol. 4, pp. 218–19. See discussion in L. V. Hicks, 'Magnificent Entrances and Undignified Exits: Chronicling the Symbolism of Castle Space in Normandy', *Journal of Medieval History* 35 (2009), pp. 52–69 (pp. 59–60).

23 Orderic, *Ecclesiastical History*, vol. 2, pp. 80–1.

24 *Normans in Europe*, ed. van Houts, no. 21.

25 For differing interpretations of feudalism see R. A. Brown, *The Normans and the Norman Conquest*, 2nd edn (Woodbridge: Boydell, 1985), p. 34; E. Z. Tabuteau, 'Definition of Feudal Military Obligations in Eleventh-Century Normandy', in *On the Laws and Customs of England*, ed. M. A. Arnold et al. (Chapel Hill, 1981), pp. 18–59; Patricia Skinner, 'When was Southern Italy Feudal?', *Il Feudalismo nell'alto Medioevo*, Settimane di Studio del Centro Italiano di Studi sull'Alto Medioevo, 47, 2 vols (Spoleto 2000), vol. 1, pp. 309–40. For why the term is problematic see E. A. R. Brown, 'The Tyranny of a Construct: Feudalism and Historians of Medieval Europe', *The American Historical Review* 79 (1974), pp. 1063–88.

26 Tabuteau, 'Definitions of Feudal Military Obligations', pp. 46–7; list of services at p. 20.

27 *Normans in Europe*, ed. van Houts, no. 16, pp. 71–2.

28 The most comprehensive study of the post-conquest aristocracy is J. Green, *The Aristocracy of Norman England* (Cambridge: Cambridge University Press, 1997).

29 R. Fleming, *Kings and Lords in Conquest England* (Cambridge: Cambridge University Press, 1991), pp. 107–44, 228–9.

30 Golding, *Conquest and Colonisation*, p. 57.

31 Ibid., p. 55.

32 *English Historical Documents,* vol. 1, no. 51; Williams, 'A Bell-House and a Burh-Geat'.

33 J. H. Round, *Feudal England* (London: Swan Sonnenshein, 1895). See the discussion in Golding, *Conquest and Colonisation*, pp. 128–37.

34 Tabuteau, 'Definitions of Feudal Military Obligations', p. 59.

35 Loud, *Age of Robert Guiscard*, p. 289.

36 M. Mollat, *The Poor in the Middle Ages: an Essay in Social History*, trans. A. Goldhammer (New Haven: Yale University Press, 1986), pp. 52–3. See also J.-P. Poly and E. Bournazel, *The Feudal Transformation 900–1200* (New York: Holmes & Meier, 1991).

37 Orderic, *Ecclesiastical History*, vol. 4, pp. 296–7.

38 C. H. Haskins, *Norman Institutions* (Cambridge, MA: Harvard University Press, 1918), p. 63.

39 M. Arnoux, 'Paysans et seigneurs dans le duché de Normandie: quelques témoignages des chroniquers (Xe–XIIe siècles) in *Villages et villageois au moyen âge* (Paris: Publications de la Sorbonne, 1992), pp. 67–79 (pp. 67–8).

40 Dudo, *History of the Normans*, pp. 52–3.

41 *Gesta Normannorum ducum*, vol. 2, pp. 8–9.

42 B. Gowers, '996 and all that: the Norman Peasants' Revolt Reconsidered', *Early Medieval Europe*, 21 (2013), pp. 71–98. See also M. Arnoux, 'Between Paradise and Revolt: *Laboratores* in the Society of the Three Orders', in *Normandy and its Neighbours, 900–1250*, ed. D. Crouch and K. Thompson (Turnhout: Brepols, 2011), pp. 201–14.

43 Golding, *Conquest and Colonisation*, pp. 74–5.

44 Fleming, *Kings and Lords in Conquest England*, pp. 228–9.

45 R. Faith, *The English Peasantry and the Growth of Lordship* (London: Leicester University Press, 1997), p. 215.

46 Ibid., p. 197.

47 J.-M. Martin, 'Settlement and the Agrarian Economy', in *The Society of Norman Italy*, ed. G. A. Loud and A. Metcalfe (Leiden: Brill, 2002), pp. 17–46 (p. 19).

48 Skinner, 'When was Southern Italy Feudal?', p. 337.

49 Two traditions exist about William's mother. He was either the son of Rollo's marriage to a woman from outside the Frankish realm, as is attested by the *Planctus*, or of Popa of Bayeux: *Normans in Europe*, ed. van Houts, no. 9 and pp. 14–15.

50 Searle, *Predatory Kinship*, p. 94.

51 For Gunnor see E. van Houts, 'Countess Gunnor of Normandy (c. 950–1031)', *Collegium Medievale* 12 (1999), pp. 7–24; Hagger, 'How the West was Won'.

52 *Gesta Normannorum ducum*, vol. 2, pp. 266–73.

53 Ibid., vol. 2, pp. 266–9.

54 C. Heygate, 'Marriage Strategies among the Normans of Southern Italy in the Eleventh Century', in *Norman Expansion: Connections, Continuities and Contrasts*, ed. K. J. Stringer and A. Jotischky (Farnham: Ashgate, 2013), pp. 165–86.

55 J. Drell, *Kinship and Conquest: Family Strategies in the Principality of Salerno Suring the Norman Period 1077–1194* (Ithaca: Cornell University Press, 2002), pp. 1, 112; Loud, *Age of Robert Guiscard*, pp. 113–14.

56 P. Skinner, '"Halt! Be Men!": Sikelgaita of Salerno, Gender and the Norman Conquest of Southern Italy', *Gender & History*, 12 (2000), pp. 622–41 (p. 626).

57 Ibid.

58 J. Drell, 'The Aristocratic Family', in *The Society of Norman Italy*, ed. G. A. Loud and A. Metcalfe (Leiden: Brill, 2002), pp. 97–113 (pp. 104–5).

59 Heygate, 'Marriage Strategies', p. 174.

60 E. Searle, 'Women and the Legitimization of Succession at the Norman Conquest', *Anglo-Norman Studies* 3 (1981), pp. 159–70 with notes at 226–92; E. van Houts, 'Intermarriage in Eleventh-Century England', in *Normandy and its Neighbours, 900–1250: Essays for David Bates*, ed. D. Crouch and K. Thompson (Turnhout: Brepols, 2011), pp. 237–70.

61 Orderic, *Ecclesiastical History*, vol. 2, pp. 218–19.

62 Ibid., pp. 214–17.

63 *Normans in Europe*, ed. van Houts, no. 36. See also discussion in Ch. 2.

64 *English Historical Documents*, vol. 2, no. 81; William of Poitiers, *Gesta Guilellmi*, pp. 158–9.

65 For an analysis of Gunnhild's career see R. Sharpe, 'King Harold's Daughter', *Haskins Society Journal*, 19 (2007), pp. 1–27.

66 Eadmer, *History of Recent Events*, trans. Bosanquet, p. 127.

Chapter 5: The Normans and the Church

1   Orderic, *Ecclesiastical History*, vol. 4, pp. 256–61 with the quotation at pp. 258–9. For the background to the disorders in Normandy see W. Aird, *Robert Curthose, Duke of Normandy (c.1050–1134)* (Woodbridge: Boydell, 2008), Ch. 4; for discussion of Ruald's testimony, see C. Watkins, 'Memories of the Marvellous in the Anglo-Norman Realm', in *Medieval Memories: Men, Women and the Past, 700–1300*, ed. E. van Houts (Harlow: Longman, 2001), pp. 92–112 (pp. 96–7).

2   Orderic, *Ecclesiastical History*, vol. 3, pp. 342–5.

3   K. Quirk, 'Men, Women and Miracles in Normandy, 1050-1150', in *Medieval Memories: Men, Women and the Past, 700–1300,* ed. E. van Houts (Harlow: Longman, 2001), pp. 53–71. For the miracle collections from Normandy see D. Gonthier and C. Le Bas, 'Analyse socio-économique de quelques recueils de miracles dans la Normandie du XI au XIII siècle', *Annales de Normandie* 24:1 (1974), pp. 3–36.

4   *Normans in Europe*, ed. van Houts, no. 23. To modern eyes, the woman

was clearly severely depressed, but the despair she exhibited was taken as a sign of possession in the Middle Ages. Despair was a grave sin as it meant giving up hope of God's salvation.

5   *Liber Eliensis: A History of the Isle of Ely from the Seventh Century to the Twelfth, Compiled by a Monk of Ely in the Twelfth Century*, trans. J. Fairweather (Woodbridge: Boydell, 2005), pp. 252.

6   S. J. Ridyard, 'Condigna veneratio: Post-Conquest Attitudes to the Saints of the Anglo-Saxons', *Anglo-Norman Studies* 9 (1987), pp. 179–206.

7   P. Oldfield, *Sanctity and Pilgrimage in Medieval Southern Italy 1000–1200* (Cambridge: Cambridge University Press, 2014), pp. 52–3.

8   V. Rameyser, *The Transformation of a Religious Landscape: Medieval Southern Italy, 850–1150* (Ithaca: Cornell University Press, 2006), p. 175. See also G. A. Loud, 'Monastic Miracles in Southern Italy', in *Signs Wonders, Miracles: Representations of Divine Power in the Life of the Church*, ed. K. Cooper and J. Gregory, *Studies in Church History*, 41 (Woodbridge: Boydell, 2005), pp. 109–32.

9   Orderic, *Ecclesiastical History*, vol. 2, pp. 80–1, 124–5; vol. 3, pp. 164–5, and vol. 4, pp. 142–3. See also M. Chibnall, 'Liens de *fraternitas* entre l'abbaye de St-Évroult et les laics (XIe–XIIe siècles)', *Les mouvances laïques des ordres religieux*, Actes de troisième colloque international du CERCOR (Saint-Etienne: Université de Saint-Etienne, 1996), pp. 235–9 (p. 238).

10 Orderic, *Ecclesiastical History*, vol. 4, pp. 338–9.

11 For the Beaumonts see D. Crouch, *The Beaumont Twins: the Roots and Branches of Power in the Twelfth Century* (Cambridge: Cambridge University Press, 1986).

12 *The Warenne (Hyde) Chronicle*, ed. and trans. E. M. C. van Houts and R. C. Love (Oxford: Clarendon Press, 2013), appendix.

13 G. A. Loud, *The Latin Church in Norman Italy* (Cambridge: Cambridge University Press, 2007), p. 87.

14 E. Cownie, *Religious Patronage in Anglo-Norman England, 1066-1135* (Woodbridge: Boydell, 1998); B. Golding, 'Anglo-Norman Knightly Burials', in *The Ideals and Practice of Medieval Knighthood*, ed. C. Harper-Bill and R. Harvey (Woodbridge: Boydell, 1986), pp. 35–48 (p. 37).

15 *Anglo-Saxon Chronicle*, trans. Swanton, E version, p. 219. The foundation of Battle as a memorial is discussed in E. M. Hallam, 'Monasteries as "War Memorials": Battle Abbey and La Victoire', in *The Church at War*, ed. W. J. Sheils, Studies in Church History, 20 (Oxford: Blackwell, 1983), pp. 47–57.

16 *Gesta Normannorum ducum*, vol. 1, pp. 84–7.

17 Dudo, *History of the Normans*, p. 77. Discussed in more detail by van Houts, '*Planctus* on the Death of William Longsword'.

18 *Gesta Normannorum ducum*, vol. 1, pp. 92–5; Dudo, *History of the Normans*, p. 84.

19 William of Poitiers, *Gesta Guillelmi*, pp. 82–3.

20 Orderic, *Ecclesiastical History*, vol. 2, pp. 10–11.

21 H. E. J. Cowdrey, *The Age of Abbot Desiderius: Montecassino, the Papacy,*

and the Normans in the Eleventh and Early Twelfth Century (Oxford: Clarendon Press, 1983), p. 111; quote at Loud, *Latin Church*, p. 137.

22 The oath is translated in full in Loud, *Age of Robert Guiscard*, pp. 188–9 and an extract is printed in *Normans in Europe*, ed. van Houts, no. 73. For an overview of the relationship between the Normans and the papacy see Cowdrey, *The Age of Abbot Desiderius*, pp. 107–76; Loud, *Age of Robert Guiscard*, pp. 186–209.

23 *The Register of Pope Gregory VII, 1073–1085*, trans. H. E. J. Cowdrey (Oxford: Oxford University Press, 2002), no. 2.52a.

24 L. Feller, 'The Northern Frontier of Norman Italy, 1060–1140', in *The Society of Norman Italy*, ed. G. A. Loud and A. Metcalfe (Leiden: Brill, 2002), pp. 47–73; Loud, *Age of Robert Guiscard*, pp. 196–7 for the wider context.

25 *Register of Pope Gregory*, no. 3.11.

26 R. Allen, '"Praesul praecipue, atque venerande": the Career of Robert, Archbishop of Rouen, 989–1037', in *Society and Culture in Medieval Rouen*, ed. L. V. Hicks and E. Brenner (Turnhout: Brepols, 2013), pp. 153–83 (pp. 158–9).

27 Allen, 'Career of Robert', pp. 156–7; Gauthiez, 'The Urban Development of Rouen', p. 23.

28 Hagger, *William: King and Conqueror*, p. 114.

29 Golding, *Conquest and Colonisation*, p. 145.

30 *English Historical Documents*, vol. 2, no 78.

31 Golding, *Conquest and Colonisation*, pp. 151–2.

32 N. Kamp, 'The Bishops of Southern Italy in the Norman and Staufen Periods', in *The Society of Norman Italy*, ed. G. A. Loud and A. Metcalfe (Leiden: Brill, 2002), pp. 185–209.

33 Malaterra, *Deeds of Count Roger*, pp. 182–4, 212–13.

34 Houben, *Roger II*, p. 21.

35 C. Potts, *Monastic Revival and Regional Identity in Early Normandy* (Woodbridge: Boydell, 1997), pp. 62–104.

36 Cowdrey, *Age of Abbot Desiderius*, pp. 116–17, 139–40; Loud, *Latin Church*, pp. 84–92.

37 Lifschitz, *Conquest of Pious Neustria*; S. K. Herrick, *Imagining the Sacred Past: Hagiography and Power in Early Normandy* (Cambridge, MA: Harvard University Press, 2007).

38 Oldfield, *Sanctity and Pilgrimage*, pp. 61–3.

39 Ridyard, 'Condigna veneratio'; P. A. Hayward, 'Translation Narratives in Post-Conquest Hagiography and English Resistance to the Norman Conquest', *Anglo-Norman Studies*, 21 (1999), pp. 67–93.

40 Eadmer, *The Life of St Anselm of Canterbury*, ed. and trans. R. W. Southern (Oxford: Clarendon Press, 1962), pp. 50–4.

41 L. Jean-Marie, *Caen aux XIe et XIIe siècles: Espace urbain, pouvoirs et société* (Caen: Mandragore, 2000), pp. 182–8.

42 E. Hall and J. Sweeney, 'The *Licentia de Nam* of the Abbess of Montivilliers and the Origins of the Port of Harfleur', *Bulletin of the Institute of Historical Research* 52 (1979), pp. 1–8 (p. 5).

43   Rameyser, *Transformation of a Religious Landscape*, p. 159.
44   Orderic, *Ecclesiastical History*, vol. 2, pp. 272–3.
45   M. Gibson, *Lanfranc of Bec* (Oxford: Clarendon Press, 1978), pp. 139–40.
46   William of Poitiers, *Gesta Guillelmi*, pp. 82–3. For a discussion of synods in Normandy see 'The Synod in the Province of Rouen in the Eleventh and Twelfth Centuries', in *Church and Government in the Middle Ages*, ed. C. N. L. Brooke et al. (Cambridge: Cambridge University Press, 1976), pp. 19–39.
47   *Normans in Europe*, ed. van Houts, no. 70; discussed by Loud, *Latin Church*, p. 137.
48   Orderic, *Ecclesiastical History*, vol. 3, pp. 26–7.
49   *The Letters of Lanfranc Archbishop of Canterbury*, ed. and trans. H. Clover and M. Gibson (Oxford: Clarendon Press, 1979), no. 41 to John; no. 43 to Herfast. For a discussion of the events and recording of the riot in Rouen see A. Alexander, 'Riots, Reform, and Rivalry: Religious Life in Rouen, c.1073–c.1092', *Anglo-Norman Studies* 33 (2011), pp. 23–40.
50   R. Allen, 'The *Acta archiepiscoporum Rotomagensium*: Study and edition', *Tabularia 'Documents'*, 9 (2009), pp. 1–66 (pp. 38, 52) http://www.unicaen.fr/mrsh/craham/revue/tabularia/print.php?dossier=sources&file=09allen.xml.
51   Orderic, *Ecclesiastical History*, vol. 3, pp. 84–5.
52   Allen, '*Acta*', pp. 38, 52.
53   Kamp, 'Bishops of Southern Italy', p. 191.
54   Allen, '*Acta*', pp. 40, 54.
55   For Odo see, D. Bates, 'The Character and Career of Odo, Bishop of Bayeux, 1049/50–1097', *Speculum*, 50 (1975), pp. 1–20.
56   *The Chronicle of John of Worcester, vol. III: the Annals from 1067–1140*, ed. and trans. P. McGurk (Oxford: Clarendon Press, 1998), pp. 12–13.
57   H. E. J. Cowdrey, 'Bishop Ermenfrid of Sion and the Penitential Ordinance Following the Battle of Hastings', *Journal of Ecclesiastical History*, 20 (1969), pp. 225–42. A translation of the Ordinance can be found in *English Historical Documents*, vol. 2, no. 81.
58   *English Historical Documents*, vol. 2, no. 101. For Gregory's letters to William and Lanfranc see *Register of Pope Gregory*.
59   William of Malmesbury, *Gesta pontificum*, vol. 1, pp. 308–9.
60   William of Malmesbury, *Gesta regum*, vol. 1, pp. 498–9.
61   Ibid., pp. 506–7. For the effects of the conquest on monasteries, see Golding, *Conquest and Colonisation*, pp. 157–65.
62   *Regesta regum Anglo-Normannorum*, ed. Bates, no. 62 dated 1066 x 1083.
63   Ibid., no. 63.

Chapter 6: Cultural Exchanges

1   Orderic, *Ecclesiastical History*, vol. 2, pp. 184–5.

2   E. Ridel, *Les Vikings et les mots: l'apport de l'ancien scandinave à la langue française* (Paris: Errance, 2009), pp. 108–14; and discussion in L. Abrams, 'Early Normandy', *Anglo-Norman Studies* 35 (2013), pp. 45–64. (p. 53).

3   E. van Houts, 'Scandinavian Influence in Norman Literature of the Eleventh Century', *Anglo-Norman Studies* 6 (1984), pp. 107–24 (pp. 108–9). For extracts from this poem see *Normans in Europe*, ed. van Houts, no. 27.

4   *Normans in Europe*, ed. van Houts, no. 14 and 'Scandinavian Influence in Norman Literature', p. 111.

5   van Houts, 'Scandinavian Influence in Norman Literature', p. 120.

6   For a concise discussion of English administration following the conquest, see Golding, *Conquest and Colonisation*, Ch. 5.

7   E. Treharne, *Living Through Conquest: The Politics of Early English, 1020–1220* (Oxford: Oxford University Press, 2012), p. 101.

8   Treharne, *Living Through Conquest*, p. 173.

9   Metcalfe, *Muslims of Medieval Italy*, pp. 106–7, 144–5.

10   For detailed discussions of the administration of the kingdom of Sicily see J. Johns, *Arabic Administration in Norman Sicily: the Royal Dīwān* (Cambridge: Cambridge University Press, 2002); H. Takayama, *The Administration of the Norman Kingdom of Sicily* (Leiden: Brill 1993).

11   For example, D. C. Douglas, *The Norman Achievement, 1050–1100* (London: Eyre and Spottiswoode, 1969).

12   Johns, *Arabic Administration*, pp. 3–4.

13   Ibid., pp. 111–12.

14   Ibid., pp. 114, 268–73.

15   Ibid., p. 284.

16   J.-C. Ducène, 'Routes in Southern Italy in the Geographical Works of al-Idrīsī', in *Journeying Along Medieval Routes in Europe and the Middle East*, ed. A. L. Gascoigne, L. V. Hicks and M. O'Doherty (Turnhout: Brepols) pp. 143–66 (pp. 144–5). There is no English translation of al-Idrīsī's work, but extracts can be found in *Roger II and the Creation of the Kingdom of Sicily*, trans. G. A. Loud (Manchester: Manchester University Press, 2012), pp. 355–63.

17   Metcalfe, *Muslims of Medieval Italy*, p. 263.

18   Ibid., p. 237. The manuscript has been digitized by the British Library http://www.bl.uk/manuscripts/FullDisplay.aspx?ref=Harley_MS_5786.

19   Johns, *Arabic Administration*, pp. 284–6; Metcalfe, *Muslims of Medieval Italy*, pp. 247–8.

20   Ben Jervis, *Pottery and Social Life in Medieval England: Towards a relational approach* (Oxford: Oxbow, 2014), Ch. 4.

21   For Southampton Domesday see http://opendomesday.org/place/SU4111/southampton.

22   B. Jervis, 'Conquest, Ceramics, Continuity and Change. Beyond

Representational Approaches to Continuity and Change in Early Medieval England: A Case study from Anglo-Norman Southampton', *Early Medieval Europe* 21 (2013), pp. 455–87.

23 N. Sykes, 'Zooarchaeology of the Norman Conquest', *Anglo-Norman Studies*, 27 (2005), pp. 185–97. See also N. Sykes, *The Norman Conquest: a Zooarchaeological Perspective*, BAR International Series, 1656 (Oxford: Archaeopress, 2007).

24 Anselm's letters have been translated as *The Letters of Anselm of Canterbury*, trans. W. Fröhlich, 3 vols (Kalamazoo, MI: Cistercian Publications, 1990–4).

25 Boulogne-sur-Mer, Bibliothèque municipale, MS 11: images are available online http://www.enluminures.culture.fr/documentation/enlumine/fr/BM/boulogne-sur-mer_048-01.htm.

26 *English Romanesque Art, 1066–1200* (London: Arts Council of Great Britain, 1984), p. 87, no. 4. Avranches, Bibliothèque municipale, MS 72: images online http://www.enluminures.culture.fr/documentation/enlumine/fr/BM/avranches_038-01.htm.

27 *The Golden Age of Anglo-Saxon Art 966–1066*, ed. J. Backhouse, D. H. Turner and L. Webster (London: British Museum, 1984), p. 69, no. 50. Rouen, Bibliothèque municipale, MS 274: images are available online http://www.enluminures.culture.fr/documentation/enlumine/fr/BM/rouen_026-01.htm.

28 C. de Hamel, *A History of Illuminated Manuscripts* (Oxford: Phaidon, 1986), p. 94; *English Romanesque Art*, p. 57, no. 5. For an image of Hugh's self-portrait see J. G. Alexander, *Medieval Illuminators and their Methods of Work* (New Haven: Yale University Press, 1992), p. 11, fig. 13.

29 C. Hicks, *The Bayeux Tapestry: The Life Story of a Masterpiece* (London: Vintage, 2007), pp. 29–39.

30 G. Beech, *Was the Bayeux Tapestry Made in France? The Case for Saint-Florent of Saumur* (New York: Palgrave Macmillan, 2005).

31 E. C. Pastan and S. D. White, 'Problematizing Patronage: Odo of Bayeux and the Bayeux Tapestry', in *The Bayeux Tapestry: New Interpretations*, ed. M. Foys, K. Overbey and D. Terkla (Woodbridge: Boydell, 2009), pp. 1–24.

32 Amatus, *History of the Normans*, p. 50.

33 Orderic, *Ecclesiastical History*, vol. 2, pp. 58–63.

34 D. Roach, 'Saint-Evroul and Southern Italy in the *Historia ecclesiastica*', in *Orderic Vitalis: Life, Works and Interpretations*, ed. C. Rozier, D. Roach and E. van Houts (Woodbridge, forthcoming 2016). I am grateful to Daniel Roach for sending me this paper in advance of publication.

35 Houben, *Roger II*, p. 113. See also E. Borsook, *Messages in Mosaic: The Royal Programme of Norman Sicily (1130–1187)* (Oxford: Clarendon, 1990).

36 Metcalfe, *Muslims in Medieval Italy*, p. 236.

37 W. Tronzo, *The Cultures of his Kingdom: Roger II and the Cappella*

Palatina in Palermo (Princeton: Princeton University Press, 1997), pp. 10, 60, 109.

38 For a survey of what we know about the Jewish community in Rouen see E. Brenner and L. V. Hicks, 'The Jews of Rouen in the Eleventh to the Thirteenth Centuries', in *Society and Culture in Medieval Rouen, 911–1300*, ed. L. V. Hicks and E. Brenner (Turnhout: Brepols, 2013), pp. 369–82.

39 N. Golb, *The Jews in Medieval Normandy: A Social and Intellectual History* (Cambridge: Cambridge University Press, 1998), pp. 33–7, 147.

40 N. Golb, *Les Juifs de Rouen au Moyen Age* (Mont-Saint-Aignan: Publications de l'Université de Rouen, 1985), pp. 9–13.

41 D. Halbout-Bertin, 'Le Monument Juif d'époque romane du Palais de Justice de Rouen', *Archéologie médiévale*, 14 (1984), pp. 77–125.

42 B. Blumenkranz, 'La Synagogue de Rouen', in *Art et archéologie des Juifs en France médiévale*, ed. B. Blumenkranz (Toulouse: Privat, 1980), pp. 277–303.

43 Brenner and Hicks, 'Jews of Rouen', pp. 372–3.

44 Golding, *Conquest and Colonisation*, p. 74.

45 J. Hillaby, 'Jewish Colonisation in the Twelfth Century', in *Jews in Medieval Britain: Historical, Literary and Archaeological Perspectives*, ed. P. Skinner (Woodbridge: Boydell, 2003), pp. 15–40 (p. 19).

46 Hillaby, 'Jewish Colonisation', p. 16.

47 D. A. Hinton, 'Medieval Anglo-Jewry: the Archaeological Evidence', in *Jews in Medieval Britain: Historical, Literary and Archaeological Perspectives*, ed. P. Skinner (Woodbridge: Boydell, 2003), pp. 97–111 (p. 99).

48 Hinton, 'Medieval Anglo-Jewry', p. 98.

49 J. M. Lilley and others, *The Jewish Burial Ground at Jewbury* (York: York Archaeological Trust, 1994).

50 Metcalfe, *Muslims of Medieval Italy*, pp. 106–7.

51 Ibid., pp. 122–4.

52 Johns, *Arabic Administration*, p. 288.

53 Olfield, 'Problems and Patterns in Medieval Migration' p. 97.

Chapter 7: Norman Histories, Norman Identities

1 M. Chibnall, *The Normans* (Oxford: Blackwell, 2000); Crouch, *The Normans*; Douglas, *The Norman Achievement, 1050–1100* and *The Norman Fate*; F. Neveux, *A Brief History of the Normans: the Conquests that Changed the Face of Europe*, trans. H. Curtis (London: Robinson, 2008).

2 R. H. C. Davis, *The Normans and their Myth* (London: Thames & Hudson, 1976).

3 G. A. Loud, 'The *Gens Normannorum* – Myth or Reality', *Anglo-Norman Studies*, 4 (1982), pp. 13–34.

4 Haskins, *The Normans in European History*, p. 243.

5   C. Potts, '*Atque unum ex diversis gentibus populum effecit:* Historical Tradition and the Norman Identity', *Anglo-Norman Studies* 18 (1996), pp. 139–52; Robert Bartlett, 'Normans of the South', BBC2, first broadcast 18 August 2010.

6   H. Thomas, *The English and the Normans: Ethnic Hostility, Assimilation, and Identity, 1066–c.1220* (Oxford: Oxford University Press, 2003); L. Ashe, *Fiction and History in England, 1066–1200* (Cambridge: Cambridge University Press, 2007).

7   Albu, *The Normans in their Histories*, pp. 6, 238–9.

8   Quoted in Johns, *Arabic Administration in Norman Sicily*, p. 255.

9   'The Battle of Standard in the Time of King Stephen', in *Aelred of Rievaulx: The Historical Works*, trans. J. P. Freeland, ed. M. L. Dutton (Kalamazoo: Cistercian Publications, 2005), pp. 245–69 (pp. 252–3). See also discussion of such speeches in J. R. E. Bliese, 'The Courage of the Normans – a Comparative Study of Battle Rhetoric', in *Nottingham Medieval Studies* 35 (1991), pp. 1–17.

10 Metcalfe, *Muslims in Southern Italy*, p. 89; Oldfield, 'Problems and Patterns of Medieval Migration', p. 106.

11 See Chapter 1.

12 *Normans in Europe*, ed. van Houts, no. 9.

13 For recent discussions of Rollo's dream see S. Sønnesyn, 'The Rise of the Normans as *Ethnopoiesis*', pp. 203–18 (pp. 207–9), and B. Pohl, 'Keeping it in the Family: Re-Reading Anglo-Norman Historiography in the Face of Cultural Memory, Tradition and Heritage', pp. 219–51 (pp. 242–5), both in *Norman Tradition and Transcultural Heritage: Exchange of Cultures in the 'Norman' Peripheries of Medieval Europe*, ed. S. Burkhardt and T. Foerster (Farnham: Ashgate, 2013).

14 Johnson, 'Origin Myths and the Construction of Medieval Identities', p. 155.

15 E. Johnson, 'Norman Ethnicity in Normandy and Italy, c. 911–c. 1204' (unpublished PhD thesis, University of Cambridge, 2006), p. 57.

16 *Gesta Normannorum ducum*, vol. 2, pp. 24–9.

17 Ibid., vol. 2, pp. 16–19.

18 Wace, *History of the Norman People*, pp. 110–11.

19 Johnson, 'Norman Ethnicity', pp. 62–3.

20 Henry of Huntingdon, *Historia Anglorum*, pp. 390–3.

21 Johnson, 'Norman Ethnicity', p. 198.

22 Dudo, *History of the Normans*, p. 47.

23 Orderic, *Ecclesiastical History*, vol. 4, pp. 224–5. My translation.

24 Dudo, *History of the Normans*, pp. 127–32; *Gesta Normannorum ducum*, vol. 1, pp. 116–19; Wace, *History of the Norman People*, pp. 67–71.

25 Wace, *History of the Norman People*, p. 69.

26 See discussion in Hicks, 'Through the City Streets', pp. 130–4.

27 Malaterra, *Deeds of Count Roger*, p. 51.

28 Hicks, 'Journeys and Landscapes of Conquest', p. 137.

29 van Houts, 'Rouen as Another Rome', p. 119.

30 N. Webber, *The Evolution of Norman Identity 911–1154* (Woodbridge: Boydell, 2005), p. 39.

31 An excellent recent discussion of the character of the Normans, particularly in relation to crusading, is N. Hodgson, 'Normans and Competing Masculinities on Crusade', in *Crusading and Pilgrimage in the Norman World*, ed. K. Hurlock and P. Oldfield (Woodbridge: Boydell, 2015), pp. 195–213.

32 Orderic, *Ecclesiastical History*, vol. 5, pp. 24–7; vol. 6, pp. 454–7.

33 Amatus, *History of the Normans*, p. 46.

34 Malaterra, *Deeds of Count Roger*, p. 52; Metcalfe, *Muslims of Medieval Italy*, p. 94. *Strenuitas* is defined in subtly different ways by various historians: see for example Loud, *Age of Robert Guiscard*, p. 5: 'a combination of energy and resolution, particularly in adverse circumstances, which enabled them to conquer'.

35 Anna Comnena, *The Alexiad*, pp. 163–4.

36 Dudo, *History of the Normans*, pp. 18–20.

37 Ibid., p. 37.

38 Anna Comnena, *The Alexiad*, pp. 366–8.

39 Wace, *History of the Norman People*, p. 69.

40 Orderic, *Ecclesiastical History*, vol. 4, pp. 212–15.

41 Ibid., vol. 6, pp. 404–5.

42 See Aird, *Robert Curthose*, Ch. 3.

43 Orderic, *Ecclesiastical History*, vol. 2, pp. 358–9.

44 K. Thompson, 'Orderic Vitalis and Robert of Bellême', *Journal of Medieval History*, 20 (1994), pp. 133–41.

45 Ralph of Caen, *Gesta Tancredi*, p. 101.

46 Hodgson, 'Reinventing Normans as Crusaders', pp. 129–32. See also W. M. Aird, '"Many others, whose names I do not know, fled with them": Norman Courage and Cowardice on the First Crusade', in *Crusading and Pilgrimage in the Norman World*, ed. K. Hurlock and P. Oldfield (Woodbridge: Boydell, 2015), pp. 13–30.

47 Ralph of Caen, *Gesta Tancredi*, p. 150.

48 Chibnall, *The Normans*, p. 3.

INDEX

225